PERGAMON INTERNATIONAL LIBRARY
of Science, Technology, Engineering and Social Studies

The 1000-volume original paperback library in aid of education,
industrial training and the enjoyment of leisure

Publisher: Robert Maxwell, M.C.

Rethinking the Process of Operational Research and Systems Analysis

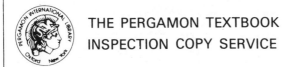

THE PERGAMON TEXTBOOK
INSPECTION COPY SERVICE

An inspection copy of any book published in the Pergamon International Library will
gladly be sent to academic staff without obligation for their consideration for course adoption
or recommendation. Copies may be retained for a period of 60 days from receipt and returned
if not suitable. When a particular title is adopted or recommended for adoption for class use
and the recommendation results in a sale of 12 or more copies, the inspection copy may be
retained with our compliments. The Publishers will be pleased to receive suggestions for
revised editions and new titles to be published in this important International Library.

This book is the second volume in a new international book series

FRONTIERS OF OPERATIONAL RESEARCH
AND APPLIED SYSTEMS ANALYSIS
General Editor: Rolfe Tomlinson

The series is aimed at helping practitioners to broaden their subject base and to advise managers and specialists in related areas of important new developments in the field.
The scope of the books will be broad and their authorship international. The subject is interpreted widely to include any scientific, applied, inter-disciplinary and systems-oriented approach to the study of real-life decision problems.
Rolfe Tomlinson is Professor of Systems and Operational Research at the School of Industrial and Business Studies at the University of Warwick, and is President of the European Association of OR Societies. He was for many years the Director of Operational Research at the National Coal Board and was then Area Chairman for Management and Technology at the International Institute of Applied Systems Analysis. The series will reflect his deep belief that scientific systems-oriented research can be of direct practical use over a much wider range of topics than at present, but only if the work is problem-oriented and seen as a collaborative effort with the problem owner.

Volume 1
EDEN, C., JONES, S. & SIMS, D.
Messing about in Problems: An Informal Structured Approach to their Identification and Management

Volume 3
STAHL, I.
Operational Gaming: An International Approach

Volume 4
KINGSMAN, B.
Raw Materials Purchasing: An Operational Research Approach

A Related Journal
JOURNAL OF THE OPERATIONAL RESEARCH SOCIETY*
Published on behalf of the Operational Research Society Limited, London

Editor: Peter Amiry, Department of Engineering Production, University of Birmingham, P.O. Box 363, Birmingham B15 2TT, England

This journal publishes contributions on any matter relevant to the theory, practice, history, or methodology of Operational Research or the affairs of the Society. It is aimed at applications in any field and encourages the submission of accounts of good, practical case studies illustrating OR in action; of reviews of the state of development of fields of knowledge relevant to OR; and of controversial articles on methodology, technique or professional policy.

* Free specimen copy sent on request

Rethinking the Process of Operational Research and Systems Analysis

Edited by

ROLFE TOMLINSON
University of Warwick, UK

and

ISTVÁN KISS
Hungarian Committee for Applied Systems Analysis, Budapest

PERGAMON PRESS
OXFORD · NEW YORK · TORONTO · SYDNEY · PARIS · FRANKFURT

U.K.	Pergamon Press Ltd., Headington Hill Hall, Oxford OX3 0BW, England
U.S.A.	Pergamon Press Inc., Maxwell House, Fairview Park, Elmsford, New York 10523, U.S.A.
CANADA	Pergamon Press Canada Ltd., Suite 104, 150 Consumers Rd., Willowdale, Ontario M2J 1P9, Canada
AUSTRALIA	Pergamon Press (Aust.) Pty. Ltd., P.O. Box 544, Potts Point, N.S.W. 2011, Australia
FRANCE	Pergamon Press SARL, 24 rue des Ecoles, 75240 Paris, Cedex 05, France
FEDERAL REPUBLIC OF GERMANY	Pergamon Press GmbH, Hammerweg 6, D-6242 Kronberg-Taunus, Federal Republic of Germany

Copyright © 1984 International Institute for Applied Systems Analysis

All Rights Reserved. No part of this publication may be reproduced, stored in a retrieval system or transmitted in any form or by any means: electronic, electrostatic, magnetic tape, mechanical, photocopying, recording or otherwise, without permission in writing from the copyright holders.

T57.6
R45
1984

First edition 1984

Library of Congress Cataloging in Publication Data
Main entry under title:
Rethinking the process of operational research and systems analysis.
(Frontiers of operational research and applied systems analysis; v. 2)
1. Operations research—Addresses, essays, lectures.
2. System analysis—Addresses, essays, lectures.
I. Tomlinson, Rolfe C. (Rolfe Cartwright) II. Kiss, Istvan.
III. Series.
T57.6.R45 1983   003   83-13433

British Library Cataloguing in Publication Data
Rethinking the process of operational research and systems analysis.—(Frontiers of operational research and applied systems analysis)
1. Operations research
I. Tomlinson, Rolfe
II. Kiss, Istvan II. Series
001.4.24   T57.6

ISBN 0-08-030829-5 (Hardcover)
ISBN 0-08-030830-9 (Flexicover)

Printed in Great Britain by A. Wheaton & Co. Ltd., Exeter

Preface

Both practitioners and teachers of OR and Applied Systems Analysis have suffered from the fact that, until the present, the subject has lacked a firm methodological base. A simple explanation for this is that the subject has its formal origins in traditional laboratory science, but that its practice lies firmly in the realm of applied social science. Both supporters and opponents of the subject have, therefore, tended to define it to suit their own purposes, and practitioners have, by and large, explained themselves in terms of "this is what I do". There has been increasing dissatisfaction with this state of affairs and in recent years a number of researchers and practitioners in different countries have set out to provide a more rigorous framework for understanding what the subject is really about; based on successful experience, rather than on hypothetical ideas as to what the subject should be. This book is the consequence of a meeting between a distinguished group of such practitioners and methodologists at a seminar at the International Institute of Applied Systems Analysis in August 1980. They found that there was a substantial agreement as to how the subject should be described and went away to write their own personal commentary on this common overview. The papers are diverse in style and intention—some are intensely practical, others are deeply philosophical. Together they provide, perhaps for the first time, a coherent, interlocking, set of ideas which can be considered as the foundations on which we may describe the subject as a science in its own right. Practitioners and teachers of OR and Systems Analysis will find the book directly useful as well as intellectually stimulating, and philosophers of science will find much in it that is relevant to their thinking.

ROLFE TOMLINSON
General Editor

MAR 7 1988

Contents

GIANDOMENICO MAJONE

Nino Majone works part of the time at IIASA, assisting with the development of the Handbook of Systems Analysis, and his chapter on "The Craft of Applied Systems Analysis" first appeared as an IIASA working paper. Majone uses the word "craft" to describe that mixture of "science" and "art" essential for a successful practitioner. This analysis of what is involved in the craft, and how we should judge quality, is central to the general theme of the book.

IAIN MITROFF

Iain Mitroff's lengthily titled chapter starts with a short, pithy, personal commentary on the seminar. It then moves on to a deep discussion of the steps necessary for a general methodology of applied systems analysis, and discusses some novel techniques for identifying underlying assumptions.

JEAN MOSCAROLA

Jean Moscarola discusses some of the findings of a group of French researchers, whose work is little known outside the French-speaking world. For some years now he, and his fellow workers, have been turning the microscope on to their own consulting activities, in a thought-provoking and professional manner. The paper sets out the many lessons learnt through this research.

GERARD DE ZEEUW

Gerard de Zeeuw discusses the second order, meta-level problems of systems analysis. In particular he emphasizes the need to make more effective use of experience, as retained in the minds of all the actors involved. At the same time it is always necessary to appreciate that any approach, however good, also has its dangers.

ROLFE TOMLINSON

In the final chapter Rolfe Tomlinson brings together the main conclusions of the seminar and discusses their implications. He emphasizes that in one sense the discussions have produced nothing that is new to successful practitioners of the subject. What is new is the development of a theory – a philosophy or a methodology – which accords with good practice and can therefore reasonably be used as a basis for further development of the subject. The main body of the chapter explores in turn the consequences that acceptance of this theory would have for practitioners, clients, teachers and researchers.

Introduction

This book is the outcome of a seminar held at the International Institute for Applied Systems Analysis (IIASA) in August 1980 under the title "Rethinking the Process of Systems Analysis". Rather than try to reproduce what was said at the seminar, much of which was necessarily ephemeral, the participants felt that they would like to go away and submit a paper which could be included in a collaborative volume, which would then truly represent the state of understanding after the discussions that took place.

The seminar was, in the first place, the result of a common concern that systems analysis, and its sister disciplines such as operational research, too often failed to achieve successful implementation because of an incomplete, and often incorrect, methodology. It was felt that analysts were making assumptions, sometimes subconsciously, that did not stand up to serious examination. One such assumption was that the "hard" part of a problem – which could be expressed in mathematical terms – could usefully be isolated from the human and organizational elements which could thus be eliminated from the analysis. Another false assumption was that implementation was an entirely separate activity from the analysis itself.

Clearly any adequate discussion of these problems demanded the involvement of experts from outside traditional OR/Systems fields. It was a case for discussion with philosophers and social scientists. It was therefore proposed to the Director of IIASA that a seminar should be held for invited scientists interested in developing an improved methodology based on experience and with a proper philosophical basis. The participants would be from a range of countries and with different professional and academic backgrounds. IIASA was already undertaking studies in the methodology of OR, and a Handbook of Systems Analysis is being developed under the editorship of Ed Quade and Hugh Miser. This seminar seemed a useful adjunct to that activity and approval was given accordingly.

Something should be said immediately about the subject of the seminar. At IIASA it is called Applied Systems Analysis, many (particularly in the UK) call it Operational Research, some Systems Analysis, and some simply Analysis. To others, each of those names can mean something quite different. To meet this problem, Rolfe Tomlinson had coined the word ORASA, which is frequently used in the book, but the confusion of names is likely to persist and we have not attempted to force a single name on our authors. The form and purpose of the activity is, however, not in question. It is the interdisciplinary, scientific, systemic study of problems and of decision-making processes, undertaken, with a view to their solution and/or improvement. Some simply call it "scientific problem solving". Throughout the book the term "systems analyst" is used within this sense and not, of course, as it is in the west, to describe someone working in commercial data processing. Sixteen persons from 8 countries attended the seminar, and some additional observers from IIASA's staff attended from time to time. Their initial training had been in many different disciplines; philosophers, social anthropologists, psychoanalysts and sociologists rubbed shoulders with "hard" economists and mathematicians. All had some experience of systems analysis and had written, or at least thought, extensively about it.

The meeting lasted one week and was structured with formal sessions in the mornings, and the afternoons were left free for informal discussion. All discussants had the chance to make a short presentation of their ideas if they wished, and were invited to suggest reading material from published papers, etc. Only two formal papers prepared especially for the seminar were circulated in advance of the meeting. One, from István Kiss and József Kindler, set out the basic dilemma which we needed to discuss. The other, by János Farkas, discussed the philosophical background.

From the eager way in which the distinguished contributors accepted the invitation we had good reason to believe that the discussions would be committed and lively. No one had guessed how stimulating they would prove to be, nor that, despite underlying differences of approach that were fundamentally at variance, there would be almost total agreement in diagnosis. It was agreed that there was a malaise, crisis, in the formulations of the subject, and there was a consensus regarding the elements needed to be included in any adequate description of adequate ORASA. It made no difference whether the foundation for concern had been empirical or philosophical – the outcome was the same. The traditional reductionist approach to analysis, developed from laboratory science, was quite inappropriate. We needed to talk in terms of intervention, action research, in which the scientist's separation between observation and observer was as inappropriate as it is unachievable. Concepts such as optimization need to be altered to "change for the better" etc, etc. The seminar felt that we were now in a strong position to establish a "true" systems philosophy, which could provide a basis for adequate training for practitioners and development of the subject.

In view of the consensus, it is perhaps not surprising that all but two of the participants accepted our invitation to present a paper for inclusion in this volume, and that all but one of these are specially written for the purpose. In the truest sense we believe them to represent the state-of-the-art, which will enable that art to extend its many successes and reduce its failures. No individual paper, except perhaps the last, attempts to provide a comprehensive overview. But together they provide a rich, many-faceted, consistent picture of an important activity for social progress. Apart from the first and last papers we could find no logical system for grouping the individual contributions and have therefore set them out alphabetically by author.

One problem that we encountered was the question of language. The meeting was in English, and we felt that to reach the widest possible audience the papers should also be in English. But many of the ideas and concepts developed in French, Hungarian or Russian do not easily translate into English. We decided to "help" individual authors so that each paper would be understood by an English-speaking audience, but not to "translate" into an English that might be grammatically correct, but might distort the ideas that are being put forward.

Finally, the editors would like to record their thanks to those whose particular efforts have made this volume possible. In particular we are grateful to Phil Ratoosh, Director of the Wright Institute and Professor of Psychology at the State University of San Francisco. In the course of a sabbatical period at IIASA Phil played a leading part in the planning and organization of the seminar, of which he was an active participant. He took part in the early stages of the editorial process and it is unfortunate that administrative difficulties made it impossible for him to continue in this role. As a psychoanalyst who previously worked as a management scientist his contribution was invaluable and we are most grateful. We would like to thank the other participants at the seminar who have not written papers for this volume – particularly Sven Persson, of Sweden, and Michael Thompson, IIASA – for their share in the success of the seminar. Finally, we should thank Hugh Miser, lately Director of Publications at IIASA, for his support and encouragement in the preparation of the volume.

ISTVÁN KISS

ROLFE TOMLINSON

1

Future Methodology Based on Past Assumptions?

JÓZSEF KINDLER and ISTVÁN KISS

1. ON THE METHODOLOGY – THE INTERNATIONAL SCENE

One of the most important developments of applied science in the last 20 years has been the increasing attention that has been given to the study of complexity. This approach has been a radical departure from traditional methods of scientific enquiry since it has not been concerned with the reductional approach of segregating a problem into its constituent elements and analysing them separately but with the process of putting related elements together and analysing their integrated effect. In connection with this, then, has been the formal development of systems theory as well as methodological developments associated with systems-based sciences devoted to complex problems, such as systems engineering, systems analysis, action research, evaluation research, etc.

These theories and methodologies demand from us a changed attitude. The essence of this is well characterized by the lecture on the fundamentals of methodology in systems analysis given by Gvishiani (in Obninsk, 1978; Kelle, 1979): "The first methodological starting principle of systems analysis could be characterized as *the idea of the organic unity of the subjective and the objective aspects within a system.* It is typical of systems analysis to modify definitely the traditional, subjective-objective relation. In this respect, systems analysis differs from the traditional acquaintance with nature where the object is rather rigidly demarcated from the subject." (Gvishiani, 1978)

Exactly the same concept was expressed by Cavallo in the Preface of a report dealing with the first 25 years of the international systems movement, which is a moderate and unbiassed survey, prepared in the course of 2 years of international cooperation. (Cavallo, 1979) In his opinion the basic question is: does science accept that man is an inseparable part of the essential problems of today? This idea however entails a new attitude; therefore we have to study how systems approach can affect the treatment of that complexity, of which man is a part, and whether this attitude contributes to the spreading of our

1

information and to the development of our capacity for collaborating with the world.

Ackoff has called the second half of our century the *Systems Age*. This deviates from analytic thinking, reductionism and the determinism of the Machine Age, and is featured by synthetic thinking, expansionism and objective teleology. Forming this new attitude demands a new paradigm and here a quotation from Martin is relevant: "those people heavily involved in systems endeavors are up to their necks in grappling with the present shift in world-views". (Martin, 1978)

But what kind of means are being employed in developing this new attitude?

Boulding, one of the founders of the systems movement, claims that general systems research is a "level of theoretical model-building which lies somewhat between the highly-generalized constructions of pure mathematics and the specific theories of the specialized disciplines". (Boulding, 1956) This may be misinterpreted in two different ways and the following 25 years have produced examples for both kinds of misunderstanding. On the one hand, it suggests that systems theory only produces theoretical constructions which have no connection with practice; on the other, that on account of its abstract nature it works exclusively with mathematical means. There are series of examples to contradict the former, e.g. the methodologies based on the systems approach like systems engineering and operational research, or the manifold applications of systems analysis. As for the latter misinterpretation, this may have been due to the fact that some representatives of mathematical systems theory regarded their own work as exclusively systems research and they stressed it accordingly. Essentially the "traditional scientific criterion" seems to verify the latter misconception too, namely: only that which is scientific which can be formalized, and formal description can only be given by means of mathematics.

Similar criticism has been expressed by Blauberg–Sadovsky–Yudin:

> "... one of the reasons why several versions of general systems theory are limited is that these conceptions emphasize formal, mathematical problems in describing systems, whereas the content basic in this theory has not yet been sufficiently worked out."
> (Blauberg Sadovsky Yudin, 1969)

The other extreme viewpoint developed in connection with mathematics is often overemphasized:

> "It is one thing to caricature ... a narrow-minded mathematical approach which would view a particular mathematical and/or quantitative structure as *the reality*. However it is quite another *not* to recognize that mathematics and logic represent high points in the achievement of our collective intellect, and that it is not the use of such achievements but their abuse which is unwarranted and dangerous." (Klir, 1979)

In systems research the choice of the tools has a double role: it helps to point out the limited applicability of tools under given conditions, and it calls attention to new non-mathematical but scientific tools for them to be developed and applied. The synthesizing feature of systems theory is indicated by the striving for integration of the quantitative and qualitative aspects of descriptions, problem solutions. There are definitions for a complex system to be one which may be analysed more than one way. (Rosen, 1979) According to Klir who represents mathematical system theory: "Within general systems research, the tools for solving the problem are of secondary importance" and "The tools need not be only mathematical in nature, but may consist of a combination of mathematical, computational, heuristic, experimental or any other desirable aspects." (Klir, 1979) The interdisciplinary feature of the systems approach finds expression in the wide range of investigational approaches and of the tools employed.

It is due to the introduction of systems thinking that the systems approach and its methodologies developed in the fifties, that is in the realization; for old problems new methods were developed, even if within a traditional branch of science. This enabled the recognition and definition of newer problems, and a new language for communication belonging to them evolved, which made it possible for representatives of problem areas previously treated as unrelated to think in common, that common thinking which is indispensible when dealing with such complex phenomena of which the recognizer and the resolver of the problem is a part. Thereupon, one of the important functions of systems research has been to remotivate consideration of concepts which, although left out, are widely recognized as needing to be grappled with. (Cavallo, 1979) It is especially interesting, that it was the methodological trends of the systems approach which created the situation in which numerous tools had earlier been employed whose usage began to be questioned. It was this experience in application which induced the heated arguments. Further, reinterpretation of concepts previously regarded as common in scientific practice, the investigation of the relation between theory and practice, and science and its application in a new correlation are being carried out. Why this change? Because instead of the traditional client-analyst relationship, participative problem solving is coming to the forefront; because the resolution of the conflict between the "ideal" concepts of rationality and optimality and the "practical" impossibilities, demands new methods and replenishing the old concepts with new contents.

What therefore is the cause of the debates and what the content? Why is it necessary to redefine certain concepts, and to replace others by new ones? And finally why did the argument over methodologies become more intensive? Let us start with the last question.

Systems engineering, systems analysis and finally, but not least, operational research belong to the group of methodologies which are applying systems approach. These methodologies are used in decision analysis in technical, economic, social, political fields as well as in planning, management etc. where they lead to a sequence of procedures like identifying and weighing the objectives, generating and comparing alternatives, implementation etc. In the course of using the procedures, the usefulness of the applied tools, and their suitability, becomes obvious sooner or later as in the majority of cases real problems demand concrete solutions. It is just the applications which created a new situation and new problems, and mainly in those countries where these methods were developed and first applied. In this connection we have to form an opinion on the current problems of operational research and systems analysis.

The situation in the field of operational research and management science may be reviewed in terms of the sarcastic lecture by the mathematician R. E. D. Woolsey at the 1978 IFORS Conference. (It should be remarked that the lectures at the plenary session of the conference were devoted to the basic problems of OR/MS and systems analysis experiences of the past, to the present problems and to the possible evolution of the future.)

"OR/MS had a utilitarian beginning, when the primary aim was to 'solve problems'. This was probably the golden age of utility and acceptance of OR/MS. Rapidly . . . the tool makers dominated the profession. There is now a counterrevolution against the tool makers being carried on by the tool users. We tool users have no illusions that we can live without the tool makers. We just realize that we have told them that their tools were unsatisfactory with no result." Today two apparently opposite viewpoints prevail: "The first totally committed to utility and elegance, the second committed to sophistication and the *hope* of utility." The two viewpoints do not always have to be in harmony, but only the two together can provide good solutions for a long time in terms of Woolsey. (Woolsey, 1978)

Other signs also point to the fact that the future of operational research, and at the same time the future of the application of mathematics to management, organizational and social sciences, lies not in the further refinement of the mathematical models but in the transformation of the working style (and this essentially implies a return to the inter-disciplinary team work in the heroic age of operational research).

It is significant, that the papers at the Soviet conference on systems analysis in 1978 in Obninsk were on exactly the same theme. (Obninsk, 1978; Kelle, 1979) They emphasized that complex social and economic problems – different from those of simple technical ones – do not allow optimal solutions, and mathematical models are only approximations which do not so much provide solutions as help to put up good questions. The papers stress those solutions in which there are conflicting objectives or several criteria, when no single individual makes a decision except on the basis of values of the groups.

The work of the All-Union Institute of Systems Research in Moscow is also remarkable from this point of view. They are developing interactive decision procedures or such models as avoid the separation between decision-makers and operational researcher/systems analyst. (Larichev, 1979) With the methods developed, they wish to ensure that the model analysing decision should serve not the modeller but the decision-maker. It is on account of this that Lapin emphasizes that systems analysis cannot be reduced to certain formalized methods. (Lapin, 1979) Actually over-formalization explains that in the United States, 20% of the decisions on major programs are based on such "scientific" methods of analysis.

As was shown in examples from the USA and USSR, and the list may be extended, there are problems in using scientific methodologies. It is evident, therefore, that there is contradiction between the exact methods of systems analysis and the decision-making in practice. What is the cause of this contradiction?

The significance of the methods in scientific research is well known. It is also known that the approach in certain scientific branches, as well as the uncritical acceptance of methods, has caused many disturbances to this day, in areas where they have been accepted mechanically. (For example the mechanical application of approaching the social phenomenon in a natural science way, like organizational research, has in many respects led to a dead-end.) At the same time, it is also true that certain methods which were worked out in other fields can be successfully applied in phenomena spheres deviating from the original. "Borrowing" methods is absolutely necessary in the research of new areas which do not dispose of appropriate methods to fit the nature of their particular subject. Criticism, checking of the assumptions, and investigation of the validity however are indispensible.

In scientific papers, but also in the daily newspapers, there are an increasing number of reports which regard the traditional method of natural science and technological approach as inadequate – on account of negative experiences – for solving different organizational, management and social problems. The modelling techniques which have become so widespread in the last 20–30 years are being especially criticized. The basic phenomenon is as follows: the scientific proposals for solution are made with a large amount of technical apparatus (formal models, computers) mainly as recommendations of an external body, and the results are never implemented. The phenomenon is repeated much too regularly, and could be explained by the unsuitability of the leaders of the organizations involved.

It can also be established as a fact, that such undesirable consequences can be attributed to the distorting method of approach, in which ideal presuppositions are made referring to man and his society. In conceiving the problem, it is common to exclude – on grounds of "scientific objectivity" – questions of interests, and problems of the value system, although these are fundamental in identifying the problem as well as in its solution.

As it is obvious that scientific information on man and his society belongs to social sciences (according to the traditional classification) it is therefore not surprising that the role and significance of social sciences are growing throughout the world. With the growth of the role of social sciences, for instance, we need to review our concepts of *rational* behaviour of human beings in organizations.

This is why the investigation of the *presuppositions* have a special role, since every modelling procedure is based on assumptions.

2. ON THE ASSUMPTIONS OF THE PRESENT METHODOLOGY

It may be useful at the start, and perhaps as a frame of reference, to reveal and define the assumptions relating to the problem. In all the material distributed at the seminar, there was some *kind of problem*, as in Churchman, *the systems thinking problem*, with Majone the *problem of pitfalls*, in Tomlinson *misconceptions*, in Blauberg–Sadovsky the *problem of the paradoxes*. However it had not been established just what the *fundamental problem* was, the genus proximum. Without this, as a consequence of the deviating interpretations functioning as concealed assumptions in the course of the discussion, new pitfalls, misconceptions would be generated. Bartee's understanding of the problem seems to be acceptable for us and this assumption of ours will now be made explicit.

> "A *problem* is defined here as an unsatisfied need to change a perceived present situation to a perceived desired situation. A *solution* to a problem is realized when the perceived present and desired situations are perceived to be the same. *Problem solving* is the activity associated with the change of a problem state to a solution state." (Bartee, 1973)

We think that this understanding of the problem and the problem solution is in harmony with, on the one hand, our experiences; on the other, it actually belongs to the Popper-like second world described by Majone:

> "Popper distinguishes three 'worlds' or levels of reality: first the world of physical objects and physical states, second, the world of mental states, of subjective preferences and beliefs; and third, a world of objective structures that are produced by human minds but which, once produced, exist independently of them (theories, artistic creations and styles, norms, institutions, problem situation, critical arguments). This 'World 3' is autonomous from the other two levels of reality, though it is related to them by a number of links and feedbacks." (Majone, 1980)

It is hard to believe therefore that in relation to our topic there are some in the East and the West who do not perceive any problems in connection with systems analysis because they are satisfied with the present situation and so they have no problems, subject preferences, and beliefs: their second world of Popper reflects everything as being in order.

For most of us, however, the situation is problematical or unsatisfactory and our motivation can be expressed by the title of the final chapter in this book, written by Tomlinson: "Doing something about the future" (Tomlinson, 1980).

This is like saying that all of us judge the situation to be problematic.

However it is not certain that we view the differences between the present and the desired situation, or the seriousness of the problem, in the same way. In fact when sketching the desired situation our standpoints may be varied. The fundamental problem may be expressed in the words of Susman and Evered in connection with a crisis in organizational science:

"The principal symptom of this crisis is that our research methods and techniques have become less useful for solving the practical problems that members of organizations face" (Susman–Evered, 1978).

In other words Blauberg–Sadovsky–Yudin also criticize abstract considerations isolated from real system investigation:

"This gap between the level of abstraction and that of concrete investigation is generally characteristic of the present state of systemic elaboration, and it inhibits the development of this work as a whole." (Blauberg–Sadovsky–Yudin, 1969)

Based on the previous statements, it may be possible that some of us regard the word "crisis" as an overstatement, claiming that the situation is not so serious. However, what we can be sure of, is that we all agree that there is a greater difference between theory and practice than in the acceptable and unavoidable. If we judge this well, *this* implies the essence and focal problem of our discussion. But what procedure is to be followed at the very beginning of inquiry?

Four possible relevant answers can be found in the history of thinking:

Francis Bacon: One must proceed purely inductively, putting all preconceived ideas, or Idols, aside.

René Descartes: One's procedure is purely rationalistic. One intellectually doubts everything which can possibly be doubted and then, from the indubitable minimum which remains, one *deduces* the remainder of one's knowledge.

Morris Cohen: Starting with the problem which initiates inquiry, coupled with scepticism with respect to traditional beliefs, one pursues hypotheses, testing them by the method of trial and error.

John Dewey: Since inquiry begins with a problematic situation, one must first observe the determinate facts, together with the indeterminate uncertainties of the situation, to suggest hypotheses respecting the possible resolution of its problematic character. These hypotheses in turn must be pursued to their deductive consequences and thereby checked operationally. (from Northrop, 1947)

In this way our discussion became a secondary decision problem for the methodology question. However this raises a host of questions. What for example do we regard as "facts", what as uncertainties?

"The potential for chaos in such a system is great, but it does not need to occur because every problem has a storehouse of knowledge and standards by which selection takes place. There is a simple control on the mechanism: the human mind, unable to tolerate chaos, moves inevitably to decrease the number of options and focus on something from which it can reason and test. Although an infinite number of claims might emerge on a single problem, they will not. Only a limited number will and soon one will be the focus, however temporarily. This characteristic of human thought is a wonderful thing and it shortens our work in finding solutions enormously, but it has its dangers. The mind may be attracted to easy claims that seem to solve problems but which have grave consequences." (Rieke–Sillars, 1975)

This excerpt is from a book on argumentation and decision-making and confirms Bartee's understanding of the nature of the problem whilst, at the same time emphasizing the tremendous significance of argumentation. This and the role of persuasion is accentuated by Majone too. "The question is not whether analysts should use persuasion in proposing new policy ideas, but which forms of persuasion may be used effectively and without violating basic principles of professional ethics." (Majone, 1980) If we accept this then there will be a double consequence of our present discussion. Firstly our present discussion is audience-centred; secondly the results – if there will be such – will have to take this into consideration in oral or written presentations.

Now what are considered to be facts and just what presumptions values and value systems our authors have can only be known from background material and from their other work and may be quite fragmentary. It may be supposed on the basis of this, that in recognizing the problem and diagnosing it, there will be many common features especially with respect to facts. However – and there are subtle causes for this – a diversity of opinion is characteristic. It is even more likely that in relation to the method of the solution – in which not only the deviating assumptions but the conditions anticipated by the participants, as well as the difference in *values* and *value systems*, have a major role – a much greater plurality is to be expected than in the former. This however, if we accept the principle of the dialectic approach proposed by Churchman or Mitroff, is no trouble. But while we consider the dialectic approach to be an excellent method for revealing the concealed assumptions, we can, with respect, imagine several solutions to solving the problem. In other words, it is not at all certain that with respect to the method of solution, a uniform standpoint can be worked out. We are therefore inclined to agree with the arguments of Van Gigch who, in his inspiring work published in 1976 (*Planning for Freedom*) propounded that "different kinds of planning spell different kinds of freedom(s). The planning paradigm consists of an 'assumptions-conditions-opportunities' triad by which the types of freedom prevailing in a system are determined. Due to the disparity among the elements of the triad from system to system, it is difficult to make intersystem comparisons of the amount of freedom which obtain."

3. TOWARDS A SOLUTION

The authors of these chapters certainly accept as a *fact* that, for example, the differences between Eastern and Western countries are not negligible. One Marxist principle about using concrete methods appropriate for different objects or systems has often been violated in the West by regarding certain procedures as generally acceptable, and by using pre-fabricated models to treat any object or system; the same approach has often caused difficulties in the socialist countries too. All this applies to concrete methods and procedures (namely to the tactical level of the methods) but does not imply that the methodology policy (and strategy) at greater depth, and built on more abstract assumptions and of much wider validity, could not be worked out. It is clear, however, that at this level we have to accept a more philosophical mode of discussion, although there are quite a few who regard this as empty speculation; in fact the positivists smell in it a brand of new metaphysics. The suspicion of the positivists has not been mentioned accidentally. It is precisely in this area that the more serious methodological pitfalls of the more subtle assumptions are concealed.

Majone mentions the burdens of the heritage of scientific method: "The received view on scientific method, which in one form or another has dominated the philosophy of science from the 1920s to the 1950s, has by now only historical interest for the specialists but it is still accepted by many researchers as a general scientific ideology. In particular, the influence of logical positivism – a key component of the received view – has been felt throughout the social and behavioral sciences, and nowhere more strongly than in the study of decision-making." (Majone, 1980)

As the close connection between systems analysis and decision-making is well known and since "during the past decade, the focus of research on system theory and systems analysis has shifted towards the analysis of large-scale systems in which human judgement, perception and emotions play an important role" therefore either on the basis of the interdisciplinary principle or on the dialectic approach method we have to take into account the large-scale systems inherently containing the human element, or the standpoint of the researchers in their *organizations*. But the positivist approach is not appropriate – from the marxist viewpoint either – for solving organizational or even social problems. We agree with Susman and Evered's claim in that "what appears at first to be a crisis of relevancy or usefulness of organizational science is, we feel, really a crisis of epistemology. This crisis has risen, because organizational researchers have taken the positivist model of science, which has had great heuristic value for the physical and biological sciences and some field of the social sciences, and have adopted it as the ultimate model of what is best for organizational science. By limiting its methods to what it claims is value-free, logical, and empirical, the positivist model of science, when applied to organizations, produces a knowledge that may only inadvertently serve and sometimes undermine the values of organizational members." (Susman–Evered)

The term *positivist science* is used for all approaches to science that consider scientific knowledge to be obtainable from only sense data that can be directly experienced and verified among independent observers.

We are primarily concerned with the assumptions lying beyond the positivist approach methods. All positivist approaches to science (P.S.) are deficient in their capacity for generating knowledge for use by members of organizations for solving problems they face. The following arguments explain this deficiency.

"P.S. assumes that its methods are value neutral", but "knowledge and human interests are interwoven, as reflected in the choice of methods and the ends towards which such methods are put".

"P.S. treats persons as objects of inquiry, even though they are subjects or initiators of action in their own right."

"P.S. eliminates the role of history in the generation of knowledge. Individuals and organizations are not born in an instant with their present structures and functions intact. Rather, present patterns of behavior can many times only be understood as the product of shared definitions held by organizational members regarding what their common endeavor is about."

"P.S. assumes that a system is defined only to the extent that a denotative language exists to describe it. However, any representational system is always less than the actual system leaving the practising manager to rely on intuition, hunch, interpretation, etc. P.S. generally acknowledges that such methods can be precursors to scientific knowledge, but it does not consider them by themselves to be legitimate scientific methods."

"P.S. is itself a product of the human mind, thus knowledge of the inquirer cannot be excluded from an understanding of how knowledge is generated." (Susman–Evered)

It is not difficult to realize that with this elucidation we have come closer to the roots, although in contrast with this some would acknowledge John Stuart Mill's viewpoint. He claimed that "the relations of the basic principles and science are not like the comparison between the foundations and the house built on it, but that of the roots and the tree. The roots fulfil their task perfectly even if it is not dug down to bring them to the daylight." (Mill, 1863)

In our case, however, we had to dig down to the roots, because as it emerged from the description, the positivist roots in contrast with the physical sciences did not fulfil their role. As Checkland remarks: "The positivist methods of science applied to the physical regularities of the universe are not problematical. However, the question as to whether social phenomena may be investigated by the methods of science is highly problematical. Is 'social science' science? It is a live issue. ... 'Systems Analysis' of the Rand Corporation variety, 'Systems Engineering' and most of the 'Operational Research' studies which get reported are positivistic in this issue.

"All these approaches have severe limitations on the face of the rich complexity of the real world and in the last decade 'Soft systems methodology' has emerged as part of the struggle to respond to these problems." (Checkland, 1979)

We consider that the theoretical and practical deficiencies in the claims of Churchman, Majone, Tomlinson, Boothroyd, Blauberg–Sadovsky, Farkas and others in applied systems sciences, looking at their roots, may be also traced back to the unsatisfactory positivist approach method.

If this is so, then essentially two policies may be worked out to avoid the consequences of the deficiencies. One is of the type "Beware of the pitfalls" or warning that in the course of systems analysis, systems research, what kind of pitfalls can be counted on. This kind of methodological policy is somewhat frightening. The question is however, whether it is worthwhile to proceed on such a path where there are so many pitfalls? There is only a little chance that however carefully we proceed we are bound to fall into one or another pitfall.

As another alternate policy some kind of new approach is necessary.

4. ON A POSSIBLE APPROACH TO BE MORE "SCIENTIFIC"

Among the authors of this book there seems to be a surprising essential agreement on the key term of "*action*" in the new approach. That this approach, built on what many call *action research*, radically deviates from the traditional approach is well reflected by Tomlinson (1980).

In this chapter, as in that written by Checkland, a subtle assumption is disclosed: namely, the norm, or perhaps the myth, of scientism. The excellent Soviet mathematician Ju. Srejder's remark is most fitting; that is, if today we call something "scientific" this just about means the same as when it was said in the Middle Ages "according to the teaching of the Church"; that is, it suggests infallibility, an aura of a convincing power and certainty. Therefore the adjective "scientific" has the same laudatory connotation as, according to Majone, the term "analysis" has.

If we accept this characterization then it already appears that there are certain contradictions. Miser, Majone, Tomlinson and others, as well as scientists from the socialist countries (Gvishiani, Blauberg) stress that there is a living, successful, activity which is not, or only sporadically, reflected in the literature.

At the same time this successful activity – whether we call it action research or something else – is pre-scientific and "has developed through personal experience and intuition". This is called "craft" in systems analysis. The dilemma is therefore the following: there is successful activity – in our case "the craft of systems analysis" – but this is not "scientific"; the scientific approach (for example current operational research) is not *successful*. It should however be just the opposite: we ought to prefer the scientific approach, because it is more useful and successful. To solve the dilemma two alternatives are available. One of these was conceived by Atkinson and is that "one must grasp the fundamental difference between the *practical-problem orientation* and *basic-science orientation* which exists in all fields of scientific endeavor.

"When *practical-problem orientation* prevails, the matters considered are always matters of obvious social significance. It is, in fact, the immediate social importance of a problem which defines the need for empirical, trial-and-check efforts to find solutions.... The guiding intention of technological research on these matters is efficient solution of the immediate problem.

"*Basic-science orientation* is different. Here the intention is to contribute to the growth of a conceptual scheme which will account for some phenomenon more adequately than does the conventional wisdom (common sense) of the time. The conceptual analysis of a general problem leads to interest in some events that may appear very trivial when evaluated in terms of social importance.

"The intention of basic research is to contribute to the growth of a conceptual scheme and that the significance of solving some immediate empirical problem is to be evaluated solely in terms of the degree to which the solution does or does not contribute in some way to the enhancement of fundamental knowledge about the phenomena being studied." (Atkinson, 1964)

In our opinion, however, the other alternative is more appropriate. According to this view the criteria of being scientific have developed on the basis of natural sciences. So the "covering law" idea may be found in Atkinson's characterization tool. "Covering law is the term which Hempel (1965) a leading contemporary philosopher of the formalist school, applied to a general law which explains a particular case by 'covering' or subsuming it. Covering laws are the basis for the only two kinds of explanation that Hempel considered as meriting the label of being scientific, that is the deductive-nomological and the inductive statistical forms." (Susman–Evered, 1978)

If we consider the norms of positivist science as the yardstick, then we may regard action research as unscientific. This was the conclusion that Susman and Evered reached too: "We find that action research is not compatible with the criteria for scientific explanation as established by positivist science. Hempel's covering-law model of explanation would not grant action research the status of a valid science. However in action research the ultimate sanction is in the perceived functionality of chosen actions to produce desirable consequences for an organization." Susman and Evered accentuate the philosophical viewpoints of action research, underlying that "While adherents of positivist science can cite several philosophical viewpoints as a foundation for legitimating its methods, action researchers can do the same with different philosophical viewpoints."

Some of the viewpoints will be enumerated in the form of key-words only; praxis, hermeneutics, existentialism, process philosophies and phenomenology.

Some of these are considered especially important on account of the lines represented here.

1. Praxis, which refers to the art of acting upon the conditions one faces in order to change them. Its significance has to be pointed out, since from a marxist point of view it was one of the basic focal thoughts of Marx as in his often quoted thesis: "The philosophers interpreted the world in different ways; the task is to *change* that." ("Die Philosophen haben die Welt nur verschieden interpretiert es kommt an, sie zu verandern." These über Feuerbach)

2. The hermeneutic viewpoint of action research is connected by two threads to the background material. On the one hand in respect of the presupposition (Mitroff, 1979) "the idea of the hermeneutical circle is that no knowledge is possible without presuppositions", on the other in respect of holistic interpretation (systems thinking). As Churchman has said, "In the social sciences, the hermeneutical circle takes the form of attempting an initial holistic understanding of a social system and then using this understanding as a basis for interpreting the parts of the system. Knowledge is gained dialectically by proceeding from the whole to its parts and then back again. . . . The hermeneutical tradition strengthens the action researcher's methodological position by forewarning him that his interpretations of a social system will never be exactly the same as held by the members of the social system. This provides the action researcher with a base for understanding his own preconceptions better and by contrast those held by system members, and also allows him to see possible solutions not seen by system members." (Churchman, 1968)

3. In Checkland's opinion the point of a soft systems methodology is Husserlian phenomenology. "Developed experimentally, this approach (i.e. soft systems methodology) turns out to be based in the alternative tradition of social science, that of Husserlian phenomenology." (Checkland, 1979)

4. Action research has much in common with *existentialism*. Both arose out of concern with limitations of rationalistic science, both assert the importance of human choice and human values, both are keyed to the importance of human action, and both avoid giving traditional causal explanations of human actions.

We can see therefore that action research may be based on philosophical theories, though doubtless these digress from the theory based on positivist methodology. If we wished to reply to Checkland's question of whether social science is a science, then our answer would be "yes", but not in the traditional positivist sense and its criteria have still to be worked out, of course, not on traditional positivist bases. The question may be asked: Is there any need for this at all? The answer is rather simple because "science" and "scientific" are "good" words, that is their connotation is positive and will remain so for a long time. This has to be taken into consideration, if we wish to view systems analysis and systems research in an "audience-centred" way and this in our opinion, on account of their function, is almost necessary.

5. CONCLUDING REMARKS

After surveying the application of the different methodologies based on systems thinking we could find quite a lot of contradictions in their usage. From one point of view this could be judged as the dead end of these methodologies; but from another – and from our viewpoint as well – it means the source of further development, that is the condition of improving these methodologies. (Gvishiani, 1979)

In the current Soviet yearbook of Systems Research there are several papers dealing with the philosophical side of the subject. Even more significantly the subtitle of the yearbook is: *Methodological Problems.* One of the papers is entitled: *Systems analysis, as a program for scientific research.* (Nappelbaum, 1980) Instead of forecasting – which would be extremely difficult in this phase of evolution, because we are now at a breaking point in it – Nappelbaum claims considering tendencies, raising questions for creating conceptions. It is necessary because the methodologies are currently under change, and this is why they are becoming the immediate subject of research. What is the reason for this process? All of these methodologies – cybernetics, operational research current the day before yesterday, management science yesterday, and systems analysis today – were developed for social demands. The wave of events lifted systems analysis to the highest position among the methodologies, and now its – or any other methodology's – shift from this position depends on how the given methodology fulfils those social demands which created them.

One of the main features of a systems analyst is the higher sensitivity of information. Considering this sensitivity, the systems analysts have to realize that the facts on the surface are only syndromatic signs of a problem but they need diagnosis, have to be reconsidered with respect to the primary information to be able to improve the methodologies, but at the same time, they cannot wait for the development of a more scientific background. This will be developed by providing systems analyses, during which they have to apply their craft knowledge. But in doing so – emphasizes Nappelbaum – never forget the cardinal feature of systems research, that it is "action-oriented" because of the human beings involved in all of the systems investigated or treated by systems approach.

From the methodological point of view systems analysis in its present form can be regarded as a subset of special methodologies. That is to say systems analysis is one version of *systems approach.*

"*Methodology* in general is regarded as a branch of philosophy, and might be deemed to compromise all philosophic mathematical and scientific methods. In contrast to this sum-total of all rational ways of pursuing knowledge there are special methodologies which emerge either out of needs of specific disciplines or out of a specific attitude towards reality. The *systems approach seems to be such a special methodology* rather than a new science or superscience. In particular it is a methodology which grows out of a holistic view, and thus not bound to a single discipline or a limited number of them. The holistic view is no novelty but requires the acceptance of certain basic assumptions." (Mattessich, 1979) Regarding the systems-oriented methodologies, the more basic assumptions are considered the deeper is the foundation of the methodology. This is why systems methodologies emancipate "thought from traditional schemata, which hindered the posing and solving of new problems of cognition. The emancipation is more effective the deeper its methodological core is perceived." (Blauberg–Sadovsky–Yudin, 1969)

The present day systems analysis has a traditional schemata as well. This traditional line of systems analysis has laid great stress *on analysis* having used mostly analytical methods and procedures which have been based on positivistic assumptions. In this sense systems analysis has been not so much *systems* analysis as *systematic* analysis and because of this strongly marked feature its scope of application has been curtailed to systems "free from man". Attempts to enlarge this narrow approach to *organizations* have not met with success.

The term itself, *systems analysis*, has some inconsistency as "analysis" conflicts with the holistic view represented by the connotation of the term "systems". The time has come to change the old term, coining a new one which is basically consistent. Perhaps "*systems inquiry*" would be appropriate as not having a "contradiction in terms" (contradictio in adiecto).

The main point, however, is that the course of systems analysis has to be changed if it is to keep its usefulness in coping with really significant human systems.

REFERENCES

Ackoff, R. L. and Emery, F. E. (1972) On purposeful systems. Aldine–Atherton, Chicago.
Ackoff, R. L. (1979) The future of Operational Research is Past. *J. Opl. Res. Soc.*, **30**, No. 2.
Atkinson, John W. (1964) An introduction to motivation. Van Nostrand Co., Princeton.

Bartee, E. M. (1973) A holistic view of problem solving. *Management Science*, **20**, No. 4.

Blauberg, I. V., Sadovsky, V. N. and Yudin, E. G. (1977) Systems Theory – Philosophical and Methodological Problems. Progress Publishers, Moscow (in English).

Blauberg, I. V., Sadovsky, V. N. and Yudin, E. G. (1980) The systemic approach: Prerequisites, Problems and Difficulties. General Systems, **XXV**, pp. 1–31. (First was published in Russian in 1969)

Blumer, H. (1956) Sociological analysis and the variable. *American Sociological Review*, **21**. (Ref. in Susman–Evered)

Boothroyd, H. (1978) Articulate Intervention – The interface of science, mathematics and administration. Taylor and Francis, London.

Boulding, K. E. (1956) In Cavallo, pp. 21–22.

Cavallo, R. E. (ed.) (1979) Systems Research Movement: Characteristics, Accomplishments, and Current Development. General Systems Bulletin Special Issue – Summer, **IX**, No. 3. (A Report Sponsored by the Society for General Systems Research)

Checkland, P. B. (1979) Systems methodology in problem-solving: some notes from experience in Progress in Cybernetics and Systems Research, **V**, Hemisphere Pub.

Checkland, P. B. (1979) Techniques in "Soft" Systems Practice, Part 2: Building Conceptual models. *J. Appl. Syst. Anal.*, **6**.

Cherns, A. B., Clark, P. A. and Jenkins, W. I. (1976) Action research and development of the social sciences, in Alfred W. Clark (ed.). Experimenting with organizational life: The Action Research Approach, Plenum, New York. (Ref. in Susman–Evered)

Churchman, C. W. (1968) Systems Approach, Dell., New York.

Churchman, C. W. (1979) The Systems Approach and its Enemies, Basic Books, New York.

Farkas, J. The hidden, lacking or erroneous presuppositions of systems theory, Background paper to this seminar. (Shortened and revised version included)

Gvishiani, D. M. (ed.) (1978) Systems Analysis and the Management of Scientific-Technological Progress. Academy of Sciences of the USSR, Moscow (in Russian).

Gvishiani, D. M. (1979) Systems Approach and the Methodological Problems of Systems Analysis, in Systems Research (Yearbook in Russian), Nauka, Moscow, pp. 7–28.

Habermas, Jurgen (1971) Knowledge and human interests. Beacon, Boston. (Ref. in Susman–Evered)

Hempel, C. G. (1965) Aspects of scientific explanation and other essays in the philosophy of science. Free Press, New York. (Ref. in Susman–Evered)

Husserl, E. (1972) Selected essays (Hungarian transl.) Gondolat Kiadó, Budapest.

Kelle, V. V. (1979) The methodological problems of systems analysis. Voprosi Filozofii, No. 3 (in Russian).

Klir, G. (1979) In Cavallo, p. 24.

Kluckhohn, C. (1951) Values and value-orientations on the theory of action. Toward a general theory of action, T. Parsons and A. Shils, eds. Harper and Row, New York, p. 395. (cited by Rieke Sillars)

Lapin, N. I. (1979) Methods of Modelling in Systems Analysis, in Systems Research (in Russian).

Larichev, O. I. (1978) Decision Making – Art and Science, Nauka, Moscow (in Russian).

Majone, G. (1980) Policies as Theories. IIASA RR-80-17, Laxenburg. Reprinted from OMEGA: *The International Journal of Management Science*, **8**.

Majone, G. and Quade, E. S. (ed.) (1980) Pitfalls of Analysis. Wiley, Chichester.

Martin, R. (1978) In Cavallo, p. 12.

Mattessich, Richard (1979) Instrumental Reasoning and Systems Methodology, D. Reidel, Dordrecht, Holland/Boston, USA.

Mill, J. S. (1863) Utilitarianism. Reprinted from *Frazer's Magazine*, London.

Mitroff, I. I., Emshoff, J. R. and Kilmann, R. H. (1979) Assumptional analysis: a methodology for strategic problem solving. *Management Science*, **25**, No. 6.

Nappelbaum, E. L. (1980) Systems analysis – as a program for scientific research. Systems Research Vol. 1979. Nauka, Moscow (in Russian).

Northrop, F. S. C. (1947) Logic of the sciences and humanities. The Macmillan Co., New York (cited by Rieke Sillars).

Peirce, S. S. (1877) Illustrations of the logic of science. First paper – The Fixation of belief. The Popular Science Monthly, 12.

Perelman, Chaim and Olbrechts-Tyteca, L. (1971) The new rhetoric – Univ. Notre Dame Press, Notre Dame (Ind.).

Rieke, R. D. and Sillars, M. O. (1975) Argumentation and the decision making process. Wiley, New York.

Rosen, R. (1979) In Cavallo, p. 33.

Susman, G. I. (1976) Autonomy at work: a sociotechnical analysis of participative management. Praeger, New York. (Ref in Susman–Evered)

Susman, G. I. and Evered, R. D. (1978) An assesment of the scientific merits of action research. *Administrative Science Quarterly*, 23 (Dec.).

Tomlinson, R. (1980) Doing Something about the Future. *J. Opl. Res. Soc.*, 31, pp. 467–476.

Tomlinson, R. (1976) Some dangerous misconceptions concerning ORASA (EURO III. Closing address). WP-79-67. IIASA, Laxenburg.

Van Gigch, J. P. (1976) Planning for freedom. *Management Science*, 22, No. 9.

Woolsey, R. E. D. (1978) Pragmatism triumphant or past sophistication and future elegance. In Haley, K. B. (ed.): Operational Research '78, Proc. of the Eighth IFORS International Conference, North-Holland, Amsterdam.

2

Systems Approach and Systems Analysis

I. V. BLAUBERG, E. M. MIRSKY and V. N. SADOVSKY

INTRODUCTION

Assessing the modern state of systems research, its potentiality and perspective for further development, it is necessary first of all to pay attention to three circumstances which to a large extent define the present-day situation in this field.

Firstly, there is a steadily (in any case within the last 10–15 years) growing requirement for conducting systems research in very different fields of science, technology and practical activity. The number of supporters of systems research has been increasing every year; specialists in different sciences, from theoreticians to policy-makers, hope to solve the problems facing them with help from its methods.

These hopes are not unfounded, because, *secondly*, systems research has by now already convincingly demonstrated its practical usefulness. Research on the global problems of the modern world, the working-out of long-term programs to solve energy, ecological, food and other similar problems, the extension of the methodology tools of systems analysis, as well as much systems-theoretical work in the sphere of the fundamental science – all these testify to the undoubted effectiveness of systems research.

But at the same time, *thirdly*, it should be noted that in spite of the evident practical results, modern systems research continues to be rather unsatisfactorily grounded from the theoretical point of view. We specially emphasize the need to tackle the problem of the theoretical foundations of modern systems research, because the history of systems research development and especially its general philosophical foundations are essentially better understood. Amidst Marxist philosophers it is generally accepted that Marxist–Leninist dialectics is the philosophical foundation of systems research methods[16, 20] and that these methods had their roots at least in classical philosophy.[28] When it comes to the building of a common systems concept capable of synthesizing a number of differently oriented systems theories and investigational results, then researchers still face some essential difficulties.

Two general systems approaches developed during the first post-war years – the general system theory of L. von Bertalanffy[5] and N. Wiener's Cybernetics[35] – which exerted an important stimulating influence upon the development of systems research. Unfortunately because of the many limitations and imperfections inherent in them, they are not able nowadays to serve as a theoretical basis for modern systems research.

Authors, who subsequently attempted to elaborate general systems theory in various ways, as a rule sought to express their ideas in a strictly scientific form, most commonly in terms of mathematics (M. Mesarović,[24] R. Ackoff,[1] R. Kalman,[18] G. J. Klir,[19] N. P. Buslenko,[6] N. N. Moiseyev,[26] A. I. Uemov[34] and many others). Nevertheless, from the outset they each largely limited their attention to systems of definite classes and types. In most cases they did not even try to elaborate foundations of systems methods as a whole. Post-Wiener variants of cybernetics (W. Ross Ashby,[2] H. von Foerster,[13] G. Pask,[20] A. I. Berg,[3] V. M. Glushkov[15] and others) were being developed in the same way. Finally, it must be stated that systems analysis (as usually understood) cannot play the role of providing a theoretical foundation to modern systems research even though today its own methods and conceptual means seem to be elaborated in detail. The fact is that systems analysis has to do only with methods of decision-making in the problems arising in sociotechnical systems[21] and this does not cover the whole sphere of systems research at all.

Moreover, the need to develop theoretical foundations for systems research is also conditioned by the fact that nowadays systems research is understood to represent a rather vast and ultimately diverse spectrum of scientific and technical disciplines, research and design studies etc. (ranging from disciplines of a rather general character like general systems theory, theoretical cybernetics and mathematical systems theory to strictly concrete models of the functioning of special systems in the fields of biology, psychology, social behaviour etc.). It is extremely difficult to establish general criteria which are relevant to this whole, and in any case it may be done only after certain crucial problems, concerning specific theoretical and methodological features of systems research methods, have been solved.

The situation has led to the rise of many critics of systems research methods in recent years (I. Hoos,[17] Y. Dror,[12] G. Majone,[30] L. Lynn,[13] D. Berlinski[14] and others). The need to reply to these criticisms and thus create conditions for the further progress of systems research (the latter is the chief aim) calls for the urgent solution of a large complex of problems connected with the theoretical and methodological base of systems research. Some of these problems will be considered in this article.

SYSTEMS ANALYSIS CRITICISM AND ITS LESSONS

In the above-mentioned critical works directed against systems research *systems analysis* is analysed as a methodology for studying and solving complex economic, socio-technological and ecological problems which face the modern world. In this way the criticism is directed not only and not mainly at individual failures in the attempt to apply systems analytical methods and procedures. As a rule, the problem raised is broader than this. The argument in question is whether systems analysis as a general approach is able to correspond to those problems towards whose solution it has been created and fashioned and in connection with which it has been demonstrating its effectiveness for many years.

Systems analysis in these critical works is often given a very broad interpretation, as if it were a synonym of "systems research methods as a whole". The book entitled *On Systems Analysis* by D. Berlinski[4] is typical in this respect: much space in it is paid to criticism of the general systems ideas of L. von Bertalanffy, E. Laszlo, M. Mesarović and others, when in fact their connection with systems analysis is rather remote. In other critical works, for instance, those by I. Hoos[17] and Majone and Quade,[30] systems analysis is understood in its own, specific, meaning of this term.

One rather essential thing should be explained at once. In this chapter we are not going to defend systems analysis from its external critics and opponents – though of course such a defence could be made. To our mind, trying to be constructive, this aspect of the polemical debate is neither decisive nor interesting for systems research specialists. Besides, there is no urgent necessity to defend systems analysis since, at present at least, none of the critics are able to suggest a methodological approach that can compete with it. Indeed, they cannot even state connected principles which would provide the basis for elaborating such an approach in the future.

Voices of another timbre are prevalent in the critical choir. Dissatisfaction with the level of theoretical inquiry and of the effectiveness of many practical applications of systems analysis are first expressed most strongly by specialists who are professionally engaged in developing some particular sphere of systems problems. In other words, we refer to criticism of a reflective character arising from attempts to generalize and to comprehend critically the accumulated experience of systems research, undertaken as a necessary precondition to improve on this experience. The publications already mentioned which have appeared in the last years (see particularly reference 30), and the discussions that have taken place at a number of symposia and conferences, testify to this. The IIASA seminar on which this book is based, having the rather symptomatic discussion theme "Rethinking the process of systems analysis", was typical in this respect. In addition to IIASA staff, well-known specialists from a number of countries engaged either in research in systems problems, practical applications of systems analysis or teaching activities connected with systems analysis, were also invited to take part in the seminar. It is worth noting here that the important feature of the seminar was striving to find some general theoretical-methodological foundations on the basis of which it would be possible to comprehend and interpret problems of systems analysis.

To our mind, the *systems approach* as its theoretical and methodological reflexion may serve *as the basis for elaboration of systems analysis problems.* Later, when speaking of the structure of systems research as a whole, we shall moreover touch upon functions of systems approach. We should like to direct your attention to the following circumstances, in order to avoid terminological confusion and to clarify our own position. The reference to a systems approach seems to be appropriate because it is within its framework that some positive experience of methodological research in the application of systems ideas to different areas of science (biology, psychology, ecology and so on) has been accumulated. On the other hand, the reflective component is not yet developed well enough within systems analysis. Overdramatization of the general situation currently established in systems analysis makes no sense . . .

In the history of science it has been noted again and again that new and promising studies usually pass through three stages of their appreciation.

1. The stage *of enthusiastic acclaim and indiscriminate overestimation* of results achieved in different fields of science. The mixing up of hopes and real perspectives is also present.

2. The stage *of scathing and largely unfair criticism* when the major attack is directed mainly against the discrepancy between the personal expectations of a particular critic and the real achievements of the emerging discipline.

3. The stage *of relatively smooth and peaceful development* accompanied by elaboration of the discipline's theoretical foundations as well as increasing efficiency of applied results.

Systems analysis now seems to be at the second stage of this process and there is no reason to doubt that it will enter the third period of its development very soon.

It should be noted that in the shower of critical comments about SA a prevailing theme is to reproach it for its ineffectiveness when applied to the study of social, economic, political and similar processes. This inefficiency may be explained by the fact that the tools of SA are evidently inadequate for the development of authentic models of complicated socio-economic systems. One cannot but admit that this criticism is a well-founded one. At the same time however it should be stressed that the same qualifications are equally valid for other approaches and should not be regarded as applicable to SA only. These obvious shortcomings reflect specific features of a common process, which is under way in various domains of science and practice, and is connected, on the one hand, with the need to gain a more exact and objective understanding of social, economic, biological, psychological, etc. phenomena and, on the other hand, with the inability of existing applied mathematics to meet all the demands created by that understanding. Both these problems are widely discussed elsewhere (and not only in the literature on systems studies) and gradually a rather encouraging convergence of previously alarmingly diverging opinions is emerging. Moreover, in many cases the way to this rapprochement has been paved precisely with the help of systems approach conceptual ideas.

As to SA itself, its status, possibilities, prospects and limitations (particularly applied systems analysis), there is still a very long way to go before the debating sides can settle their differences. In fact the reverse process is taking place, and a relative concord is giving way to a more and more explicit divergence of opinions about problems of crucial importance, and this is happening not only between systems analysts and external opponents but also amongst the most ardent supporters of systems ideas. In this connection it seems to be appropriate to draw some conclusions relating to the criticism of systems analysis which is under way now.

It is typical that in the dissenting studies examined here the main lines of criticism are focused around a range of problems of paramount importance for the future of systems studies methodology. All these problems, without a single exception, were known to people active in systems studies some 10–15 years ago (see [7, 31, 33, 34, 37]). We refer here to the problems of wholeness, of system boundary demarcation, of adequate reflection in a system representation, the ties connecting the system with the environment, and the structural representation of the environment etc. To repeat, all these problems have been formulated years ago although, for various reasons which we will comment upon later, they were not researched as intensively and productively as they should have been.

At the same time if we are going to limit ourselves to reducing all the existing difficulties to already established theoretical and methodological problems, we would find it most difficult not only to envisage the future prospects for systems studies development but even to answer a much simpler question, namely to explain the success and effectiveness of systems studies, and SA in particular, which have been demonstrated in a variety of research fields and in management practice in recent years. Indeed it is exactly these achievements that have provoked such a wide acceptance of systems methodology. Such a question does not have to bother an external opponent of SA but the answer to it is one of the major prerequisites *for systems analysis rethinking* and for finding ways to perfect it.

Thus even the above examination of the overall situation in which systems analysis now rests indicates that for an effective conceptualization and reconceptualization one must: first, investigate relations between various forms and kinds of systems studies; second, consider – along with the purely methodological questions – certain organizational aspects of the formation and development of the systems analysis activity; third, digress from time to time into history of systems studies. Naturally, we shall not be able to touch upon all these problems here and will concentrate our attention on the "hottest spots" of the problematique of modern systems research.

STRUCTURE OF MODERN SYSTEMS RESEARCH AND THE PROBLEM OF "WHOLENESS"

To solve the problems formulated above, it is necessary to classify the main types of systems studies with respect to the level of generality, their tasks and function in the realm of scientific and practical activity. To our mind it is essential to develop an adequate typology of this kind because above all it makes it possible to formulate questions about *the internal interactions inside the scope of system studies* which take place between the various forms of knowledge, scientific activity, technical art and, equally important, between people with different professional backgrounds. Earlier in some of our papers (see e.g. [8, 32]) we have proposed to this end to make a distinction between the philosophical systems principle, the systems approach and systems analysis. Let us shortly describe these directions of the modern systems research.

By *the systems principle* we mean a principle in compliance with which a phenomenon of objective reality, as viewed through the relations of the systems wholeness and interactions of the components which constitute it, creates a specific epistemological prism or a specific reality "dimension" ([20], p. 10). In such an interpretation the systems principle is indeed a philosophical one embracing the conceptions of the wholeness of objects, of the reality of the relation between the whole and its parts, of the system-environment interaction as of one of the prerequisites of systems existence, of the structural nature of any systemic object, etc. It is quite obvious that the systems principle pedigree can be traced right back to classical philosophy (see [28] for more details). As to methodological considerations, reliance upon the systems principle provides a researcher with a certain general conception, with a certain vision of the essence of complicated transient objects. This conception turns out to be closely connected both with the historico-philosophical retrospection, as revealing the makings and application of various epistemological-cognitive conceptions and with modern problems covering the methodology of science. However to carry these general methodological ideas consistently through in a specific scientific study one has to provide them with a much more concrete and detailed expression cast into specific methodological constructs. Development and advancement of such constructs is a main objective of the *systems approach*.

The *systems approach* is one of the forms of methodological knowledge and is directly connected to analysis, synthesis and design of objects as systems. It is essentially interdisciplinary and supradisciplinary by nature. Among the major systems approach problems are: 1. The problem of development of conceptual tools, both meaningful and formal, permitting one to represent objects as systems; 2. The problem of generalized systems modelling, as well as the problem of modelling oriented toward the different kinds or different properties of systems, e.g. system dynamics, system goal-seeking behaviour, system development, system hierarchical structure, system control processes etc.; 3. The problem of analysis of the methodological foundations of the various systems theories. Every problem from this list, whilst having a distinct methodological flavour typologically, is not beyond the scope of concrete scientific knowledge as we have it through the present methodology of science. However for its validation and development the systems approach calls for some philosophical knowledge and has to rely in particular upon the systems principle.

Finally, *systems analysis* being the latest form of systems study and one which is especially distinguished for its applied orientation, may be regarded as the advanced offspring of operational research and, to some extent, system engineering – which were a great success in the fifties and sixties. Along with its predecessors, systems analysis is first and foremost a mind of scientific and technological activity applied to the analysis and design of complicated and over-complicated objects. When it proved impossible to justify an analytic solution, whether in terms of principle or practicality – as was the case e.g. for environment protection, adequate food provision on the world scale, global modelling and other similar problems – there was no way out but to consider the problems as complex problems calling for the use of the entire range of existing techniques (heuristic methods and devices included). Following this argument, systems analysis is a specific type of scientific and engineering art which may bring in impressive results in the hands of an experienced professional, and may equally result in a near waste of effort when practised mechanistically and unimaginatively. (Unfortunately the latter fault occurs rather frequently.)

From the methodological viewpoint, the remarkable effectiveness of systems analysis at the early stages of development can be attributed chiefly to a conscious use of the integrated systems representation of the problems and of the situations analysed and designed i.e. the utilization of the concept of *wholeness*. At the time it was a conceptual breakthrough because whereas a holistic vision of phenomena and processes was already fairly well entrenched (though not universally) in the realm of philosophical and methodological thought, it was, still somewhat alien and speculative to thinking in engineering and applied science. Nevertheless it is this realm (that of engineering and applied science) which is the main sphere of systems analysis. The conscious study of objects to examine if they possessed characteristic wholeness immediately broadened the scope of applied knowledge and practical systems development, for it has encouraged the analyst to take into consideration and to predict interrelations between systems components which had previously been completely neglected. Why then, has the effectiveness of systems analysis lessened and why have many systems analysts chosen to look back to simpler, basically analytical (rather than holistically-synthetic), purely formal (rather than meaningful) approaches? In our opinion, the heart of the matter is not only in the growing complexity of the objects being studied with the help of SA, or the problems to be treated by it. First and foremost the explanation lies in the fact that the "wholeness" concept exploited in earlier studies has gradually exhausted its heuristic potential. It has been in fact a *concept* of wholeness wholly lacking in adequate definition, – not a *concept* of wholeness within the rigorous, philosophical theoretical meaning of the term that earlier studies have been trying to capitalize on.

To account for this idea let us refer to J. van Gigch "Applied general systems theory".[14] This author quotes Hegel's statements concerning the interactions of the whole and its parts in a chapter devoted to the main principles of general systems theory. He writes in particular that the works of Hegel contain some ideas which form the basis of general systems theory, for example:

1. The whole is more than the sum of its parts.
2. The whole defines the nature of its parts.
3. The parts looked at apart from the whole can not be properly described.
4. The parts are constantly interconnected and interdependent.

It is doubtful if one can accept this as a proper interpretation of Hegel's view of the problem. Firstly, it should be noted that the authorship of some of these statements can not be directly ascribed to Hegel: for example, the thesis of non-summativity of the whole originates from Plato and Aristotle. It is particularly important that the cited statements were not regarded as indisputable truths, either before Hegel or later,* and this circumstance itself needs clarification.

It should be noted that an effective application of the concept of wholeness as a definite methodological tool in a concrete scientific study requires far

---

* Here it is instructive to recall J. J. Rousseau's objection to L. M. Deschamps in connection with his approach to the problem of whole and parts (incidentally, in the French historico-philosophical literature of the nineteenth century L. M. Deschamps was often regarded as a forerunner of Hegelian learning): "We judge with the help of induction within certain bounds, we judge about the whole by its parts. But it seems to me that you do just the opposite in deducing knowledge about the whole. I am not able to understand this . . ." (see (11, p. 13)). Let us venture to state that arguments like this would be accepted with sympathy by a considerable number of specialists who work in concrete spheres of knowledge.

more than a mere affirmation of the holistic nature of the object under investigation and to the conclusions which follow. To make the most of the concept of wholeness when dealing with some phenomenon, process or problem, one has to recognize the need for, and to skilfully exploit, various complex research procedures, e.g. to provide a combination (or, even better, a symbiosis) of analytical and synthetic research strategies, to understand the need for, and explicitly curtail, the reductionism in a research policy, to identify different kinds of wholeness, to differentiate methodologically additivity, super-additivity and sub-additivity principles in holistic objects of cognition etc. (see e.g. [6]).

The analysis of these research procedures is being carried out using the systems approach, the main purpose of which is to expand these procedures in such a specific methodological form that they would be ripe for effective assimilation by scientific (both fundamental and applied) knowledge.

That is why if we are willing to proceed by treating (in the form proposed above) systems approach as a supradisciplinary, methodological orientation bringing together the philosophical systems principle, on the one hand, with interdisciplinary systems research and development, on the other, we would be amply justified in affirming that one of the most important factors for the development of SA is the recognition of the need for close links between SA and the systems approach and the working out of the best lines of advance to this end. This will open the way to enrich ASA with existing philosophical and methodological ideas and enable the subject to capitalize on a rich and highly structured concept of wholeness, rather than a simply intuitive conception of wholeness.

THE PROBLEM OF THE INTERRELATION OF SYSTEM AND ITS ENVIRONMENT

Together with the necessity for a profound understanding of specific features of the problem of wholeness, a methodologically based solution to the question of the *interrelation of a system and its context (environment)* – an issue which has received growing attention in recent works on systems analysis – is equally important for the further progress of systems analysis.

Whatever version of SA may be adopted in a particular case, the system conceived in the course of the study is always designed to conform to a quite definite objective to be pursued with the help of it. That is why the main analytical efforts are always centred either around goal setting, i.e. at the stage preceding system identification, or around its structuring, policy formulation etc., i.e. at the stage of system analysis after the system has been identified. As to system identification, demarcation of its boundary, selection of the relevant fragments of the environment etc., all this is performed on the basis of one most crucial assumption (whatever particular procedure used at this stage in any particular case). It is assumed that separating the system out from the environment, taking into account the relevant parts of that environment, would have practically no effect on the behaviour of the environment and specifically would not change its organization. Moreover it is implicitly assumed that the goal-oriented system to be designed will radically surpass the environment with respect to its orderliness and will embody in itself a kind or *organized enclave* in a relatively underorganized environment. As to the problems of interrelation, they are treated at the systems analysis level as the problems of interaction between systems components or subsystems. To put it differently, the whole range of SA tools is brought together for the study of a *single* system. And this is not accidental. It reflects a totally justifiable desire to make the most effective use of the heuristic potential of the already discussed concept of system wholeness and its relative independence from the environment (its autonomous nature).

The fundamental nature of the difficulties related to this assumption and weaknesses of the concepts based on it did not become immediately apparent. It becomes evident only as, due to ASA proliferation, the systems environment acquires a much greater degree of organization (systemic organization in some cases) and the creation of new systems produces a kind of second order chaos. A methodologically similar situation arises in the case when newly designed large scale management and information systems get involved in an interaction with traditionally functioning objects and systems. By way of illustration we may refer to the case of computer telecommunication network design, where *normal system operation* turned out to rely upon its legal, economic and similar compatibility with traditional communication means, the problem being aggravated by great discrepancies in regulatory statutes for their functioning in different European countries. Moreover the new system is not designed as an alternative to the former, but rather has to supplement it under the conditions of partial function overlap.

Thus we are dealing now with the change of the methodological relevance of the problem which has been known in principle in its own right, but has acquired an utterly different significance in the course of ASA development. Attempts to bypass the context problem by extending the scope of relevance fail (critics of systems studies are quick to point this out) due to awkwardness and unmanageableness of the resulting system, and consequent loss of the very advantages ASA is called to provide. Meanwhile in recent years the theoretical problem of system-environment interrelations was being attacked rather sluggishly, partly because this problem has been considered to be of greater importance to applied studies.

We may therefore conclude that if the problem of the interrelation of the system and its environment is to be solved adequately, as well as the problem of wholeness, systems analysis needs to be enriched with the principles and methods of the systems approach.

To put it another way, if we are to succeed, i.e. to meet prearranged effectiveness criteria, systems analysis as a certain form of science being to some extent an integration of science and art, has to undergo two changes. In the first place it has to build on the firm foundation of the systems approach and, secondly, to develop a frame of reference which can be carried forward into the future, utilizing some form of theoretical generalization and accumulation of experience. In current practice systems approach principles are used in systems analysis only to a limited degree. General systems concept are used with a great regularity when social, economic, man-machine and other similar systems are studied as only one instance of the particular class; this constitutes one of the main fields *of the application of SA*. An intensive search for ways of reinforcing *the instrumental aspect* of these investigations has resulted lately in the emergence of various new research tools – systems dynamics, heuristic programming, simulation etc. – which are however developing as a number of (explicitly or implicitly) competitive programmes (see (27)), deprived of the unifying theoretical foundation.

In this respect it should be noted that a popular emphasis is quite often given by describing SA as an "art". Of course it goes without saying that any practical activity calling for decisions under uncertainty has to rely at least partly upon intuitive heuristic considerations. In this respect any research activity is not evidently an exception, though it does not give us grounds to consider it as art. Accordingly, no radical advancement of SA can alter this fact and should not even try to do so. But it is quite another matter when the role of art becomes over-inflated, covering most of the problem and leaving to scientific techniques nothing but an instrumental support of the various analysis stages merged into a shallow framework which has remained intact for the last 10–15 years (goal setting – option generation – system design etc. with minimal variations). In this case, a lack of introspection concerning assumptions and difficulties in model interpretation is the price to be paid for this excessive role of art. Nowadays it becomes quite obvious that any further strengthening of the instrumental SA foundation will result in a noteworthy increase of systems analysis effectiveness only if it is simultaneously matched by a significant progress in the development of the theoretical foundations.

Quite a few obstacles of real substance hamper this process. One is related to the problem of identification of the class of objects for which systems analysis offers a theoretical explanation. Taking into consideration the already mentioned integrative function of systems analysis (with respect to its "scientific" and "art") components, we cannot but agree with a statement that "systems analysis theory evidently should be primarily a theoretical explanation of the systems analysts *activities* and to a much lesser degree and only indirectly of the objects of these activities" (36. p. 18).

In conclusion one more remark should be made. When speaking of the necessity for a single, general, foundation for systems analysis or systems research (the latter is essentially wider than the former) we should keep in mind that a general theory is only one of the forms, though it is the most effective form, in which there can be set out the similar basis of a research area. One does not always succeed in classifying investigations starting from some single theoretical nucleus, even in developed scientific disciplines with long and great traditions. Let us take for example the physics of elementary particles, the chemistry of polymers and even evolutionary ecology. We cannot really state that in all these fields there are what we may call a single general theory which is the foundation for unifying investigations. The situation is rather the opposite: the existence of some general theory of the same kind may be created in the more or less remote future.

For the present we can state that mechanisms for the organization of knowledge which provide some unity across corresponding disciplines are situated and function in other than theoretical dimensions. The zone of activity of these mechanisms *is not the main line of research*. It applies to the work connected with creation of handbooks, curricula and textbooks, reading-books and other so-called secondary scientific sources.[25] This work, being concerned with forming a *single body of knowledge*, differs of course by its nature from activity connected with a general theory covering corresponding areas. Pressures of time, and the need to produce concrete results, lead to a situation when basic texts and handbooks are achieved at the expense of conventional concessions, omissions in the theoretical impositioning, or the description of various viewpoints and approaches etc. But one should also keep in mind that although in traditional science this organization of knowledge is often regarded as subsidiary and artificial, it also plays the *main unifying part* in the overwhelming majority of the applied fields of science. We are now beginning to have a plethora of handbooks on systems analysis, and increasing efforts are being applied to the development of teaching courses and to discussing their contents – all this possibly indicates that systems analysis has reached the level on which formal energetic organizational action is needed. The situation is rather obvious, so it needed not be laboured. But the reflective side of this situation, one being characteristic especially for systems research, is worth attention. The fact is that the study and comparative analysis of the forms of presentation and organization of knowledge concerning systems of various types represent one of the most important directions for methodological search within the framework of systems approach. Besides, together with abstract constructions and epistemological elaborations, there grows a proliferation of attempts to address empirical forms of the organization of knowledge including forms specific for applied tasks. From this viewpoint systems analysis, being interdisciplinary and having a great variety of problems as well as approaches to their solution, is a really fruitful field for tests and applications of abstract systems constructions and models.

REFERENCES

1. Ackoff, R. L. Towards a System of Systems Concepts. *Management Science*, **17**, No. 11, 1971, pp. 661–671.
2. Ashby, W. R. An Introduction to Cybernetics. Chapman and Hall, London, 1956.
3. Berg, A. I. *et al.* Cybernetics. *Philosophical Encyclopaedia*, **II**, Moscow, 1962, pp. 495–506 (in Russian).
4. Berlinski, D. On Systems Analysis. An Essay Concerning the Limitations of Some Mathematical Methods in the Social, Political and Biological sciences. MIT Press, Cambr. (Mass.), 1976, **XI**, 186 pp.
5. Bertalanffy, L. von. General System Theory: Foundations, Development, Applications. The Penguin Press, Allen Lane, 1971, **XXII**, 311 pp.
6. Blauberg, I. V. and Yudin, B. G. The concept of Wholeness and its Role in Scientific Knowledge. Znaniye Press, Moscow, 1972, 48 pp. (in Russian).
7. Blauberg, I. V. and Rudin, E. G. Development and Essence of Systems Approach. Nauka Publishers, Moscow, 1973, 270 pp. (in Russian).
8. Blauberg, I. V., Sadovsky, V. N. and Yudin, B. G. Philosophical Principle of Systemicity and the Systems Approach. Soviet Studies in Philosophy, **XVII**, No. 4, 1979, pp. 44–68.
9. Buslenko, N. P. Complex Systems Modelling. Nauka Publishers, Moscow, 1978, 399 pp. (in Russian).
10. Churchman, C. W. The Systems Approach. Delta Books, NY, 1969, **XI**, 243 pp.
11. Deschamps, L. M. Truth or Reliable System, vol. I. AzTNII Press, Baku, 1930 (in Russian).
12. Dror, Y. Ventures in Policy Sciences: Concepts and Applications. Elsevier, NY, 1971, 321 pp.
13. Foerster, H. von. On Self-Organizing Systems and Their Environment. Self-Organizing Systems. Ed. by M. C. Yovits and S. Cameron. Translation from English. Foreign Literature Publishing House, Moscow, 1964, pp. 113–139 (in Russian).
14. Gigch, John P. van. Applied General Systems Theory. Harper & Row, NY, 1978.
15. Glushkov, V. M. Introduction to Cybernetics. Ukrainian SSR Academy of Sciences Press, Kiev, 1964, 324 pp. (in Russian).
16. Gvishiani, D. M. Materialist Dialectics. – Philosophical Foundation of Systems Research, Systems Research Methodological Problems: Yearbook, 1979, Nauka Publishers, Moscow, 1980, pp. 7–28.
17. Hoos, I. R. Systems Analysis in Public Policy: A Critique, Berkeley University, California Press, 1974, 259 pp.
18. Kalman, R. E., Falb, P. L. and Arbib, M. A. Topics in Mathematical System Theory. McGraw-Hill, New York, 1969.
19. Klir, G. J. An Approach to General Systems Theory. Van Nostrand Reinhold Comp., NY, 1969, **XII**, 323 pp.
20. Kuzmin, V. P. Systems Principle in K. Marx's Theory and Methodology. Politizdat Publishers, Moscow, 1980, 322 pp.
21. Larichev, O. I. Methodological Problems of Practical Application of Systems Analysis. Systems Research. Methodological Problems: Yearbook 1979, Nauka Publishers, Moscow, 1980, pp. 210–219 (both in Russian).
22. Lilienfeld, R. The Rise of Systems Theory: An Ideological Analysis. Wiley, NY, 1978, 292 pp.
23. Lynn, L. E. The user's perspective. Pitfalls of Analysis. Ed. by G. Majone and E. S. Quade. Wiley, Chichester, England, 1980, pp. 89–115.
24. Mesarović, M. D., Macko, D. C. and Takahara, Y. Theory of Hierarchical Multilevel Systems. Academic Press, New York, 1970.
25. Mirsky, E. M. Inter-Disciplinary Research and Disciplinary Organization of Science. Nauka Publishers, Moscow, 1980, 273 pp.
26. Moiseyev, N. N. The Simplest Mathematical Models of Economic Forecasting. Znaniye Publishers, Moscow, 1975, 63 pp.
27. Nappelbaum, E. L. Systems Analysis as a Program of Scientific Research: Structure and Key-Concepts. Systems Research. Methodological Problems: Yearbook, 1979. Nauka Publishers, Moscow, 1980, pp. 55–77.
28. Ogurtsov, A. P. On Understanding of the Systems Nature of Scientific Knowledge. (Antiquity and New Times), Systems Research: Yearbook, 1974. Nauka Publishers, Moscow, 1974, pp. 154–186 (all in Russian).

29. Pask. G. An Approach to Cybernetics. L. Hutchinson, 1961.
30. Pitfalls of Analysis. Ed. by G. Majone and E. S. Quade. Wiley, Chichester, England, 1980, **VIII**. 213 pp.
31. Sadovsky, V. N. Foundations of General Systems Theory: Logical and Methodological Analysis. Nauka Publishers, Moscow, 1974, 279 pp.
32. Sadovsky, V. N. Systems Principle, Systems Approach and General Systems Theory. Systems Research: Yearbook. Nauka Publishers, Moscow, 1978, pp. 7–25.
33. Shchedrovitsky, G. P. Principles and General Scheme of Methodological Organization of Systemic-Structural Research. Systems Research. Methodological Problems: Yearbook, 1981. Nauka Publishers, Moscow, 1981, pp. 193–227.
34. Uemov, A. I. The Systems Approach and General Systems Theory. Mysl Publishing House, Moscow, 272 pp. (all in Russian).
35. Wiener, N. Cybernetics or Control and Communication in the Animal and the Machine. NY, 1948.
36. Yudin, B. G. Some Specific Features of Systems Research Development. Systems Research. Methodological Problems: Yearbook, 1980. Nauka Publishers, Moscow, 1981, pp. 7–23.
37. Yudin, E. G. Systems Approach and Principle of Activity. Methodological Problems of Modern Science. Nauka Publishers, Moscow, 1978, 391 pp.

3

The Deliberative Context of Systems Analysis

HYLTON BOOTHROYD

This chapter is in four parts: an indication of how it relates to the general culture of operational research and systems analysis, some comments about the origin of the ideas I presented to the IIASA Seminar, an outline of the presentation itself, and some post-seminar comments.

THE WORLD OF ORASA

There has been a continuous ORASA culture since the late 1930s. In the UK, the USA, and Sweden the original ORASA cultures grew from the direct investigational support of decision-makers by full-time scientists who carried out observational/analytical studies of operations. This grounding of ORASA in investigation-plus-recommendation remains strongest in North America, the UK, and Scandinavia. This chapter is about the theoretical foundations of the investigational practice of ORASA. It is part of a slowly-developing personal enquiry into what constitutes an adequate description of ORASA: an enquiry that has already led me to criticize three widely influential subsidiary themes in thinking about ORASA.

At an early stage in the history of ORASA a potent subsidiary theme emerged: enquiry into mathematical and computational problems posed by some types of model produced by some types of investigation. For various reasons there was an explosion of interest in such enquiry, to the extent that many participants and funding-sponsors came to believe, wrongly, that ORASA consists principally of enquiry into mathematical and computational problems. Indeed, there seemed to be a widespread phantasy that the truth about real systems could be discovered by ratiocination largely divorced from observational investigation. Those engaged in investigation and recommendation have not been seriously misled by this view of ORASA-as-mathematics, apart from a widespread tendency to confuse optima-within-a-

33

model with optima-for-real. But many of those with no direct experience of investigation have become prisoners of this view.

A second subsidiary theme was that ORASA is only a tantalizingly short step away from a science of decision-making. In the USA, Churchman and Ackoff wrote extensively towards this goal, and in countries with a Marxist constitution the hope for a good scientific outcome to human problems is often an explicit article of faith. Those engaged in investigation and recommendation have long suspected that ORASA-as-science is a good but incomplete account, and some have been disheartened and embarrassed when ORASA studies have led to conflict or to recommendations later discovered to be wrong. The problems partly come from confusing the use of scientific methods with the possibility of constructing a scientifically-justified deductive decision technology.

A third subsidiary theme was that ORASA as a social process would only be satisfactorily described if it was re-conceptualized in terms of the behavioural and social sciences. On this theme ORASA practitioners are divided: some are dismissive, others are hopeful but find the behavioural sciences to be too extensive and too fragmented to consider re-interpreting their practice in those terms.

So this chapter stands somewhat apart from the traditions of ORASA-as-mathematics, ORASA-as-science, and ORASA-as-social-science. This means I differ in theoretical standpoint, though not I think in spirit, from Churchman; that I see the seminar contributions of Mitroff and Checkland as providing views on possible conceptual contents of ORASA enquiries where I am silent; and the contributions from the USSR, Hungary and Poland as the beginnings of a similar process of making the descriptions of ORASA fit the reality of practice more faithfully and more fruitfully.

THE ORIGINS OF THE PRESENTATION TO THE IIASA SEMINAR

In 1956, as a young mathematician, I joined the 40/50 strong operational research group in the UK state coal industry; the group was committed to extensive programmes of measurement and modelling, both to improve operations and to improve planning. I soon discovered that much of the mathematics that was needed was below graduate level, much was beyond anyone's mathematical ability, and relatively little was both challenging and feasible. That was not a hardship to me. I was soon completely won over to the idea of science-in-action. Until I joined it, I had never realized that such a satisfying investigatory activity existed.

It was only slowly that I realized that I had no understanding of economics, that I had neither the means nor the ability to think analytically about psychological and social factors, and that the flow of commissions for study needed a level of imagination, confidence, risk-taking and negotiation skills that was largely unknown to the teams which then went on to carry out the studies.

By 1966, when I moved into the university world, I had begun to be aware of two particular problems and the university soon presented me with a third:

(a) clients were inclined to treat the findings of investigations as complete and final, rather than as a stage in a joint process of exploration and experiment – this was related to their picture of science as providing definitive final answers on both facts and desirable choice of action;

(b) in the literature of operational research and systems analysis the implicit picture of decision-making was quite unlike the untidy, episodic nature of the experience of making decisions about the conduct of investigations – the words and concepts we used in practice to guide our own professional behaviour were not the words and concepts we offered to our clients;

(c) within the university world, most people who had not themselves advised on action based on research were quite unable to visualize its nature or its value – it was at times like living among a race of the blind!

The end results of a lengthy period of wrestling with these problems were a working paper widely circulated in the UK in 1974, a summary of some key points given in a paper to IFORS in 1975,[1] and a major re-working of the paper into the book, *Articulate Intervention*.[2]

Although *Articulate Intervention* is only about 150 pages long, it is dense with terse arguments about a wide range of matters which are germane to systems analysis. Apart from its density, it is tough reading in one other respect: the analytical point of view is quite unlike that of previous writing for systems analysts and is used with no attempt to link it with a presumed starting point anywhere else. It may be useful therefore to put on record some of the ideas which I experienced as fundamental unlockings of the problem of describing ORASA in the order in which they occurred, starting from a simple science-in-action point of view:

(i) all theories have the logical status of conjectures;[3] this means that when we complete a piece of scientific or mathematical investigation the results cannot be guaranteed to be final and unchangeable; so every idea we work with must remain subject to criticism; but this is true of all theories, not just scientific ones, so the collection of ideas-in-use-for-decision-making has a unity of logical status within which some ideas have been more thoroughly researched than others;

(ii) life is saturated with theories;[4] every piece of thinking about action is made against a background of uncountably many ideas about the nature of reality and the likely outcome of actions; the theories can be of great generality, or so direct and simple and specific that they are considered to be facts;

(iii)   many economic and social theories are simply interest-group slogans masquerading as theories;[5] life is not lived simply as the product of theories but partly also as the product of wants, volitions, laws, contracts, and social customs which are logically expressible as proposals but not as theories;

(iv)   the morally justifiable goal of minimizing suffering is profoundly unlike the goal of maximizing happiness;[6] taken far enough this implies that we ought not to retain the ideal of a calculus whereby decisions are determined without further review and criticism, particularly if we value freedom within the framework of a society which meets our basic needs;

(v)   life is saturated with proposals;[2] every piece of thinking about action is made against the background of uncountably many ideas about obligations, preferences, and values; for the actors involved these have the status of proposals rather than theories;

(vi)   intellectual history has a stable programmatic nature which can be considered in its own right independently of the actions which cause its development;[7] organized life similarly has a stable, but changing, portfolio of theories and proposals whose programmatic development can be considered in its own right;[2]

(vii)   human conduct is considered and resolved upon a platform of understanding – we can usefully call this combination of reflection and decision the "deliberation" of action;[8] in using the word "deliberation" I want to evoke the idea of thinking as combining theories and proposals – not just thinking about what-is but thinking about what-to-make-be;

(viii)   the man who makes the platforms of others explicit is in danger of his life;[8] so, for example, I expect some people to dismiss what I write as unuseful to them, but I also expect some to attack both me and what I write because they feel threatened.

This was the undeclared background against which I suggested that for preliminary reading my fellow seminarians might look at Chapters 2 and 3 of *Articulate Intervention* on programmes and actions. Finally, the time came to squeeze what I was to say into a linear form for oral presentation. To my surprise something new came out, at least initially: the idea that I could order my thinking around the central place of natural language in the deliberation of actions.

AN OUTLINE OF THE PRESENTATION TO THE IIASA SEMINAR

Our central concern is to say useful things about systems to clients. On the one hand, we particularly offer formal analysis, the construction and exploration of explanatory models, and the use of scientific methods. On the other hand, we find ourselves needing behavioural, social, and political explanations to describe our relations with clients and to discuss our conduct of systems analysis. There is tension here. What we particularly offer does not provide an adequate ground for theorizing our own goings on. But if we try to ground ourselves in behavioural, social, and political points of view we risk usurping the prime place we currently give to the explicit content of our analysis.

I therefore propose that we ground our understanding of systems analysis neither on the analytic methods we use, nor on a behavioural, social, and political viewpoint. I propose rather that we start from the fact that we, and our clients, use language to talk about action: that their and our cognitions are central to our experience of systems analysis. If we take this as a central point of view, we can then turn on the one hand to our familiar approaches through scientific modelling and we can turn on the other hand to behavioural, social, and political concepts, but we shall remain clear that the contributions of both will derive from the practice of language and representation and that the contributions will be commissioned, conducted, included and rejected by the practice of language.

Our aspiration as systems analysts might then be summed up in a single diagram (Fig. 1):

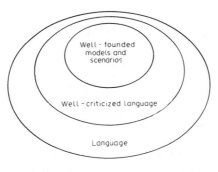

FIG. 1

The practice of language has many aspects, of which we might particularly note that it is used:

to reflect and argue about what is, what is going to be, and what could be,
to deliberate what to do,
to persuade and to negotiate.

Of these, it is the deliberation of action which provides the original context for the commissioning of systems analysis, and the context to which the outcomes of systems analysis are most evidently offered.

A key question is whether for deliberating action our language in principle needs anything more than well-founded theories. In a perfect world, would actions be a logical consequence of knowing? In the end, can a science *of* decision-making be a science *for* decision-making? The classical form of the question is: Does *is* imply *ought*? My answer is, *No*. Theories do not seem to me to imply action. To stand alongside *theories* in language, I need *proposals*, which cover not only possible actions and conditional actions, but also our proposed evaluations of the actions and their imagined consequences.

My view of deliberation is then that at any point in time there is an active set of imagined actions, imagined consequences, theories, and proposals drawn from a much wider, indefinitely large set. The content of the wider set will range itself on a dimension from the completely articulated to the completely unarticulated, and on a different dimension from unshakeable core to disposable non-core. The whole process through time, together with the real actions and real consequences, constitutes an "action programme".[2]

ORASA can be conceived of as intervention into action programmes. Schematically we might use a simple diagram (Fig. 2):

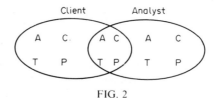

FIG. 2

to suggest that useful systems analysis is possible if there are enough differences between clients and analyst to provide a useful contrast and enough similarities for them to work together.

It is then possible for systems analysts to define their role as some or all of the following:

(a) joining clients in articulating and elaborating the components of reflection before action;
(b) reflecting on the quality of components and acting to improve them;
(c) elaborating the means for deliberative argument;
(d) participating in deliberative argument.

COMMENTS ON SOME ISSUES ARISING FROM THE IIASA SEMINAR

There is an open-ended set of issues raised by the material in the presentation. Of these, I think it most useful to comment further on the idea of natural language as the context for ORASA and then to comment on the status of the ideas of "deliberation", "action programme", and "intervention".

In putting natural language at the centre I was doing much more than using a presentational device. It is at the centre for several strong theoretical and practical reasons:

(i)   life is like that; the cognitive content of deliberation and the process of deliberation may be enhanced by ORASA on the one hand and behavioural and social sciences on the other hand, but their acceptance and integration will be not on their own terms but on the terms of the deliberative goings-on to which they are directed;

(ii)   natural language is a powerful and flexible tool by which deliberative concerns can be switched with extraordinary ease; the cognitive and explorative products of ORASA are offered against a presumed closed set of anticipated cognitive needs and anticipated explorative needs; the conduct of ORASA has suffered by a tendency to regard its output as having timeless relevance and validity; the designer of negotiation support systems needs to take into account the dynamics of deliberation;

(iii) anyone who participates in the deliberation of cooperative action quickly learns that although we aim to treat low-level decisions and routine decisions by rules, there is nevertheless a constant passage between obeying rules and questioning their current validity; criticism appears not to be satisfactorily exercisable as a deductive activity – it is an imaginative and creative activity for which natural language is naturally well-suited;

(iv)   we have no logically defensible way of assuring an actor that he can hereafter rely permanently on the rightness of our theories to determine his actions; there must always be room for over-ride by him.

The idea of systems analysis arising out of deliberation and contributing to deliberation was found useful by the seminar. It tied in with the experimental work of Mitroff[9] and the soft-systems view of Checkland.[10] As a result of this and other debates it now seems reasonable to postulate:

(a)   a deliberative point of view will always be experienced as consistent with the practice of systems analysis;

(b)   some analysts will find a deliberative point of view supportive and heuristically useful in suggesting new categories of analytical activity; other analysts will simply note it without finding it either supportive or suggestive.

The idea of mapping the content of deliberation on to the formal components of action programmes was not explored by the seminar, and indeed an explicit mapping of a sample of deliberation is something I have only occasionally attempted myself. There are various reasons for this:

(i)   even a short segment of deliberation carries with it an endless cloud of implicit theories and proposals – deliberation takes place in an environment that is saturated with theories and proposals that are left unspoken, unwritten, unremembered, and mutually unaccessed between actors;

(ii) the explicit content of sentences in which action is being considered usually combined features of theories and proposals intimately interwoven – they are distinguishable only by rewriting into clumsy, non-fluent separate statements.

Nevertheless, an analytical approach to the deliberation of action seems unavoidably to require analysts to distinguish is/ought content. The most notable progress in the analysis of deliberation is that of Eden.[11] Otherwise the notion of "action programme" is at present little more than an organizing principle that occasionally comes vividly to mind when one realizes that a debate is hopelessly confounding *is* and *ought*.

The use of the word "intervention" causes some unease, and leads systems analysts to be reluctant to describe their own activities in that way. On the one hand, some systems analysts in the UK, deeply integrated into the goings-on of industrial companies, feel that the word "intervention" suggests a remoteness and distance which quite mis-describes their position; for them, the right word is "participation". On the other hand, systems analysts at IIASA, deeply aware of the sovereign independence of member states, feel that the word "intervention" suggests a wholly improper interfering attitude towards their counterparts and clients in member states; for them, the right word is "analysis". In between, there is a substantial group of analysts for whom the word "intervention" correctly suggests that the world will go on without them unless they negotiate a contributory analytical role with the intention of changing the content and/or the process of deliberation.

I understand and sympathize with these points of view. However, I am clear that my use of the word "intervention" includes all three. The analyst who sees himself as a full participant has to provide a continuing flow of useful reliable contributions to deliberation or he will cease to be a participant. The analyst who sees his work as the uncontroversial documentation of how a system works also expects that there is a possibility that sometime, somewhere, someone will open his document and find it useful. I am certainly not writing this for an IIASA publication in the expectation that no-one will ever be in the slightest degree affected by it!

So, I think that the meaning of what I have written, holds over the full spectrum of systems analysis, from participant to detached commentator. On the other hand, I acknowledge that very few of us could announce ourselves as interventionists without being misunderstood! For the present, there is therefore a difference between the language of self-analysis and the language of self-presentation. For the foreseeable future we will continue to present ourselves as operational researchers, or applied systems analysts, or whatever other name is in good standing in our environment. But I hope that we do not intend to practice our craft without leaving a mark somewhere!

REFERENCES

1. Boothroyd, H., Describing operational research. In *Operational Research '75* (ed. K. B. Haley), North-Holland, 1976.
2. Boothroyd, H., *Articulate Intervention: the Interface of Science, Mathematics and Administration*, Taylor and Francis, 1978.
3. Popper, K. R., *The Logic of Scientific Discovery*, Hutchinson, 1959.
4. Popper, K. R., *Objective Knowledge*, Oxford, 1972.
5. Robinson, J. and Eatwell, J., *An Introduction to Modern Economics*, McGraw-Hill, 1973.
6. Popper, K. R., *The Open Society and Its Enemies*, Routledge, 1945.
7. Lakatos, I., Falsification and the methodology of scientific research programmes. In *Criticism and the Growth of Knowledge* (ed. I. Lakatos and A. Musgrave), Cambridge, 1970.
8. Oakeshott, M., *On Human Conduct*, Clarendon, 1975.
9. Mitroff, I. I., present volume.
10. Checkland, P. B., present volume.
11. Eden, C., Jones, S., and Sims, D., *Thinking in Organisations*, Macmillan, 1979.

4

Rethinking a Systems Approach

PETER CHECKLAND

INTRODUCTION

The fact that it is rare for anyone firmly to declare themselves *against* "a systems approach" probably indicates the weakness rather than the strength of the idea conveyed by these words. The phrase is so loosely used, and means such different things to different people, that many potential opponents probably regard "a systems approach" not as impregnable but as not worth attacking. I shall argue that the notion can be sufficiently sharply and lucidly expressed that debate about its strengths and weaknesses becomes meaningful and is worth encouraging. This paper will consider briefly the nature of systems thinking and "the systems movement" within which the ideas are used consciously; it will try to indicate the meaning of "a systems approach" among the many activities which go on in the systems movement and describe the implications and significance of recent practical research which has established "soft" systems methodology for tackling the ill-structured problems which abound in the real world; and it will argue that the implications of this work are that the traditional concept of "a systems approach" now has to be re-thought. For the work not only illuminates the meaning of "a systems approach" in its first manifestations (in "systems engineering" and "systems analysis") it also gives it a new meaning and links systems thinking more firmly to the concerns and problems of social science. Finally, we examine the question: what does the successful application of a systems approach in real-world problem situations imply about the nature of social reality?

SYSTEMS THINKING, THE SYSTEMS MOVEMENT AND "A SYSTEMS APPROACH"

This section will summarize briefly arguments which have been rehearsed at greater length elsewhere.[1, 2, 3, 4]

Systems Thinking

In considering the nature of systems thinking it is worth reflecting upon the fact that the noun "system" yields two adjectives, and that the use of systems ideas in problem solving has usually implied one of these – "systematic" – and has neglected the other – "systemic". Systems engineering[5] and systems analysis as developed by the RAND Corporation[6] (this latter being implied in most of the work of the International Institute for Applied Systems Analysis, IIASA[7]) are both highly *systematic*. Soft systems methodology[1, 8] aspires to be *systemic*, and the rethinking entailed in moving from a systematic approach to a systemic approach is the subject of this paper. But in order to understand that shift, and to relate it to the systems movement as a whole, it is necessary to consider the *systemic* origins of the systems movement, which may be seen historically as an attempt to develop holistic thinking which is complementary to the reductionist thinking of the method of natural science.[1, 2]

The most fundamental systems idea is that of "emergent properties". Such properties are those of some entity regarded as a whole – they are meaningful only in terms of the whole, not in terms of its parts. The smell of ammonia and the functional capabilities of a bicycle are examples of such properties. The ammonia smell, as a concept, has no meaning in terms of the properties of the nitrogen and hydrogen which make up the ammonia molecule: it is a meaningful concept only in terms of the entity ammonia. Similarly, the properties of a bicycle relate only to the assembled whole, not to its individual parts. My student who remarked to one of her colleagues "you're certainly more than the sum of your parts, you're an idiot", had understood the idea completely.

Given the basic idea that it might be useful to assume that the universe contains many wholes having emergent properties (both natural and man made) we may regard systems thinking as the attempt to develop an epistemology built upon this concept. Systems thinking tries to develop an epistemology which can both describe the universe and attempt to elucidate some of its mysteries; its basic notions are that whole entities (having *emergent properties*) are *hierarchically* arranged, the entities being characterized by processes of *communication* and *control*, this latter in the control engineers' sense of processes which seek to maintain the integrity of the whole in the face of a changing external environment.[1] Historically it is not surprising that this kind of thinking was developed – before being generalized to cover entities of any kind – by the so-called "organismic biologists" (Woodger, Haldane, Lloyd Morgan, Henderson, Cannon, Bertalanffy) who doubted whether the biological organism could be investigated adequately by the purely re-ductionist methods of science.

Systems thinking, then, emerging from biology in the 1920s and then further developed by control and communication engineers in the 1940s, provides a complementary tradition to that of the 350-year-old tradition of natural science. Summarizing savagely, we may present scientific thinking as the brilliant working out of the consequences of adopting Descartes' second rule for using the mind.[9] When faced with complexity, suggested Descartes in 1637, divide it up into separate parts and treat these one by one. The method of science does precisely this; it represents the triumphant working out of this principle. But it is not an all-powerful enquiring system, and in particular can hardly cope with the kind of complexity associated with, for example, biological organisms as whole entities or with real-world problems as opposed to those defined by scientists within laboratories.

Systems thinking is a response to the impotence of reductionism in the face of great complexity.

In all ages there have been systems thinkers, of course, thinking in terms of the emergent properties of wholes, but the *conscious* development of systems ideas and the language to express them stems only from the late 1940s. The *systems movement* is only 35-years-old.

The Systems Movement

In order to build a picture of the whole of the activity which constitutes the systems movement, it is necessary to make a number of distinctions which yield a map of it.[3] This "map" does not purport to describe the systems movement unequivocally, since any particular piece of systems work may well span several of the map's categories. But it does provide the minimum necessary categories needed to enable any piece of work to be "placed" and related to others. It is a typological rather than a representational map.

The first distinction is made between the development and/or use of systems ideas as such and the development and/or use of systems ideas in other disciplines. Within the former category we may now distinguish between the development of systems ideas theoretically and their development in practice. Finally within this latter category we may distinguish work which seeks to aid decision-making, work on the engineering of "hard" (concrete) systems and work on problem solving using the idea of "soft" (conceptual) systems. These four distinctions yield the categories of systems-based work shown in Figure 1.

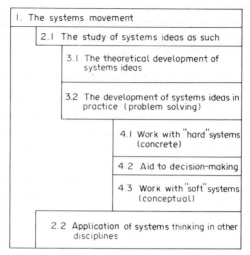

FIG. 1. *Categories of systems-based work needed to understand the Systems Movement as a whole*

Examples of work which does fall to a considerable extent into one category, and so illustrates that category, would be:

2.1 Developing General System Theory.[10]

2.2 Developing a systems-thinking-based physical geography[11] or conceptualizing Social Work in systems terms.[12]

3.1 Developing the logical entailments of "all possible machines"[13] or establishing hierarchy theory.[14]

4.1 Developing systems engineering.[5]

4.2 Developing RAND systems analysis.[15]

4.3 Developing "soft" systems methodology.[1]

A Systems Approach

The seven categories illustrated are sufficient to provide understanding of any systems-oriented activity observed in the real world and also to provide the basis of a definition of what is meant by "a systems approach". The phrase suggests *a way of going about tackling problems*, analogous to the phrases "an experimental approach" or "a mathematical approach" (with both of which approaches it is not incompatible). Tackling problems using a systems approach implies not being reductionist, examining the complexity of the problem situation using the ideas of "organized complexity" which systems-thinking embodies. The description "a systems approach" will most often be associated with the use of categories 2.2 or 3.2 in Figure 1, and the phrase is probably most used in connection with work based in 4.1 and 4.2. It is worth examining the nature of the systems approach embodied in systems analysis, systems engineering and most operational research, and comparing it with that emerging in the more recent work on "soft" systems methodology.

HARD SYSTEMS THINKING AND ITS "SYSTEMS APPROACH"

Both systems engineering (SE) and systems analysis (SA) imply a value system which rates most highly the achievement of some practical end. In this they resemble technology rather than science, whose prime value is the gaining of new knowledge.[1] Both SE and SA aim to achieve practical results: a system engineered to meet some defined need in the case of SE, a rational appraisal of the alternatives facing a real-world decision taker in the case of SA. Analysis of a dozen accounts of the methodology of SE and SA published between 1955 and 1976[4] shows that all reduce to the same core proposition, which may be taken as the defining characteristic of "hard" systems thinking:

> problems can be expressed as the search for an efficient means of reaching a defined objective or goal; once goals or objectives are defined, then systematic appraisal of alternatives, helped by various techniques, enables the problem (now one of selection) to be solved.

"Hard" systems thinking is any structured problem solving which bases itself on this goal-seeking schema. It is a powerful framework, and it is manifestly successful in a large number of real problems. When President Kennedy in his "Message to Congress on Urgent National Needs" (1961) set the American nation the objective, "before this decade is out, of landing a man on the moon and returning him safely to earth", no matter how extensive the resources required to do it, it was NASA's systems engineering which was able to ensure that the objective was achieved. When the American Department of Defence asks the RAND Corporation to appraise various radar systems, the RAND systems analysts are well able to produce a cost-benefit analysis of the alternatives.

Further reflection, however, suggests that these are very limited problems indeed. They are well structured problems. That is a way of saying that they are capable of being expressed as a search for an end which is taken as given. It is their structure which makes *systematic* work possible, which defines from the start what will be recognized as "a solution". But what if ends are themselves problematical? Methodology which requires the means-end schema is fundamentally excluded from the myriad problems of the real world, which are unstructured problems in which objectives cannot be taken as given. What should be done about inner-city problems? How should we design our schools? How can a "satisfactory" balance be achieved between industrial development and preservation of the natural environment? What level of the risks associated with nuclear power ought we to tolerate? These and countless problems like them find "hard" systems thinking inappropriate. They are the kind of ill-defined, unstructured problem which "soft" systems thinking attempts to tackle.

SOFT SYSTEMS THINKING AND ITS "SYSTEMS APPROACH"

"Soft" systems methodology provides a structured way of tackling ill-structured problems without imposing on them either the means-end dichotomy of "hard" methodology or, indeed, any other assertive schema of this kind. It takes as its starting point not a problem but a *situation* in which at least one person has at least a sense of unease, a feeling that some elements are problematical and hence worth exploring. The methodology moves from *finding out* about the situation to *taking action* within it, and does so not by relying on experience, which is probably the most popular method of making this transition, but by doing some careful, formally organized systems thinking *about* the problem situation.

The initial conceptualization is in terms of the following elements: a "problem solving system" which aspires to bring about "improvement" in a "problem content system"; and the roles: "client", "problem solver" and "problem owner". The occupant of the client (or "sponsor") role causes the study to happen, but he may not be regarded by the problem solver as the problem owner. The problem solver is free to assign any person or persons he wishes to that role, and it is always insightful to consider several possibilities.

In many versions of a systems approach, including RAND systems analysis and Churchman's conceptualization,[16] it is assumed that the systems thinking is at the disposal of a client who is also the problem owner. We have found it very useful to separate the two roles.

It is of course the case that one person or group of persons may occupy more than one of the three roles. Later in the study a fourth role, he who can cause things to happen, or not happen, in the problem situation becomes important as feasible improvements are formulated. This is the basic initial framework within which soft systems methodology is used. Its stages will now be described briefly.

After an initial expression of the problem situation has been assembled (for which guidelines are available[8]) the would-be problem solver names some hopefully relevant "human activity systems",[17] *relevant*, that is, to exploring the problematical situation. These systems are named in "root definitions", and models are built of the systems named. Techniques are available both for formulating root definitions and for building models of human activity systems[18, 19] The models should exhibit alternative ways of viewing the human activity regarded as relevant to problem solving. (For example, models of the human activity whose real-world manifestation is NASA might be based on perceiving it as an engineering activity, as a political activity –

Kennedy's justification for the moon landing was political – or as part of "showbiz", given NASA's commitment to the televizing of its more spectacular exploits.) When built and checked for logical coherence, the models are brought into the problem situation and used *to provide structure for a debate* with persons involved in the situation, who ought if possible to include the "problem owners" implied by the choice of relevant system. The debate is set up by formally *comparing* the models with the real-world problem situation. This frequently entails enriching the expression of the problem situation, and this may cause new relevant systems to be selected and new root definitions to be formulated. The purpose pursued in the debate is the definition of changes which persons in the problem situation regard as meeting two criteria simultaneously: that they are systemically desirable, given the systems thinking embodied in the root definitions, models and comparison, and culturally feasible for these particular persons in their particular historical setting. If changes meeting the two criteria can be found (if not, more radical, or more conservative root definitions may be needed) then action may be taken in the problem situation to implement them: the new problem becomes that of seeking implementation, and the cyclic learning process begins again.

The methodology outlined in the previous paragraph (and extensively discussed in [1]) was arrived at experientially through an action research programme now underway for a decade. The process followed was that of the cycle shown in Figure 2.

FIG. 2. *The Autopoietic System of the Action Research*

This self-constructing (autopoietic) system is of course an organisationally closed system; at the start of the research a forcible entry was effected by taking hard systems engineering methodology as given, applying it to unsuitably soft problem situations, doing what the situation seemed to demand when the hard methodology failed, and generalizing the results from a number of studies. About 150 studies, mainly in problem situations of modest size within organizations of various kinds, have now been completed by Lancaster University researchers, by their associated University-owned consultancy company ISCOL Ltd., by members of the Open University Systems Group, and others.

The crucial characteristic of the methodology lies in the nature of the concept at its core: the notion of the "human activity system". In the case of the systems, natural or man-made, with which hard systems thinking deals, it will be possible to achieve descriptions of them on which all agree: these might be publicly testable descriptions of a machine which a systems engineer proposes, for example, or accounts of the logical structure of the decision taker's problem with which the RAND analyst is trying to help. In the case of the human activity systems of soft-systems thinking, however, there will be many possible accounts of them, all valid according to different *Weltanschauungen*. (NASA is, among many other possibilities, *validly* an engineering system, a political system or a "showbiz" system according to three different images of the world which an autonomous observer is free to adopt.) Hence the methodology is crucially different from systems engineering, RAND systems analysis and classic operational research. Its models are *not* models of part of the real world, they are "ideal types", models of pure perceptions of parts of the real world; they are used in the construction of a systems-based learning process which is made formally explicit.

Thus the two systems approaches implicit in hard and soft systems thinking are rather different. The systems approach of systems engineering and systems analysis is a systematic progress towards definition of the system which achieves the objective, the alternative which best meets the defined need: the paradigm is fundamentally one of *optimization*. The systems approach of the more recent work, however, is a systemic exploration of perceptions: the paradigm is one of *learning*. The relation between the two would seem to be that the hard paradigm is a special case of the soft: occasionally, in a minority of real-world problems, a root definition can reduce to an "objective" which can be taken as given, and learning reduces to optimizing.

The soft methodology, orchestrating an examination of the social process which Vickers calls "appreciation",[20] can also be seen as an enquiring system which maps interestingly on to Churchman's treatment of such systems[16] (apart, that is, from his assumption that the client or sponsor is also the problem owner).

Churchman examines texts by five historical figures – Leibniz, Locke, Kant, Hegel and the American philosopher Edgar Singer – taking them to be would-be designers of systems to produce sure knowledge. Using a basic Leibnizian model of a system which builds nets of contingent sentences which, being neither tautologous nor self-contradictory, are candidates for "likely truths", he examines: a Lockean enquirer which seeks consensus among the community of enquirers; a Kantian/Hegelian (dialectical) enquirer which brings in its designer's *Weltanschauung* as well as the operation of the system itself, and opposes every world view to its "deadliest enemy" in the search for higher-level truth; and a Singerian enquirer which accepts enquiry as never ending and summons "an heroic mood" to go on both defending the status quo and attacking it.

In these terms the debate stage of soft systems methodology explores the possibility of a Lockean consensus, but does so by means of a Kantian/Hegelian structure in which the debate is fed and structured by systems models which represent constructed images and counter images based on opposed root definitions. Overall, the acceptance that, unlike a RAND analysis or a systems engineering project, a soft systems study is never finally complete, shows the methodology to be a Singerian enquirer. Certainly those who have used it have no doubt of the appropriateness of Singer's "heroic mood"! In the language here developed, the systems approach of the soft school sees the approach as a form of Singerian never-ending enquiry; the hard systems approach, on the other hand, reveals itself to be a Lockean enquirer which can assume a consensus on the objective to be achieved or the system to be engineered.

This essential difference between the systems approaches of hard and soft systems thinking could in principle be explored by using systems methodology. The evaluation and development of systems analysis includes the rethinking of the whole concept of systems analysis now going on. This rethink presents us with a problem situation of the soft variety to which soft systems methodology could be applied. The Appendix records an attempt to do this.

SYSTEMS THINKING, SOCIAL SCIENCE AND SOCIAL REALITY

Clearly, systems thinkers employing a systems approach to problem solving, whether working within the hard or the soft paradigm, are prepared to intervene – in their different ways – in what in everyday language we call "social systems". Further illumination of the idea of a systems approach ought thus to be obtainable by relating the two versions of "a systems approach" discussed above to some of the history of social science. We may usefully ask: What theories of social reality are implicit in hard and soft systems methodology? How does the history of, for example, the sociologists' attempts to deal with the complexity of social phenomena illuminate the nature of hard and soft systems thinking?

This is not a common strategy. The literature of the systems movement, like that of management science, has shown itself remarkably indifferent to, not to say ignorant of, the state of developments in sociology, even though anyone using systems methodology (or the techniques of management science) is seeking to secure change in a social system. Writing in 1976 Bryer and Kistruck[21] claim not to have found a single attempt by a systems theorist to justify his approach in sociological terms. What follows summarizes an attempt to do precisely that.[1]

Intellectual Traditions in Sociology

Were sociology able to point to a significant body of empirically-derived publicly-repeatable results, then its literature would contain substantive accounts of the laws governing social interactions. What it does offer, however, is a plethora of discussions of the nature of social theory and the relations between it and philosophy. This does not necessarily establish the waywardness of sociologists, rather it reflects the peculiar difficulties faced by a science which cannot assume that repeatable happenings characteristic of an external reality can be discovered by disciplined observation. The nature of social reality and the proper ways of investigating it scientifically are still problematical issues in sociology.

The unresolved issue might perhaps be summarized as the question: is sociology to be the study of objective social facts which transcend the individuals who make up a society, or is it the study of the individual subjective understandings which persons acquire of their social situations? Both strands of thinking are heavily represented in the literature. The tradition of *functionalism* sees social reality as consisting of social structures which transcend individuals; the so called *action approach* gives primacy to the individual actors who pursue their own activity and in so doing create social reality as a process.[22] The literature may be seen as a debate conducted from these two stances; at the level of philosophy they are the stances of *positivism* and *phenomenology*.

The major founding figure of the first (functionalist) tradition, Emile Durkheim, urges in *The Rules of Sociological Method*: "Consider social facts as things".[23] The sociologist, in his view, should discover the law-like patterns in which societal constraints affect individual behaviour. Sociological explanation is then either causal or functional, the latter being an account of how a particular social fact or characteristic meets a societal need, a need of the social collectivity rather than of the individuals. Durkheim's theoretical and empirical work (he investigated, for example, such social facts as the suicide rates of societies) founds the tradition which becomes "structural functionalism" or, more generally, "functionalism". This stance, with its view of a social system as a set of relationships persisting through time as a result of functional sub-systems which contribute to the equilibrium-maintaining processes of the system as a whole, is normally taken to be the paradigm example of the application of systems thinking within social science. That this is a limited view emerges from consideration of the alternative tradition, that deriving from Max Weber.

Weber (1864–1920) was a contemporary of Durkheim (1858–1917) but his writings surprisingly make no mention of Durkheim or his work, even though they share a methodological interest in the use of "ideal types" for analytical purposes and oppose each other on substantive issues. Weber opposes the reification involved in Durkheim's approach; for him the basic concept of sociology is the single deliberate action by an individual directed to affecting the behaviour of others. Sociology's concern is the scientific understanding of the subjective meaning associated with such action. Weber's aim was to create an interpretive social science based upon analysis of meaningful action by the method of *Verstehen*, placing oneself in the role of the individuals observed, and interpreting using generalizations about typical pure processes of action.

Philosophically, the Durkheim tradition of "social facts" is underpinned by the philosophy of positivism, according to which all true knowledge is based in empirical data.[24] Weber's interpretive social science links philosophically to phenomenology. In the former tradition there is a fairly clear distinction between two kinds of work: developing the philosophical base and the working out of practical methods. In the alternative tradition of phenomenology the distinction is much less clear. There is no phenomenological equivalent of, for example, Merton's paradigm for functionalist analysis.[25]

The most important figure in the development of the phenomenological stance, which yields primacy to the mental processes of observers rather than to sensorial evidence of an external world, is Edmund Husserl (1859–1938). Husserl starts from the proposition that philosophical thinking needs to be reformed because it starts not from the basic data of consciousness but from concepts which already presuppose various theories. He wishes to eliminate these in-built assumptions. He returns to Descartes' initial position of extreme doubt in which Descartes doubts everything except that he is himself thinking his doubt. For Husserl Descartes' doubt was not radical enough, the "I am" of Descartes being for Husserl only "a pure possibility generated by the meaning-constituting activity of transcendental subjectivity".[26] Distinguishing between the "natural attitude" in which, in order to live our everyday lives, we make common-sense judgements about the reality of the world and its events, and the phenomenological attitude, in which common-sense belief is suspended. Husserl tried to develop a new method for philosophical thinking based on the latter. Borrowing an expression from his own original discipline, mathematics, he speaks of putting the real world "between brackets" as he seeks the universal types among the data of pure consciousness.[27]

Husserl wrote mainly about the methodology of his philosophy; the development of a phenomenological orientation to sociology was taken up by Alfred Schutz (1899–1959).[28, 29] Schutz, like Weber, takes as a problem the need to reconcile the individual free to attribute meaning to what he observes with the requirements of a rigorous scientific method; and he turns to Husserl for a theory of subjectivity. But where Husserl considered the lived-in everyday world of experience only as a preliminary to making "the phenomenological reduction" to the pure data of consciousness, Schutz took the lived-in world, the *Lebenswelt*, to be his main concern: his programme is to discover the structure of that world, to investigate the types of everyday taken-for-granted knowledge and to find out how they are socially structured and distributed. For the individual his stock of knowledge, a sedimentation of previous experiences and his definitions of them, will be relevant in three senses: thematically, motivationally and interpretationally relevant according to how typical or atypical we judge our current experiences to be. When Schutz writes that the task of social science is:

> to investigate to what extent the different forms of systems of relevancy in the life-world – motivational, thematical and, most of all interpretational systems – are socially and culturally conditioned

we can perceive links both with Vickers' notions of appreciative systems[20] and with the content of soft systems methodology. There, the debate with actors in the problem situation (at the "comparison stage") is set up by comparing some pure systems models with expressions of the problem situation itself: the task is precisely to elucidate the thematic, motivational and interpretational relevance of these particular "relevant systems" for these particular actors in their particular situation.

This brings us near to a position in which we can attempt to relate hard and soft systems methodology, and their underlying assumptions, to the general framework of sociological theory. But finally, in outlining that framework, it is useful to mention briefly the contribution of Wilhelm Dilthey (1833–1911), philosopher of hermeneutics, the theory, art or skill of interpreting and understanding the products of human consciousness.[30] Dilthey, whose work Husserl recognized as an anticipation of phenomenology, sought to establish that the subject matter of the human sciences was intrinsically different from that of the natural sciences, being concerned not with external facts but with expressions of the human mind which become cultural artefacts. His interpretive method for understanding society and history, the "hermeneutic circle", is a means of learning to perceive social entities as both wholes and parts. A preliminary overview of subject matter guides an examination of what the parts denote; this clarifies the concept of the whole, which at the end of the cycle must be perceived so that all the parts can be related to it. Thus there are no fixed or absolute starting points, only an iterative cycle which gradually leads to increased understanding of social reality. The hermeneutic circle opposes a Cartesian faith in any self-evident starting point – such as is manifest in the hypothesis-to-be-tested of positivist natural science, in the objective to be achieved in RAND analysis, and in the system-to-be-engineered of systems engineering methodology.

To summarize this bare outline of some major intellectual traditions within sociology: we have in phenomenology and hermeneutics an attitude towards social science which takes as its prime datum not the world external to observers of it, but the observer's own mental processes. This extension of the interpretive tradition of sociology offers a "human-culturalistic" approach to compare and contrast with the "positivist-naturalistic" approach of the Durkheimian tradition.[31] In the former, human beings in the social process are constantly creating the social world in interaction with others. They are negotiating their interpretations of reality, while those multiple interpretations at the same time constitute the reality itself. There is no "pre-given universe of objects" but one which is "produced by the active doing of subjects" (Giddens[32]).

The Two Approaches and their Models of Social Reality

We are now in a position to elucidate the models of social reality which the hard systems approach (RAND systems analysis, systems engineering and operational research) and the soft systems approach (soft systems methodology) embody within their theory and practice. This can be done by trying to place these approaches on the two dimensional typologies of social theory which appear with some regularity in the literature of social science. Runciman[33] contrasts the axis holism-individualism with the axis positivism-intuitionism; Robertson's axes[34] are subjectively-objectively and sociality-culturality. For my purpose the most useful typology is that recently advanced by Burrell and Morgan.[35] Their axes are on the one hand: regulation-radical change, and on the other: subjective-objective. This choice gives the framework of Figure 3, in which the four quarters yield the sociologies of "functionalism", "interpretive sociology", "radical humanism" and "radical structuralism".

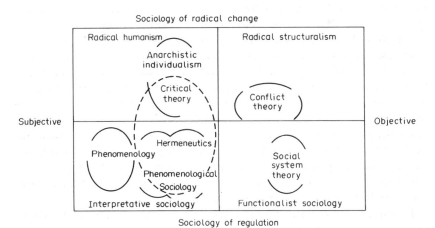

FIG. 3. *A Typology of Sociology (after Burrell and Morgan*[35]*)*

They place "social system theory" in the cell which combines a concern for regulation with a would-be objective approach to social phenomena. The

Durkheim tradition resides here. Burrell and Morgan specifically mention Bertalanffy,[36] Parsons[37] and Katz and Kahn[38] as relevant systems theorists. It is clear that it is in this area that we find the social theory implicit in systems engineering, RAND systems analysis and formal OR, with their emphasis on being scientific and their supposition that the world contains systems which can be observed, modelled, and optimized. But this is only one of many possible social theories, as the Burrell/Morgan and the other typologies demonstrate.

The social theory of soft systems methodology, with its emphasis on the *process* of learning and its acceptance that its models of human activity systems are models of perceptions, not models of complex reality, clearly lies in the left hand cells of the typology, with hermeneutics and phenomenology. But the position would not be too far left of the centre line because the methodology will over a period of time yield a picture of the common structurings of the social collectivities within which it works. Also, given the would-be problem solver's complete freedom to select relevant systems which, when compared with the expression of the problem situation, embody either incremental or radical change, the area occupied must include some of the subjective/radical cell. Here the extension of the area towards the "radical change" axis will be limited by the desire to achieve action in the real world; in practice, defining changes which are "culturally feasible" has led so far to rather conservative use of the methodology – but this is a matter of practice so far, rather than principle.

This analysis illustrates sharply the difference between the systems approaches of hard and soft systems thinking. It does not seem possible to establish the proposition that they are identical; the possible link between them is that in certain instances of real-world problem solving, shared assumptions, overlapping *Weltanschauungen*, common "appreciative settings" among persons in the problem situation may lead to agreement to analyse rationally a particular decision, to optimize a particular system. Sometimes a Singerian enquiry may find itself with a Lockean consensus: the hard paradigm is a special case of the soft.

A modest test of the coherence of this examination of the social assumptions of a systems approach emerges from the fact that the social theory of soft systems methodology – the dotted area of Figure 3 – occupies the area in which Burrell and Morgan locate the "Critical Sociology" (or "Critical Theory") of the theorists of the Frankfurt School.[39, 40] This was not noted until the analysis had been completed, and derives some interest from the fact that the leading theoretician of the Frankfurt School, Jürgen Habermas, has mounted an attack on systems theory as he perceives it, regarding it as one more example of the cultural manipulation of Western society by the science-and-technology-dominated purposive-rational mode of thought.[41] Critical Sociology is certainly intrinsically opposed to hard systems methodology, Habermas arguing that although the model of a self-regulating system could in principle be restricted to analytical purposes and not used for *design*, in fact "the transferral of the analytical model to the level of social organization is implied by the very approach taken by systems analysis".[42] And that approach, for Habermas, leads to a negative Utopia he seeks to avoid by achieving the "communicative competence"[43] which enables "public unrestricted discussion, free from domination, of the suitability and desirability of action-orienting principles and norms".[42] This clearly distances Habermas from hard systems thinking; what of the alternative paradigm?

Mingers has recently made a detailed comparison between Habermas' Critical Theory and soft systems methodology.[44] He finds a major difference stemming from Critical Theory's overtly political stance, systems methodology having no theory of how the structure of society (for example its stratification) might limit fundamentally the debate the systems approach sets up. But the similarities are perhaps more significant: both take seriously the problem of human action, at once purposive/rational (hence capable in principle of being engineered) and "natural", or unchangeable; both conclude that hard systems analysis, tied to technical rationality, cannot cope adequately with the multi-valued complexities of the real world; and both, denying the inevitability of the divorce between rationality and values which characterizes natural science, try to bring the two together in rational communicative interaction.

So the case can be made for mapping the social theory of soft systems methodology on to the dotted area indicated in Figure 3.

MATCHING SITUATION AND METHODOLOGY

Conclusion

I have argued:

- that the phrase "a systems approach to tackling problems" is usually applied to that part of the systems movement containing hard (systematic) systems methodology – RAND analysis, systems engineering etc. (areas 4.1, 4.2, of Figure 1).
- that their paradigm of optimization links with an implied functionalist social theory.
- that recent work on soft systems methodology offers a new view of "a systems approach" (area 4.3 of Figure 1) and develops a systemic process of enquiry whose aim is learning rather than optimization.
- that soft systems methodology's implicit social theory is phenomenological (offering a formal way of following the hermeneutic circle).

– that the hard systems approach is a special case of the soft systems approach.

Finally, in completing this examination of a systems approach it is useful to examine it from the point of view: the problems tackled, rather than: the problem-solving methodology used. This further illuminates the notion of "a systems approach".

Any belief in the value of coherently-organized enquiry assumes that the world, both "natural" and social, is not capricious but shows regularities. In the case of systems thinking the observer chooses to make systemic intellectual constructions and anticipates useful learning from attempting to map them on to real-world complexities. This suggests a way of looking at the types of phenomena or problem situations which the world may contain. Such phenomena and/or situations can be expected to show interconnectedness, and this, we may anticipate, will lead to there being several different types of phenomena or situations:

Type 1. Situations or phenomena characterized by interconnections which are part of *the regularities of the universe.* Examples would be frogs, foxgloves, ecological systems, systems of chemical reactions.

Type 2. Situations characterized by interconnections which derive from *the logic of situations.* Examples would be arrangements to manufacture or assemble products, or situations dominated by a decision about to be taken in order to achieve a known objective.

Type 3. Situations in which interconnections are cultural, situations dominated by *the meanings attributed to their perceptions by autonomous observers.* Most real-world problem situations are of this type, both on the small scale (e.g. how should we behave towards ageing parents?) and on the large (e.g. should the nuclear deterrent be abandoned?).

In this perspective it is clear that the hard systems approach was developed in, and is suitable for use in, situations of Types 1 and 2. (Natural science deals with phenomena of Type 1). The soft systems approach is for use in the kind of situation in which it was developed, which were of Type 3.

The most frequent error in using a systems approach is to try to treat Type 3 situations as if they were Type 2. The logic of situations does of course play a large part in the real-world, but it is not necessarily a determining part, and methodology based on the assumption that it is, is bound eventually to pass the problems by.

In any case, examination even of a situation "*clearly*" of Type 1 or Type 2 can most usefully start with an examination of the *context* in which a Type 1 or Type 2 situation is perceived. *This context will itself be a situation of Type 3,* since the decision to see a situation as "Type 1" or "Type 2" excludes other possible attributions of meaning. This emphasizes again that the hard systems approach and its methodology needs to be seen as a special case of the soft systems approach and soft systems methodology.

ACKNOWLEDGEMENTS

Versions of this paper were given at the International Institute for Applied Systems Analysis, Austria, August, 1980, and to the first National Meeting of the UK Systems Society, London, September, 1980. The experiences which have led to the position described here have been shared with many colleagues and several generations of Masters and Doctoral students; I am grateful to them all for their involvements.

REFERENCES

1. Checkland, P. B. *Systems Thinking, Systems Practice.* Wiley, 1981.
2. Checkland, P. B. Science and the Systems Paradigm. *International Journal of General Systems,* **3** (2), 1976.
3. Checkland, P. B. The Shape of the Systems Movement. *Journal of Applied Systems Analysis,* **6**, 1979.
4. Checkland, P. B. The Origins and Nature of "Hard" Systems Thinking. *Journal of Applied Systems Analysis,* **5** (2), 1978.
5. Hall, A. D. *A Methodology for Systems Engineering.* Van Nostrand, 1962.
6. Optner, S. L. (Ed.) *Systems Analysis.* Penguin Books, 1973.
7. Quade, E., Brown, K., Levien, R., Majone, G. and Rakhmankulov, V. Systems Analysis: an outline for the state-of-the-art publications. IIASA RR-76-16, also *Journal of Applied Systems Analysis,* **5** (2), 1976.
8. Checkland, P. B. Towards a Systems-Based Methodology for Real-World Problem Solving. *Journal of Systems Engineering,* **3** (2), 1972.
9. Descartes, R. *Discourse on Method* 1637. Many translations are available: e.g. F. E. Sutcliffe, 1968, Penguin Books.
10. Bertalanffy, L. von. *General System Theory,* Braziller, 1968.
11. Chorley, R. J. and Kennedy B. A. *Physical Geography: a Systems Approach.* Prentice-Hall, 1971.
12. Pincus, A. and Minahan, A. *Social Work and Practice: Model and Method.* Peacock Publishers, 1973.
13. Ashby, W. R. *An Introduction to Cybernetics.* Chapman and Hall, 1956.
14. Pattee, H. H. (Ed.) *Hierarchy Theory: the Challenge of Complex Systems.* Braziller, 1973.
15. Quade, E. and Boucher, W. I. (Eds) *Systems Analysis and Policy Planning: Applications in Defence.* Elsevier, 1968.
16. Churchman, C. W. *The Design of Inquiring Systems.* Basic Books, 1971.
17. Checkland, P. B. A Systems Map of the Universe. *Journal of Systems Engineering,* **2** (2), 1971.
18. Smyth, D. S. and Checkland, P. B. Using a Systems Approach: the Structure of Root Definitions. *Journal of Applied Systems Analysis,* **5** (1), 1976.
19. Checkland, P. B. Techniques in Soft Systems Practice, Part 2: Building Conceptual Models. *Journal of Applied Systems Analysis,* **6**, 1979.
20. Vickers, G. *The Art of Judgement.* Chapman and Hall, 1965.
21. Bryer, R. A. and Kistruck, R. Systems Theory and Social Science. Working Paper 735/76, Warwick University School of Industrial and Business Studies, 1976.
22. Cohen, P. *Modern Social Theory.* Heinemann, 1968.
23. Durkheim, E. *The Rules of Sociological Method.* (1895) (Translated by S. A. Solovay, J. H. Mueller; Free Press, 1964.)
24. Kolakowski, L. *Positivist Philosophy.* Penguin Books, 1972.

25. Merton, R. K. Manifest and Latent Functions. (1957) in Demerath, N. J. and Peterson, R. A. (Eds). *System, Change and Conflict.* Free Press, 1967.
26. Roche, M. *Phenomenology, Language and the Social Sciences.* Routledge and Kegan Paul, 1973.
27. Husserl, E. *The Idea of Phenomenology.* (1907). (Translated W. P. Alston, G. Nakhnikian; Nijhoff, 1964.)
28. Schutz, A. *Collected Papers Vols I, II, III.* Nijhoff, 1962, 1964, 1966.
29. Luckmann, T. (Ed.) *Phenomenology and Sociology.* Penguin Books, 1978.
30. Makkreel, R. A. *Dilthey: Philosopher of the Human Studies.* Princeton University Press, 1975.
31. Morris, M. B. *An Excursion into Creative Sociology.* Columbia University Press, 1977.
32. Giddens, A. *New Rules of Sociological Method.* Hutchinson, 1976.
33. Runciman, W. G. *Social Science and Political Theory.* Cambridge University Press, 1963.
34. Robertson, R. Towards an Identification of the Major Axes of Sociological Analysis. In J. Rex (Ed.), *Approaches to Sociology.* Routledge and Kegan Paul, 1974.
35. Burrell, G. and Morgan, G. *Sociological Paradigms and Organisational Analysis.* Heinemann, 1979.
36. Bertalanffy, L. von. General System Theory. (1956). In *General System Theory.* Braziller, 1968.
37. Parsons, T. *The Social System.* Free Press, 1951.
38. Katz, D. and Kahn, R. L. *The Social Psychology of Organisations.* Wiley, 1966.
39. Connerton, P. (Ed.) *Critical Sociology.* Penguin Books, 1976.
40. Jay, M. *The Dialectical Imagination.* Heinemann, 1973.
41. Habermas, J. and Luhmann, N. *Theorie der Gesellschaft oder Sozialtechnologie.* Suhrkamp 1971. (See also: F. W. Sixel "The Problem of Sense: Habermas-v-Luhmann" in J. O'Neil *On Critical Theory.* Heinemann, 1976.)
42. Habermas, J. *Toward a Rational Society.* Heinemann, 1971.
43. Habermas, J. On Systematically Distorted Communication and Towards a Theory of Communicative Competence. *Inquiry,* **13**, 1970.
44. Mingers, J. Towards an Appropriate Social Theory for Applied Systems Thinking: Critical Theory and Soft Systems Methodology. *Journal of Applied Systems Analysis,* **7**, 1980.

Appendix to Chapter 4

The Changing Process of Systems Analysis: An Outline Systems Analysis

Author's Note: During the meeting "Rethinking the Process of Systems Analysis" at IIASA 25th–29th August 1980, stimulated by the papers presented and by the importance of the topic under discussion, I reflected upon the event itself by carrying out a brief systems study of it using the "soft systems methodology" I had discussed earlier in the paper "Rethinking A Systems Approach". The outcome of that outline study was presented to the final discussion and is summarized here.

INTRODUCTION

A meeting at which knowledgeable practitioners from several countries discuss the process of systems analysis with a view to "rethinking" it, may itself be regarded as a problem situation – one perhaps susceptible to systems analysis? If so, it is not systems engineering or RAND-style systems analysis which will be appropriate, since there is here neither a client seeking an efficient means to a known-to-be-desirable end nor an obvious system-to-be-engineered. It is this kind of unstructured problem situation in which (and for which) soft systems methodology was developed.[1] What follows is therefore a brief (and immediate) outline "soft" systems analysis of the problem of rethinking the process of systems analysis.

METHODOLOGY

In soft systems methodology a would-be neutral "rich picture" of the problem situation is assembled. In the light of it a few relevant human activity systems are selected, "relevant" that is, hopefully, to bringing about useful change. These relevant systems are named in "root definitions" and models of the systems are then built which can be compared with the expression of the problem situation. The purpose of the comparison is to provide a structured debate about change, change which people within the situation deem both desirable and feasible.

In the outline study presented here, the picture of the problem situation suggested that what was needed was a way of viewing a complex many-stranded debate within the systems movement, a debate which begins to

61

resemble a "paradigm shift", in Kuhn's terms.[2] Two relevant systems were selected; in order to progress rapidly, their root definitions were set out in terms of their necessary elements as expressed by the mnemonic CATWOE.[3] The comparison was then done at the level of the root definitions, omitting model building in the interest of speed. The comparison stage comprised bringing together the CATWOE elements of the two root definitions and their equivalents in real-world systems analysis. It was not possible to take the study further, since what was now required was a debate involving the real-world owners of this problem situation (rather than recommendations based only upon the analyst's own value system). However, it is suggested that this small study does provide a useful framework in which the issue of the future of systems analysis can be discussed coherently.

RICH PICTURE

The rich picture here consisted of the many pages of notes through which I had sought both to follow and contribute to the discussions. The flavour of it can be conveyed through some of the significant quotations I had recorded:

1. Mathematics is not enough . . . how can SA cope with ethics . . . this being essential when people starve in a world of plenty.
2. Criticism is essential . . . best done via dialectics. 30 years ago OR was the Antithesis to the then ways of managing . . . now we hear people saying "that problem is not OR".
3. The systems analyst places his expertise at the disposal of the legitimate authority in the situation; he works within the decision taker's values.
4. There is need for professionals to develop the *craft* skills . . .
5. SA seeks to improve "procedural rationality", the process of decision making, rather than individual decisions.
6. There is a gap between theory and practice . . . the "tool makers" dominate the profession.
7. As *professions* emerge so do what they define as "problems". The amateur landscape gardener of genius was known as "Capability" Brown, not "Problematical" Brown. He explored the capabilities of a piece of terrain, not "solved" its "problems".
8. SA frequently serves political masters; but the logic of politics is not the logic of SA.
9. There is a long history of advisors – priests, lawyers, court jesters – now we have systems analysts. Criteria for "good" or "bad" SA are not clear, so examining its process is essential. If SA is to adopt "fallibilism" (rather than "falsification", which seems inappropriate) then we need the "conventional" definition of "false" from *the community of workers*. Note that the other advisor-professions value highly the procedures not the solutions . . . note the lawyers' concern for the "due processes" of law.

10. SA is in a paradigm shift. Social paradoxes (man in nature/man in society) lead to logical paradoxes – the system of systems, the set of sets. ... Dialectical thinking might provide a new paradigm but obstacles to its adoption arise from the condition of society.

11. Because SA leads to action (not learning) its theory is important, because that theory will "validate" the action. SA joins clients in articulating and elaborating the components of *reflection before action*.

12. SA needs better descriptions of methodological guidelines in context. IIASA needs curriculum designers and text book writers as well as research specialists. You have to be able to agree with oneself.

13. (In reply to the last sentence) No! No! No!

14. The direction now is towards "systems studies" in which many scenarios are studied rather than the alternatives for one decision.

15. The emphasis is moving to "actors" not "organization", "legitimacy" not "efficiency".

16. It is often said the field needs a Newton. It's a poor metaphor; it needs a Jung or a Freud.

17. We need to ask what a dialectical theory of management would be like. Dialectical debate needs assumptions to be surfaced and mapped.

18. A seminar of medical practitioners would not be like this.

ROOT DEFINITIONS OF RELEVANT SYSTEMS

The very existence of a discussion like the one in question implies "an analyst" and "a real-world and its problems", a world in which the analyst wishes to make useful intervention. He is assumed to possess a particular set of reasonably unified concepts and procedures, as is shown by the fact that they have a name meaningful to many people: "systems analysis". At a very basic level, then, a relevant notional human activity system is that shown in Figure 1.

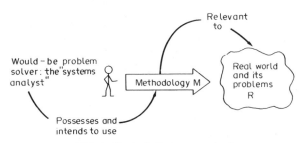

FIG. 1. The basic "relevant system"

Obviously in such a system an important factor will be *the relation of M to R*, since it is unlikely that useful intervention will follow from too great a mismatch: a mathematical methodology M, for example, will have little impact on an R which consists of aesthetic problems. With that in mind, and noting that our problem theme is the nature of systems analysis, we may make a root definition of the basic system in which R is taken to contain systems, to be systemic, and M is a systematic examination of those systems. This implies systematic examination of systems in the real world as a means of problem solving. This root definition, which we may call Paradigm 1, is clearly mappable on to classic systems analysis and systems engineering.

Expressing Paradigm 1 in this way immediately directs thoughts to counter definitions based on different world views. If we transfer the systemicity within the root definition from R to M, for example, we have Paradigm 2, a root definition in which a systemic M investigates a problematical R. Clearly this version will map on to soft systems thinking rather than hard. Let us proceed with these two root definitions.

COMPARISON

Following the process of soft systems methodology within this study, we can elaborate the root definitions which I have called Paradigms 1 and 2 by enumerating the CATWOE elements. If we examine the *real-world* versions of these for *"text-book"* applications of classic systems analysis/systems engineering and soft systems methodology, we can by this means set up the "comparison" stage of the chosen methodology. This will take us very quickly through a first iteration of the methodology stages, and also yield analytical clarity. Taking this approach does not deny that the exigencies of *actual* – rather than "text book" – applications lead to what is often a rather messy dealing with both hard and soft considerations.

[The reader will have noticed that I am myself in this study using the methodological guidelines of soft systems methodology flexibly. It is an example of what Naughton[4] calls the use of "strategic rules" rather than the "constitutive rules" which define the methodology.]

Table 1 sets out the comparison of Paradigms 1 and 2, done in the way described.

When we compare the columns for Paradigms 1 and 2 with the sample quotations which express the problem situation, we see that *virtually all the points they make either assert Paradigm 1 (for example quotations 3, 7, 8) assert Paradigm 2 (2, 14, 15) or contemplate a shift from one to the other (1, 5, 10, 17)*.

The next methodological step in this study (which happens to be using a "Paradigm 2" methodology – soft systems methodology) would be to draw the problem owners into the debate on the comparison between the root definitions and the expression of the problem situation, the preliminary comparison being that summarized in Table 1 and the preceding paragraph. This is not here possible, of course, so it is necessary to end this first iteration at

TABLE 1. *"Catwoe" elements*[3] *for the root definitions paradigms 1 and 2*

			Paradigm 1. Hard systems thinking	Paradigm 2. Soft systems thinking
C	"Customers"	Victims and beneficiaries of what the system does	Decision-makers who command real-world systems	Participants who debate the differences between the models and the expression of the problem situation
A	"Actors"	Those who carry out the system activities	External analysts and engineers	Those who choose to take part: analysts and/or problem owners
T	"Transformation"	What input does this system transform into what output?	Information into advice to decision-makers	Information into specific learning for the "actors"
W	"Weltanschauung"	The world view which makes it meaningful to consider this system	R is systemic M is systematic Optimization is possible	R is problematical M is systemic Learning is possible
O	"Owners"	Those who could demolish this notional system, could prevent it from acting	Decision-makers/clients	"Actors" as defined above, or the analyst
E	"Environmental constraints"	The things in its environment which this system takes as given	Power structures and value systems of the decision-maker-clients	As little as possible compatible with achieving change in the problem situation

this point. Although the work of only an hour or two, however, this study serves to sharpen discussion of issues related to the future development of the process of systems analysis. And it leaves us with a slightly sharper way of expressing the problem. It leaves us with the question: what are the intellectual and institutional problems of a changing mode of enquiry as it moves from the professional appraisal of a relatively well-defined problem to a dialectical enquiry which orchestrates the interaction of clashing value systems?

REFERENCES

1. Checkland, P. B. *Systems Thinking, Systems Practice.* Wiley, 1981.
2. Kuhn, T. S. *The Structure of Scientific Revolutions.* Chicago University Press, 1962.
3. Smyth, D. S. and Checkland, P. B. Using a Systems Approach: the Structure of Root Definitions. *Journal of Applied Systems Analysis,* **5** (1), 1976.
4. Naughton, J. Theory and Practice in Systems Research. *Journal of Applied Systems Analysis,* **8**, 1981.

5

*Thought and Wisdom**

C. WEST CHURCHMAN

I still remember the astonishment I felt when, about 2 years go, I was called to jury duty in Marin County, California. A group of us formed a panel, and a random selection process asked one person after another to answer some questions. One of the questions (apparently of central importance) asked the prospective juror whether he or she could separate in his mind the process of judging whether a certain young man was guilty or innocent of an armed robbery of a restaurant, from the processes that would follow (e.g. imprisonment or release).

To me the answer was perfectly obvious: of course not. Here was a system, one of the components of which a jury trial, and another component was the so-called criminal justice system which I'd long since decided was fraught with inequities. The jury trial had a reasonable chance of throwing the young man into the jaws of this criminal justice system. How could I conceivably stand up and declare that the two processes – the trial and the subsequent justice system – were systemically separable?

But to my astonishment, one after another of my fellow citizens unhesitatingly answered the judge in the affirmative. Indeed, none of them even asked his honour to explain what the question meant (to a systems philosopher its meaning is quite obscure). Not all the candidate jurors were selected. (One loving wife of a police officer actually believed that officers make more accurate witnesses than non-officers – a devotion beyond the call of marital duty, I'd say.) But none was rejected because he declared he could not separate the trial from its possible aftermaths.

So I sat there with considerable nervousness as to what I should say when called upon. My uppity ego was telling me to tell the judge "I am a systems expert and the question is absurd since the answer is obviously 'no'. All social systems are strongly nonseparable with respect to their components, and this one is clearly no exception. If your honour would take the time to read a few of my books, you'd know this is so and not bother us by asking foolish

* A revised version of this paper first given at IIASA became the first lecture in the ninth and final Gaither Lecture Series, given at the University of California, Berkeley, May, 1981.

questions." My more cautious (cowardly?) ego asked whether such a reply might not evoke a "contempt of court" sentence. "But I *am* contemptuous of the court", said the brave ego. Luckily the random number system wisely never got to calling me.

When I got home, I thought I could see why everyone else was so quick to say "yes". To them, it must have seemed obvious that the young man had entered the restaurant at a certain time and used a gun to demand money, or else he had not done anything of the kind. The past contained one of these two facts, and the jury trial was being used to determine which fact had occurred. It was not being used to draw inferences about what should happen in the future to the young man; that would be up to the judge, parole officers, prison officers, etc.

But to me this piece of ontology was quite deceptive. One could believe, reasonably enough, that history contains an episode at a certain place and time (the happenings in the restaurant at 6.15 p.m. on a certain date), but decide *not* to undergo the process of discovering whether history contains it. To use perhaps too superficial an example, I do believe that beneath the surface of my front yard there are some old gold pieces, or else not. But nothing would induce me to take shovel in hand to try to find out, even if I had found a letter in the house from some prior resident saying he had buried them there.

The point is that once you dig for facts or coins, you change a lot of other things as well, and these changes may not be ones you want. Of course, I think most of the potential jurors would recognize one feature of the situation that makes fact-finding nonseparable from the aftermath, namely, that they determine the fact incorrectly, a common enough mistake on the part of juries no matter how sincere and "objective" they try to be. But I suppose that most of them believed the error could be as much one way as the other: to incarcerate the innocent is (for them) about the same as freeing the guilty. Indeed, they are not alone in this regard: science's typical way of expressing its findings in terms of a sample mean plus or minus an error term expresses the same idea. In the case of science, one often doesn't know the "other things" that people will create from the findings, but surely a guilty man free in the streets is a totally different event from an innocent man in a cell. Since I'm fairly sure that the system that holds people in cells – innocent or not – is incredibly inequitable, how can I wilfully join a subsystem – the jury trial – that so often puts people there?

I really should not have been too surprised at the behaviour of my fellow jurors, because I've been living a lifetime among fellow academics who firmly believe there is a clear distinction between the determination of facts and the determination of ethical values. I suspect they have no adequate defence of the argument just given which connects the two determinations ("should this particular fact be determined?" is an ethical issue); but I also suspect they have never posed the issue in this manner. What has been strange to me is that operational researchers, city planners, policy analysts, and others of their kind, also believe that the separation of fact-determination from ethical-determination is real. Indeed, many of them do not seem to believe that the determination of ethical values belongs in their business, which is essentially an inquiry into plans.

To illustrate, during the past 16 years at Berkeley, the Center for Research in Management has presented a series of lectures in Systems Science, the first having been given by Charles Hitch[1] in 1965. With one exception, none of the lecturers addressed the question of the proper determination of ethical values at all, even though I believe that every one of them assumed some ethical foundation in his work. Hitch assumed that there should be a well designed military administration in the USA. Schultze[2] assumed that there are good and bad (evil?) budget designs. Rivlin[3] assumed that social experimentation should be conducted for the good of the country. Macy[4] implicitly assumed that public broadcasting, if "properly" conducted, is a "good thing", well worth fighting for. Vickers[5] believed that our social world is in peril, and society needs redesigning of responsibilities to reduce the peril. Simon[6] said that the use of artificial intelligence to bring some of us up to the level of being "satisficed" is a good thing. Raiffa,[7] whose topic surely called for an ethical discussion since he dealt with arbitration and negotiation, cleverly shied away from all ethical issues except those dealing with his version of logical consistency. The exception was Jantsch[8] who did discuss at some length the relationship between matters of morality and his theory of universal evolution. But he lets method (paradigm) lead, and problems come second.

The story of the Gaither Lectures is repeated in many other contexts: city planning departments which practically forbid classroom discussion of ethics, operational research texts which never mention ethical issues the student may confront in the future, public policy schools which ignore the ethical foundations of policy, and so on. Schools of Business Administration in the USA often have departments which teach courses on law and society where ethical issues are addressed, but ethics is handled by case methods or exercises, rather than reading the history of ethics.

If I may add one more mystery to the story, the avoidance of the issue of how to determine ethically justified values is a fairly recent occurrence in the so-called "scientific" community. In the classical age of Greek science, from the pre-Socratics through Plato, Aristotle, and on into the Hellenistic period, the issue was central to all science. Much more recently, the age that saw the creation of modern science, and most especially the seventeenth and eighteenth centuries in the West, regarded the issue as among the most important ones that science must face. I leave it to those who are more astute than I in understanding historical causes, to tell us what happened in the nineteenth century that turned the intellectual community away from basic ethical issues. I sometimes suspect that my most beloved and admired Kant had a lot to do with it. Rather, it was Kant's idea that the creation of knowledge of the phenomenal world[9] is totally different from the creation of moral knowledge that did the trick. The post-Kantian scientists then concluded that intellectually one could dwell in the first world and simply have "non-scientific" opinions in the second, a conclusion that I am sure Kant never intended.

The title of this chapter is "Thought and Wisdom". Here I would like to suggest one notion of the topic, namely, that wisdom is thought combined with a concern for ethics. This is a highly intellectual idea about wisdom, and may indeed emanate from thought itself. In any event, it leads me to say that the science of Leibniz, Spinoza, Hume, and Kant of the seventeenth and eighteenth centuries was far wiser than the so-called science of the twentieth century.

I now would like to spell out in more detail the very common philosophical position that in effect is one version of the epistemology of planning.

To give this epistemology a label, I'll call it bounded systems thinking. It begins with the ontological assumption that the world of human affairs consists of problems and possible solutions: problems really exist, and the first task is to identify and describe them, a task that is not radically different from an entomologist's description of insects in a given volume of earth.

These planners differ from the natural scientist in the manner in which they assign importance to the problems they find. Problems, for them, become important to the extent that people are legitimately concerned about them. If possible, it is objectively neater if people's concerns are based on a certain kind of legitimacy, say, economic cost. I recently served as chairman of a USA National Academy of Sciences committee on how to get more USA drivers to wear their safety belts (apparently only one in seven does so at the present time). It was only natural for the committee members to try to show that the concern about safety belts was legitimate, and to many of them the proof of the legitimacy was the economic cost to the nation and its industries of the failure of drivers to wear them. Apparently, basing legitimacy on economic costs seemed to most of the committee members a calmer, more thoughtful approach than simply getting angry at the carelessness of people who got themselves and others killed by their failure to wear safety belts.

Now the reason, I think, that these planners want to formulate the problem first, is that such a step provides feasible boundaries to the ethical issues, which need no further defence. "All will agree that needless waste of economic resources is highly undesirable, and that remedies must be found to reduce or eliminate the waste." The keen interest the USA has taken in productivity is just another example of this kind of thinking.

I don't believe I've ever seen a textbook in operational research or planning that did not state that the first task was to formulate the problem, including the text that I and a number of other authors wrote in 1957.[10] We are to search among the insect population for those that do the most damage, and then make models and gather data to tell us how to minimize the harm they create. By behaving in this manner, we also reduce to a minimum our responsibility to defend our planning activities on an ethical basis.

IIASA is a good example of the kind of planning I've been describing; indeed, it has been organized by "problem areas", without any explicit justification: energy, food, human settlements, etc. Its Charter announces that it will address the problems of peace in the world, as though the problems of peace could readily be separated from the problems of war. Perhaps a very naive political question is to ask an Institute devoted to studying human systems to explain what kind of system the Institute is, and to justify its existence or nonexistence on the basis of its reply.

One takes a step from thought towards wisdom if one asks thought itself to examine one of its most precious assumptions. To do this, suppose we explore in a "what if" mode for awhile. What if problems are not like insects that populate a volume? What if the so-called problems are all tightly interconnected, every problem being an aspect of all the others?

I can ask one of my mentors, Anaxagoras, to illustrate this speculation. In the sixth and fifth centuries B.C., many brilliant Greek physicists were asking about the nature of the reality we humans inhabit. They proceeded in their inquiry by the method of analysis, which means breaking down reality to irreducible elements, and then showing how the elements can be used to explain all the complicated objects we observe: tables, buildings, grass, lakes, mountains, etc. The process is very similar to the method that systems analysis uses in building its models out of "elementary" variables. Water, or water–air–earth–fire, or other possibilities were explored by these "pre-Socratic" thinkers. Anaxagoras took a non-analytic approach. He said, in effect, that no matter how far one goes in breaking an object down to parts and subparts and sub-subparts, the resulting piece of reality still contains everything: "in every thing is everything". He did add one strange exception: not every thing has a "rational principle" ("nous"), a point I'll return to in a moment.

Hence, the "what if" I'd like to explore is this: in every so-called problem of humanity is to be found all other problems, no matter how minutely we analyse.

We can also add Anaxagoras' exception: in every problem is to be found all other problems, except the rational principle. The "rational principle" I take to mean the ethical principles that justify any approach we take to better the social condition. That is, we need an "unbounded" systems approach which must include a study of the ethics of humanity, not within a problem area, but universally.

I should now add that the speculation I'm trying to design does *not* exclude problems from the reality of the planner. Indeed, all planning begins with a problem. There is a close analogy here with the beginning of *Kant's Critique of Pure Reason*, where Kant says "That all knowledge begins with experience, there can be no doubt". The unwary are apt to conclude "here's just another empiricist", except that Kant immediately goes on to tell us that knowledge must contain more than experience, e.g. nonexperiential universals. By analogy, my speculation says that all planning begins with a problem, but should not be confined to the problem statement. Furthermore, the beginning should not be a clear problem formulation, but rather should be an utterance of moral outrage. John Dewey once said that problems arise from "felt needs", but I think this is much too mild a statement. Problems arise for all of us personally when we see people being badly treated by other people; for example, helpless people treated in ways that arouse our moral feelings. One very sad aspect of a great deal of planning research is that the roots of the "Request-for-Proposals" are cut off at the very start; no wonder the plant withers and dies as proposals, interim and final reports are written.

For example; the problem of world-wide starvation is morally outrageous: that a species that has the resources to feed every member adequately and the intelligence to do so, in fact lets millions starve. But my speculation says that this problem should unfold into other problems, of national politics, of world trade, of religion, of culture, etc. To try to define "starvation" carefully at the outset tends, I think, to prevent the unfolding, so that we planners remain stuck in the bounded problem region.

I should also add to the picture the idea that moral outrage does not judge the importance of problems in terms of numbers, either numbers of people or numbers of dollars. Recently, I was asked to write a piece about Locke, California, a town that was founded by the Chinese railroad workers of a couple of generations ago. Now there are only about twenty of the eighty-year-old men left. The state planners want to make Locke into a state historical monument for tourists, while a developer from Hong Kong wants to make it a kind of "Chinese Disneyland". No one had asked the old men what they wanted until a young man decided to make a video tape of the town. The old men wanted to be left alone to die in their town, with no tourists and no redesign. One could not help feeling moral outrage that the lives of the old men were being treated as means only by the state planners and the developers. No matter that there are "only" twenty old men who will live for "only" 5 to 10 years more. The moral outrage is still quite strong. I might add, of course, that if the numbers are very high, as in the case of murdered Jews in World War II, or starving kids in the world today, then moral outrage may be accompanied by moral astonishment and horror.

The point is that the problem of Locke will eventually unfold into the larger and larger systems problem, to the problems of the aged in our society, to the problems of resources for all the needy, and so on. The beginning, the image that starts us on the pathway of understanding, need not be very "large" at all.

The speculation I am trying to depict has an awesome quality which is caught by the etymology of the verb "to decide", the meaning of which comes from the Latin verb "to cut". A decision cuts away all the other possible threads of human life, most of them never to occur in the reality of one person's lifetime. This seems patently true to most of us as we reflect in ageing on our decisions about marriage, children, jobs, education, friends, and enemies. Imagination has no difficulty in showing us what "it might have been", and as imagination performs its task of designing a film about our other possible lives, mood accompanies the film with feelings such as "Thank God it never happened", "What if it had happened?", or "What joy there would have been".

The awe arises from the reflection that we humans were born into a world where decisions to act cut off the realization of all sorts of possible designs of human living, finally and forever. Speculative history can draw upon this reflection as a rich source: a history where Lincoln decided not to go to Ford's Theatre, or Caesar not to cross the Rubicon, or Hitler to invade England early in World War II.

Now it is perfectly reasonable for thought to argue that all decisions we humans believe we make are not real. Indeed, thought of the past had some pretty strong arguments for the position that "decision", in the sense of wilfully cutting off possibilities, is illusory. For a rationalist like Spinoza, who believed that all reality is perfection, the existence of an event in reality is like a theorem in geometry. One cannot decide to make triangles with interior angles summing to less than two right angles. In the same manner, one cannot decide whom to marry. All events are inferences from the perfection of God. Leibniz, who has much in common with present day operational researchers, said in effect that God built a gigantic model (e.g. a nonlinear program), which described possible universes, and since this God was a perfect computer, He could use the model to calculate the design of an optimal universe, which He then implemented (having no politics to prevent implementation).

The end of the nineteenth century witnessed a severe battle between "merchanists" and "vitalists" about the reality of freedom of choice. The fight was really between some leading physicists and some philosophical biologists; the latter, e.g. Henri Bergson, wanted to use a non-physical "vital force" to define life. But the physicists realized that the vitalists were ruining their game, because in the physics of the nineteenth century, the aim was to state the laws of nature without exception. If the vitalist won out, the poor physicist would have to state the Second Law of Thermodynamics with the added clause "except when vital forces are around".

Today, the fight has virtually disappeared. I will cite two intellectual reasons and one humanistic why this is so. First, most philosophers have come to the conclusion that the universe was not created by a perfect designer, nor does it operate according to perfect laws. One suspects at times that Jantsch's enthusiasm for his evolutionary principle may be leading the way back to a Spinozistic viewpoint, with evolution as the perfect force instead of deduction. But I found in my friendship with Erich, that every time I tried to interpret his work in the context of the history of philosophy, he most emphatically denied the interpretation.

Second, we logicians have discovered that contraries (propositions that cannot both be true) exist only in the context of a given language and its rules of sentence-formation and deduction. In broader languages, the contrariness disappears. Thus, Euclid's famous Parallel Postulate is false in so-called non-Euclidian plane geometries, but both Euclidian plane geometry and non-Euclidian plane geometry hold true for surfaces in three dimensional geometry (where "straight line" is the shortest path between two points on the surface). In the same manner, Singer[11] showed how in a more general language of science than either the language of mechanics or biology, one could legitimately say that all events are determined and that some events are freely chosen; "the world behaves in accordance with deterministic (including statistical) laws" and "the world in part behaves in accordance with teleological laws of choice" are *not* contraries.

For me, the humanistic change is more to the point. To say that all human decisions are pre-determined is a pure cop-out, for it removes from humanity's concerns the responsibility of the plight of the world, its poverty, pollution, overpopulation, and military threat. This point is probably in the spirit of the Vickers' lectures, because he takes responsibility to be an essential part of the structure of organizations, including nations. I'd be inclined to say that the failure of the intellectual argument for determinism is morally outrageous.

I began my discussion of an Anaxagoras' hypothesis with "what if?" Now I would like thought to carry the speculation into reality, because there is an argument that convinces me that the nonbounded approach to systems is the correct one.

In defence of its correctness, I call as witness an old problem of systems analysis, namely, the inventory problem. In one of its "simplest" examples, the problem asks how many items should be ordered by a retail store and placed on the shelf to respond adequately to consumer demand. The problem is deceptively simple, because it seems to be a mere matter of the comparison of two costs: the cost of over-ordering so that unsold inventories sit unproductively on the shelf, and the cost of being out of the item when a customer is there and ready to purchase it. The simplicity fades away when we ask how we should measure the first cost. What does it cost the store to keep one thousand dollars worth of inventory on the shelf for a day. The obvious answer is this: it costs the store the amount it could have made by using the thousand dollars for money-making purposes. But this response is ambiguous, because the thousand dollars could be used in lots of ways: it could be gambled at the race track, invested in bonds or risk stocks, or to hire a brilliant consultant for a day. The question, then, should be modified as follows: "What is the best use of the one thousand dollars?" But this question asks how a firm should best use its capital, especially in the form of cash. Since cash can be transformed into other forms of capital, the question is what should be the capital structure of the firm.

In other words, the "simple" problem of inventory requires for its answering the answering of what appears to be a much more complicated problem, namely, how the firm's capital should be managed. It is easy to see that the question of purchasing for inventory also requires for its answering the determination of the firm's marketing policies, since we need to know not what demand customers do make, but rather the optimal demand pattern the firm can create through pricing and advertising.

So the very often neglected problem of data-determination in operational research leads us to the same conclusion as did the Anaxagoras speculation: in a problem as simple as the question of the amount to purchase for inventory, is to be found all the other problems of the firm. In any specific problem, one finds the connectedness to all the other problems, and it is the nature of the connectedness that is central to the planning of an organization.

I think that our failure to examine and plan around connectedness accounts for the plight of the human being today. Of course, the problem is how we are going to go about the task of determining the connections. Some systems analysts want to build very large models, but I don't see how the size of the model necessarily answers the question of the determination of the "opportunity" costs I've just been discussing.

There are several interesting epistemological consequences of opportunity costing. One is that the method of analysis called reductionism completely fails, because as we pursue the question of how much the keeping of inventory on a shelf really costs, the pathway leads us, not to simpler issues, but to more and more complicated ones.

The second point is that an opportunity cost is not an empirical datum, or "fact". There's simply no way to observe it. Nor is it a mere "appearance", because it's real enough: what I sacrifice when I give up an opportunity to do x because I do y instead is a real sacrifice. The exhaustiveness of appearance and reality in the old fashioned ontology of centuries of philosophy simply disappears. Opportunity costs are "neither of the above".

It is reasonable enough to ask how we do in fact determine opportunity costs in practice. One answer I've already suggested and rejected: that we determine them by bounding the problem. If I go to Reno and have the opportunity of playing blackjack or craps, I can perform an expected-return analysis of these two options and select the one with the largest score. But this doesn't answer the question whether I should be in Reno in the first place.

I do know how some of our ancestors suggested we solve the larger problem: namely, by trying to understand the nature of God. A perfect intellect would have no problem with the fact that every problem of decision-making, no matter how small, is connected to every other problem, no matter how large. Both Leibniz and Spinoza seem to have viewed God in this manner. But neither seems to have asked whether a being that is simultaneously omniscient and omnipotent can also be perfectly benevolent.[12] There seems to be growing evidence in political history that the more technologically powerful and knowledgeable a nation becomes, the less its benevolence with respect to the helpless people of the world.

I also realize that opportunity costs are determined by politics, by the use of political clout in getting Congress and other legislative bodies to allocate funds, or in getting managers of firms, or hospitals, or educational institutions to support programs.

No doubt this discussion raises far more questions than it begins to respond to. That's because my intellect is on the side of question-asking. I realize that there are many who believe that what we need in today's messy world are some down-to-earth, specific answers as to how we're going to feed the starving, reduce militarism, clean the environment, and increase health. We question-askers are very much afraid that, as in the past, so in the future, these very practical, realistic, feasible responses to the questions, if carried into action, will make the world worse than ever.

REFERENCES

1. Charles J. Hitch, *Decision-making for Defense*, Berkeley, CA: University of California Press, 1965. Gaither Lecture Series in Systems Science, University of California, Center for Research in Management, Berkeley, April 5, 7, 8, 9, 1965.
2. Charles Schultze, *The Politics and Economics of Public Spending*, Washington, DC: The Brookings Institution, 1968. Gaither Lecture Series in Systems Science, University of California, Center for Research in Management, Berkeley, April 11, 12, May 15, 16, 1968.
3. Alice M. Rivlin, *Systematic Thinking for Social Action*, Washington, DC: The Brookings Institution, 1971. Gaither Lecture Series in Systems Science, University of California, Center for Research in Management, Berkeley, January 12, 14, 26, 28, 1970.
4. John W. Macy, Jr, *To Irrigate a Wasteland*, A Quantum Book, Berkeley, CA: University of California Press, 1974. Gaither Lecture Series in Systems Science, University of California, Center for Research in Management, Berkeley, February 5, 6, 12, 13, 1973.
5. Sir Geoffrey Vickers, *Responsibility — Its Sources and Limits*, The Systems Inquiry Series, Seaside, CA: Intersystems Publications, 1980. Gaither Lecture Series in Systems Science, University of California, Center for Research in Management, Berkeley, April 15, 22, 29, and May 6, 1975.
6. Herbert A. Simon, *The Sciences of the Artificial Revisited*, 2nd ed., Cambridge, MA: M.I.T. Press. Gaither Lecture Series in Systems Science, University of California, Center for Research in Management, Berkeley, January 28, 30, and February 1, 1980.
7. Howard Raiffa, title of book to be announced, Cambridge, MA: Harvard Press, forthcoming. Gaither Lecture Series in Systems Science, University of California, Center for Research in Management, Berkeley, November 20, 21, 24, and 25, 1980.
8. Erich Jantsch, *The Self-organizing Universe*, The Systems Science and World Order Library, Pergamon Press, Oxford, 1980.

9. Immanual Kant, *Critique of Pure Reason*, 1781.
10. C. West Churchman, Russell L. Ackoff and E. Leonard Arnoff, *et al.*, *Introduction to Operations Research*, John Wiley, NY, 1957.
11. Edgar A. Singer, Jr, *Experience and Reflection*, University of Pennsylvania Press, Philadelphia, PA, 1957.
12. G. W. Leibniz seems near to examining the question in *Discours de Metaphysique*.

6

Policy Analysis for Advising Rulers[1]

YEHEZKEL DROR

I. SCOPE AND PURPOSE

This chapter considers main issues of policy analysis for advising Rulers, as a task of much importance by itself; and as a "pure type" situation which serves to bring out broad features, problems and requirements of policy analysis.

My basic propositions, using the terminology of the book as a whole, are that advancement of policy analysis for advising Rulers should constitute a main dimension of rethinking the process of operations research and systems analysis. And, that consideration of the needs of advancing policy analysis for advising Rulers serves to identify and explore broader needs of increasing the utility of policy analysis for handling complex and intricate policy issues.

My treatment deals with "policy analysis" in the sense of a profession-craft clustering on providing systematic, rational, and science-based help with decision-making – including problem identification, options development, comprehensive impact evaluation, alternative future guesstimation, goal development and so on (Dror, 1971). The chapter deals with policy analysis for advising Rulers, looking at policy analysis both as a process of deriving advice to Rulers; and as a structure, in the sense of policy analysis units working for and near Rulers. The term "Ruler" is used in the clinical and technical sense of real heads of government, never mind their formal titles. With some adjustments, the concept "Ruler" also covers collegial and collective ruling bodies, such as Cabinets.

With some changes, main findings and recommendations of this paper apply to a larger set of issues and circumstances. Thus:

– The term "Ruler" can be expanded to include other top level decision-makers in central government and, with additional adjustments, top level decision-makers in public and private organizations, such as enterprises and local government.

79

- Large parts of the paper, especially those dealing with methodology, apply to policy analysis for advising Rulers from a distance, such as by independent Think Tanks and by party research organizations. In such cases, special problems of communication between the Ruler and the analysis unit arise. Thus, it seems that, in the absence of a policy analysis outfit near the Rulers to serve as a liaison between the Ruler and policy analysis from a distance, the latter will have difficulties to become relevant to Ruler's concerns and to communicate its findings to the Ruler in a useable form. Such special issues are not directly dealt with here, but much of the discourse applies.
- More difficult are adjustments and applications of my analysis to the variety of Third World countries. In some of them, primary problems of nation building and independence maintenance, as well as features of political culture, together with scarcity of professional infrastructure, pose special difficulties to policy analysis for advising Rulers. Many Third World countries face a painful paradox, because policy analysis, together with realistic vision, is essential for them in order to achieve very high aspirations; while, at the same time, these countries pose strong barriers to correct utilization of policy analysis as an aid to critical decision-making. Exploration of special problems of policy analysis in Third World countries in general and for advising their Rulers in particular, are left for another occasion.
- Parts of the evaluation of contemporary policy analysis inadequacies and of proposed progress towards what is called "advanced policy analysis" apply to broader issues of the usefulness of policy analysis for handling complex problems, at a range of decision levels. Thus, to move to the converse of Rulers, an interesting problem exists of policy analysis for citizens at large, to permit progress in the direction of more enlightened public opinion, both as a goal by itself and as a condition for good policy-making in democratic societies.

In contradistinction to such expanded applications of the core ideas of this paper, a number of issues are excluded or neglected, even if in reality they cannot be completely compartmentalized from policy analysis for advising Rulers. Thus, I do not consider various supportive functions for Rulers, fulfilled by other types of advisers, such as: emotional support; purely political advice; help with ideology; and mass-media handling assistance. Also, I do not discuss specialized advice, such as in economics, science and technology, intelligence, and governmental reorganization; though some interfaces between such specialized advice functions and policy analysis are touched upon.

This is a technical chapter, dealing with policy analysis to help Rulers. A prior question is, which Rulers should be aided; better technical support for a crazy or criminal Ruler will only increase the evils he is inflicting. Probably, fanatic Rulers in any case cannot tolerate the rationality-base and professional autonomy of policy analysis, depending instead on servile instruments. But, this may be too optimistic an assumption, especially as the spectrum of evil, but quite instrumental-rational, Rulers is too much of a historic reality to be ignored. Therefore, policy analysts, as other persons of knowledge, carry heavy moral responsibility when deciding for whom to work. Such moral and ethical problems of policy analysis require separate treatment (Dror, 1983, introductory part).

This paper is based on close study of realities of policy analysis for Rulers, both from the inside and from a scholarly perspective, in most of the Western Democracies and in a number of Third World countries. But, regretfully, I am not familiar with relevant facts in the Communist countries. Therefore, applicability of my study in these countries has to be judged by professionals who know the situation there.

Policy analysis for advising Rulers is a delicate and problematic subject, as well as quite a neglected one. To advance policy analysis for advising Rulers, concerted efforts by multiple groups with various experiences and mixed disciplinary backgrounds in a diversity of political contexts, are needed. Also essential is careful pilot testing and experimentation with novel designs and methods. This discussion is devoted to encouraging such shared work in the slowly growing informal college of practitioners and scholars of advanced policy analysis.

The order of progression is as follows: First, to provide some of the background against which policy analysis for advising Rulers should be considered, I comment briefly on some causes for the crucial importance of Rulers and of their decisions in contemporary highly-industrialized societies, exposing some of their essential and expanding functions, including those in which policy analysis should be of help. These pointers at the challenges of policy analysis for advising Rulers lead into the main body of the chapter, namely! a more extended discussion of main aspects of policy analysis which need radical changes to become relevant to Rulers' decisions, including a number of indicative proposals for advancing policy analysis in the identified directions. It concludes with some observations on reality and prospects, including partial exposition of barriers hindering advancement of policy analysis for advising Rulers and ways for overcoming them. All this, as a concise *tour de force* into *terra incognita*, poses more questions than providing answers.[2]

II. IMPORTANCE OF RULERS AND THEIR DECISIONS

To claim that Rulers and their decisions are very important in highly-industrialized countries (and even more so in less developed ones) is not to state the obvious. If the fate of nations is viewed as determined by *Fortuna*, either in the sense of exogenous events or/and in the sense of uncontrollable domestic trends and infrastructures then all governmental policies, including Rulers' decisions, are of little moment. Alternatively, if governmental decision-making is seen as a collective process with little specific impact by any one person, including top level politicians – then Rulers' decisions are of little consequence. These two perspectives fit parts of reality. But, my strong impression is that – within the perspective of policy-making, as distinct from a bio-evolutionary view of *Homo sapiens* as a zoological specie – the impact of Rulers' decisions is real and significant. More than that, despite many expectations to the contrary, the importance of Rulers' decisions seems to be on the increase. This trend is related to Rulers and Rulership as a role and an institution, with variations depending on the particular individuals fulfilling the Rulership role. The trend is not a result of individual accidents and particularities, but of broad societal and political objective variables.

Without presuming to present here a grand theory of the crucial importance of Rulers in highly-industrialized countries and its causes, let me mention a few aspects explaining and illustrating this phenomenon, as a background to discussion of policy analysis as helping Rulers in fulfilling their augmented functions. There are significant differences in this matter between various countries, and also within the sub-set of highly-industrialized countries as discussed here. But, main relevant factors operative in most of these countries during most of current history can be identified. These include the following, in no strict order, but moving from broader and more diffuse causes of high importance of Rulers to narrower and more specific ones:

Socio-psychological needs. While this matter is far from adequate conceptualization and even further away from understanding, and while the intensity of relevant variables differs between countries and periods, there seem to exist strong individual-psychological and mass-psychological needs for very visible political personalities, and Rulers in particular. The need for Rulers to help with maintaining and reconstructing self-identity and collective identity in a period of cultural and political turbulence serves to illustrate a little more concretely socio-psychological necessary and presently augmented functions of Rulers (Erikson, 1975, p. 22).

Giving directions to Society. A main cause for the great and increasing consequence of Rulers' decisions is the expansion of governmental responsibilities for giving directions to societies, as a necessary response to changing circumstances. In a growing number of countries there is an increasing need for societal architecture, in the sense of bringing about significant structural changes in important facets of society. Energy (Häfele, 1981), welfare (OECD, 1981), re-industrialization (Netherlands Scientific Council for Government Policy, 1980) and labour markets (Scharpf, 1981) serve to illustrate domains needing societal architecture in Western highly-industrialized societies. This increasingly essential governmental function cannot be carried out without active, powerful and effective power centres – the core of which includes Rulers and a main *modus operandi* of which are Rulers' decisions. Important to understand in this connection is the architectonic and radical-change nature even of attempts to reduce the scope of governmental activities, going on in a number of countries. To design and implement effectively such a trend-shift, excellent governmental capacities are needed, with much of the burden for such an endeavour falling necessarily on Rulers' decisions. It may sometimes be possible to reduce the quantitative scope of activities of central governments, but – under present and foreseeable conditions – not their qualitative importance. When the scope of governmental activities increases, as is the case at present in a number of countries and may become so in more, then the burdens on Rulers of giving directions to society may indeed impose a mission all-but-impossible with present tools.

Charisma. Present problems in quite a number of countries require policy shifts and societal architecture which cannot be undertaken without power-concentrations and consensus-building, often beyond the capacity of coalitions between partisan interests. This objective need for charismatic power produces a favourable setting for Rulers that have relevant potentials (Tucker, 1981).

Policy entrepreneurship. Policy changes are essential in most countries to meet shifting challenges. Normal bureaucracies usually are unable to produce options going against the grain of their policy traditions. In a large majority of countries, urgently needed are far-reaching paradigmatic policy innovations, depending on top-level policy-learning and entrepreneurship, in turn building up the power and importance of Rulers who can meet these needs.

Power Brokage. Increasing oligopolization and molecularization of power create vacuums requiring powerbrokers, who construct meaningful configurations through coalition building and rebuilding. Rulers are in a uniquely suitable position to fulfill this function, which in turn significantly reinforces their power. This role takes different shapes according to regime, but is essential in all countries.

Mass media. The focusing of attention by mass media, especially television, on heads of government serves to build up their power and functions, even in cases where their formal position is one of *prime inter pares*.

Crisis management. International and domestic turbulence cause many crises, with crisis management emerging as an important mode of government. In crises, Rulers' decisions fulfill central roles, both because crisis management is usually concentrated in their hands and because many of the usual checks-and-balances are suspended, in part because of time pressures. Therefore, the frequency of crisis, including the "crisis" nature of a number of economic circumstances, adds to the importance of Rulers (Preisl and Mohler, 1979).

Inter-departmentality. Objective needs for charisma and policy entrepreneurship may remain latent and unnoticed and have little effect on the actual functions of Rulers, who do not know how to build upon such potentials. The situation is different in regard to the widely recognized necessity for inter-departmental integration, that goes far beyond traditional coordination. The costs of non-integration become very obvious in all countries, especially in intensely interacting issue-clusters that must be looked at as systems, such as: defence, foreign policy, intelligence; economics, social policy, human resources; as well as in respect to pervasive, inherently multi-departmental, issues such as science and technology, energy, and environment. Such visible needs for overall governmental perspectives serve to augment strongly the roles of Rulers in looking out after multi-departmental and inter-departmental policy integration.

Summit meetings. Summit meetings are very fashionable for dealing not only with foreign relations, but also with economic, technological and other problems. This increases the importance of Rulers, who not only go to summit meetings, but benefit from their ritual and mass media glory and build on them higher stature back home.

In different societies, various mixes of these and other factors operate to make Rulers' decisions more important. Further examination of relevant variables leads to the conclusion that all-in-all the factors increasing the importance of Rulers as a core element of societal problem-handling capacities will continue to grow. Global scarcities, economic realities, societal developments, cultural propensities, domestic-political trends, scientific-technological innovations, demographic tendencies – all add up to problems overwhelming present capacities to govern and requiring radically improved policy innovation, societal architecture, direction-giving, consensus-mobilization, value clarification, grand policy shifts and political will. To meet such expanding requirements, outstanding Rulers' decisions are essential. To contribute to these – this is the challenge posed before advanced policy analysis for advising Rulers.

Before taking up my main subject, namely changes required in policy analysis to meet such needs and requirements, some warning against over-expectations is necessary:

(a) Despite the growing importance of Rulers, they are one among a number of core components of governance embedded in society. Therefore, improvement of the performance of Rulers is only one of a number of urgently needed redesigns in governance. In many countries, the improvement of Rulers' decisions is the most urgent upgrading in governmental capacities; but, it probably always must be supplemented by other changes, to achieve in the aggregate needed effects. In some countries, it may be more urgent to redesign other aspects of governance, though probably under contemporary conditions improving the performance of Rulers is an important need in all countries.

(b) Policy analysis for advising Rulers is only one approach among many to improving performance of Rulers. Changes in their constitutional power and standing, variations in their length in office, innovations in the recruitment and career patterns of Ruler-candidates – these serve to illustrate the range of possible approaches to upgrading of Rulers' performance. The relative advantages of policy analysis for advising Rulers include its inherent utility; its relatively higher feasibility, in comparison to political changes in position and recruitment of Rulers; and the speed with which it can provide positive fruits. But, its utility is strictly limited by other factors, such as the personal qualities of Rulers brought up by the political system.

These subjects are outside the scope of this chapter and therefore will not be further considered here. But they should be kept in mind, so that advancement of policy analysis for advising Rulers is seen in correct proportions, as an important contribution to the capacity to govern, but not as a breakthrough. Certainly, it is not a panacea for the present problems of governance, though it is part of a promising treatment cluster.

III. REQUIRED CHANGES IN POLICY ANALYSIS

Aim

To examine fully required changes in policy analysis so it can serve as a main aid to Rulers' decisions requires further elaboration of the functions of Rulers and their decisions. And, then, systematic exploration of potential contributions of policy analysis to each and all of these functions, leading to identification of changes needed in policy analysis to fully realize this potential.

In the present chapter, constraints of space require compressed treatment of the subject, by jumping over some phases of the examination and by focusing on concise presentation of main examples of required changes in policy analysis. In doing so, I take up diverse illustrations, to demonstrate various dimensions of required changes in policy analysis and to bring out the overall configuration of needed innovations, at least in rough outline.

The basic conspectus of policy analysis for advising Rulers can be formulated as *islands of professional excellence near and for Rulers, which provide essential and unique help based on advanced policy analysis methods.*

I deal with required changes in policy analysis under four categories, according to the main elements of the above formulation. Within each part, I examine a few items, altogether sixteen, which are numbered consecutively throughout.

The first category relates to *islands of professional excellence*. It includes three items, namely: (1) institutional feature of policy analysis for advising Rulers; (2) systemic functions of policy analysis for advising Rulers, within the broader organizational and socio-political environments; with special attention to (3) the power ecology of policy analysis for advising Rulers, which characterizes it thanks to location in the central antechamber of power.

Power ecology leads directly to the second main category, namely *near and for Rulers*. Examination of this quintessential feature proceeds through exploration of (4) single-person focus of policy analysis for advising Rulers; as well as (5) debugging, debunking and iconoclasm as the main modi operandi, with important implications for underlying models of policy analysis.

The next phase of our proceeding bring us to the third of the categories into which this part of the paper is divided, namely the *essential and unique help* which policy analysis can and should provide for Rulers, illustrated by: (6) Comprehensive and long-term perspectives, with relation to societal architecture and national planning in their different forms: (7) diagnostics, in the sense of broad estimations of situations and problem perception, leading to appropriate decision agenda setting; (8) innovative and unconventional decision inputs, including devil's advocacy, counter-accepted and counter-intuitive views, novel options and analysis-vision interfaces; and (9) policy learning functions. Because of the interdependence between policies and institutions, policy analysis for advising Rulers must also consider (10) policy implementation institutions, as essential for improving Rulers' decisions as expressed in their actual impact on reality. In contradistinction to such broad contributions, policy analysis for advising Rulers is also characterized by (11) providing help with special Rulers' operations, such as crisis management and bargaining and negotiations. To illustrate possible help by policy analysis in facing changing and increasingly important tasks of Rulers, I proceed to discuss (12) budgeting. To balance the treatment of help which advanced policy analysis may render Rulers, I conclude this sub-set of subjects with a discussion of (13) dangerous dysfunction potentials of policy analysis for the quality of Rulers' decisions.

Having thus surveyed a variety of facets of policy analysis for advising Rulers, the fourth category is reached, which brings us to a main crux of the subject, namely *advanced policy analysis methods*. This category is covered by considering (14) a number of broad methodological requisites and possibilities, with an illustrative variety of needed advancements in policy analysis approaches, methods, tools and instruments. To supplement this list, two special methodological issues, which underline the particularities of advanced policy analysis, especially for advising Rulers, are discussed, namely: (15) Social sciences in policy analysis; and (16) politics in policy analysis.

These sixteen blocks, as divided into four categories, do not add up to a complete edifice of policy analysis for advising Rulers. But, they provide a skeleton which brings out the main outlines of required rethinking of policy analysis and can serve as a partial basis for it.

In presenting a massive range of requisites for rethinking policy analysis, which really add up to proposing a quantum leap towards advanced policy analysis in general and advanced policy analysis for advising Rulers in particular, I may be accused of building up a straw man (or woman) in order easily to shoot him (her) down. Such a critique argues, that actual policy analysis is much better equipped for helping Rulers than I assume and that the main problem, as far as one exists, is that Rulers do not want the help of policy analysis.

There does exist a serious difficulty in Rulers underdemanding policy analysis; and inadequate political support is a main cause for failure of professional advisory units for Rulers (Boston, 1980). But I strongly disagree with the claim that contemporary policy analysis is well qualified to render significant help to Rulers. Visits to more than thirty offices of Rulers in Western and Third World countries; workshops with politicians and senior advisors from even more countries; intense contacts with policy analysts in a variety of contexts; examination of teaching programs in policy analysis and related subjects; and perusal of the growing literature in these areas – all produce and support findings on the inadequacies of contemporary policy analysis for systematically helping Rulers' decisions. Personal experiences with trying to aid Rulers decisions with the help of available policy analysis craftmanship-knowledge further reinforced these findings.

The fact that a few outstanding policy analysts excel at handling very complex problems, without any proportion to shared "public knowledge" (Ziman, 1968) in policy analysis as a discipline-profession and in ways not explained or at least indicated in their own writings, cannot compensate for the weaknesses of the discipline. The requisites of policy analysis for advising Rulers, as an improvement of capacities to govern, cannot be met by accidental appointment of single policy analysis stars to influential positions. Such persons are a blessing when available and an essential ingredient for advancing policy analysis as a craft and as a profession-discipline, but do not constitute a sufficient basis for meeting needs, such as illustrated by policy analysis for advising Rulers.

Turning now to the sixteen illustrative facets of policy analysis which require changes and advancements to adequately aid Rulers' decisions, the reader is reminded that these are overlapping and interdependent aspects of an integral design for advanced policy analysis. Therefore, movement back and forward in considering the subject is recommended.

POLICY ANALYSIS FOR ADVISING RULERS AS ISLANDS OF
PROFESSIONAL EXCELLENCE

A main dimension of policy analysis for advising Rulers is brought out by the formulation of "constitution an island of professional excellence". Some involved characteristics include:

1. Institutional Features

The fundamental institutional problem of policy analysis for advising Rulers is, how to meet the preferences and prejudices of a variety of changing and diverse Rulers, while preserving minimum essential requisites of advanced policy analysis. Problems of institutionalization of policy analysis for advising Rulers can be looked at as a particular, very important, instance of what I call "self-imposed rationality": Rulers are asked and expected to recognize their own limits and, therefore, to institutionalize arrangements that help in augmenting their capacities and off-setting their weaknesses. In this sense, one can also speak about Rulers binding themselves, according to the metaphor of Ulysses and the Sirens (Elster, 1979). Historic, cultural and political conditions significantly influence possibilities to move in such a direction. As emerging in some countries, constitutional and legal status for policy analysis units near Rulers can help. But, realistically speaking, in the foreseeable future institutionalization of policy analysis units and their real effects depend on discrete Rulers, the insights of such Rulers into needs for such units, and the Ruler's self-discipline in abiding by institutional arrangements essential for rendering him needed, though often not sweet, help.

Sometimes, institutionalization requisites cannot be met. The personality of some Rulers may contradict minimum needs of policy analysis so intensely as to inhibit any useful work. Short of such extreme, but not scarce, cases, a maximum effort must be made to elasticize the institutional features of policy analysis for advising Rulers, so as to permit adjustment to diverse Rulers and different conditions, while preserving essentials. Therefore, when exploring institutional features of policy analysis for advising Rulers, a broad range of alternative arrangements should be aimed at, with special attention to minimum requisites without which this function cannot operate usefully (though other, less demanding, forms of advisory services may be feasible and useful).

Following this, I explore briefly some institutional issues of policy analysis for advising Rulers, moving from essential minimum requirements to more advanced arrangements.

A minimum must, is the institutional establishment of a distinct policy analysis unit near the Ruler, as a kind of professional "islands of excellence". The task of this unit must be kept distinct from other functions of Rulers' departments and the professional inputs of the unit into Rulers' thinking and decision-making must be kept distinct from other needs of Rulers, such as already mentioned emotional support, partisan-political advice and more. It is the scope of activity and the special professional nature, which constitute the novelty of policy analysis for advising Rulers, as compared with the multitude of advisers to Rulers known in history and contemporary reality alike (Cohen, 1980; Goldhamer, 1978).

- The unit must enjoy significant autonomy in its operations. Thus, selection of subjects to be worked on should, in part, be up to the unit. The unit should be able to withstand pressure to deal only with current issues, devoting parts of its resources to broader examination of fundamental choices and basic policy assumptions. Also, the unit needs leeway to study sensitive subjects. Issues of explosive political potential and problems requiring extensive study fit better Think Tanks further away from Rulers. But, policy analysis units for advising Rulers must be able to tolerate and even support and sometimes initiate such studies – as part of their institutionalized autonomy and professional responsibility. This, subject to appropriate diplomatic skills and due care in considering possible implications.

- Related is the necessity for a professional core of persons to staff the policy analysis unit. Difficult is the question, whether and how much of this staff should be attached to a particular Ruler, moving in and out with him, or should be semi-permanent, serving in the unit for a number of years overlapping more than one Ruler. Available experience is too limited to permit a reliable answer to this very important question, but some elements of a range of acceptable solutions can be indicated:

(a) The policy analysis unit must be staffed with highly qualified professionals. Other selection criteria, such as personal and political acceptability to the Ruler, can be added, but not as substitutes for rigid professional capacities.

(b) The half-life of the staff should approximate 3 to 5 years in the policy analysis unit. If Rulers change more frequently, continuity of at least parts of the staff in office over a number of Rulers is essential.

(c) When Rulers change at longer intervals, changeovers of most of the policy analysis staff together with the Rulers is acceptable. But, continuity of some of the staff is highly desirable, to preserve institutional memory and transfer experience from one set-up to another.

These alternatives provide limited elasticity to accommodate various administrative and political traditions, while also requiring adjustments in the latter in a number of countries, as a *sine qua non* for useful policy analysis for advising Rulers.

- Subject to such minimum requisites of high-quality policy analysis for advising Rulers, elasticity in main features and operations is a condition for success and survival. This applies not only to the supreme test of survival as an institution when Rulers change, but also to alterations in the needs, preferences, perspectives and propensities of one and the same Ruler. Thus, in Western Democracies, Rulers' concerns change not only with variations in the situation and intra-personality dynamics, but also in correlation with the electoral cycle, as demonstrated in many studies of economic policy and approaching elections (Tufte, 1978). Often, the impacts of turnover, time and political cycles are much broader, many of Rulers' concerns and outlooks changing quite a lot from the honeymoon first few months (Bunce, 1981) till the Rulers' approaching willing, or more often, unwilling evacuation of the Rulership position. This has complex implications for policy analysis for advising Rulers, which must combine two contradictory needs: to adjust to changing perspectives of Rulers; and to influence Rulers' decisions so as to reduce fluctuations which ruin essential policy consistency.

- Strict secrecy in respect to all work is absolutely necessary. Any leakages or indiscretions, also by former staff members, stand a high chance of ruining the work and liquidating the usefulness, and even the very existence, of the unit. A special case involves studies which the Ruler is interested to publish and to have supported in public by the unit, so as to mobilize support and to inform public debate. Degrees of acceptable involvement of the unit in such activities vary with circumstances, but should always be restrained so as to avoid transformation of the main tasks from decision improvement to decision marketing.

- The minimum size of a useful policy analysis unit for advising Rulers is probably somewhere around 10 to 15 persons, with 25 to 30 being a preferable number. Larger units must be subdivided and take on a somewhat different nature. In presenting this number, I refer to the policy analysis functions. When additional tasks are undertaken, such as current decision management, follow-up and implementation monitoring, etc. still the minimum critical mass for policy analysis as such must be preserved and protected against dilution with other functions.

- The composition should include a mixture of various professionals, mainly policy analysts and various subject and methods experts with a variety of experiences. A good decision psychologist should be an integral part of any policy analysis for advising Rulers unit – because of some of the soon to be discussed special functions of the unit, such as Rulers' decisions debugging. A scientific advisor may well be integrated into the unit, with a double function of adding a perspective to policy analysis as a whole, while advising the Ruler on science and technology policy, with direct access to the Ruler as a possibility. Other special advisory functions should either be fused with the policy analysis unit, or operate separately with coordination to be worked out according to concrete circumstances. In doing so, care must be taken to avoid too many centrifugal forces and specialized sub-groups from disrupting the essential unity and cohesion of the policy analysis entity.

- An infrastructure of policy research "Think Tanks", consultants, brain-trusters and resources persons, ad hoc study groups, university institutes, institutes for advanced study and similar policy analysis and policy thinking capacities dispersed in society should be lightly coupled to the policy analysis unit. This, to help in data collection and in-depth analysis of problems which require massive work, as well as for handling problems that require more distance from current pressures and emotions.
- The policy analysis staff must preserve some degree of personal autonomy in recruitment base and alternative job opportunities, otherwise over-socialization into court politics is hard to avoid. The choice of the head of the policy analysis unit is critical. His personality, professional qualities, innovativeness and, last but not least, his standing *vis-à-vis* the Ruler – determine the fate of policy analysis for advising Rulers.
- The unit can be subdivided into nuclei for specific problem areas, such as domestic affairs and foreign-defence issues. But, as already noted, it is necessary to have at least a partly integrated unit, with a central core, internal mobility and elastic work teams. This is essential in order to achieve cross-fertilization, comprehensive perspectives and adequate attention to very important interface problems and overlap domains.
- Relations with political advisers require careful attention, preferable solutions involving close contact, but a mutually respected and understood difference in perspective.
- Policy analysis should be compartmentalized from political marketing, mass media contacts, pressure group handling, etc. Individual analysts may be exposed to such activities, to improve their sense for reality – but on a limited basis and not on behalf of the policy analysis unit. This, with limited exceptions, as already discussed.
- To protect important policy analysis contributions against being overtaken and displaced by current pressures and crisis conditions, some internal institutional rigidities are essential. Thus, specific procedures and roles should be responsible for look-out and longer-time perspectives, search for unconventional opinions, encouragement of innovation, self-evaluation and more.
- Relations with regular governmental departments, including both their political and their civil service components, are another crucial problem.

The need is for a mixed cooperative-adversary relationship. Too much hostility will result in information blackouts and bureaucratic-political warfare; too much cooperation may undermine the autonomy of the policy analysis activity and corrupt some of its main functions. Building up an informal network for collecting information and canvassing opinions is important and, often, essential for success.

- Contacts with the Ruler should, in part, be institutionalized with fixed meetings, assured briefing opportunities and some personal contact between all analysts and the Ruler. Parts of the communication can proceed through a very senior assistant to the Ruler or some kind of chief-of-staff to the Ruler. But frequent direct access to the Ruler by the head of the policy analysis unit is a must.
- The work climate of policy analysis units for advising Rulers needs careful handling, to avoid emotional overloads and preserve a collegial and clinical-professional culture.
- Constant learning should be institutionalized, with a memory system, explicit self-evaluation exercises and periodic overview by select outsiders. To increase innovativeness and preserve initiative and high-energy, the half-life-time of staff members should be around 3 to 5 years, as already mentioned.

These observations do not present a manual for setting up policy analysis units for advising Rulers: many details must be worked out and adjusted to particular circumstances. But they hopefully do convey some of the flavour of necessary institutional features of useful policy analysis for advising Rulers.

2. Systemic functions

Policy analysis for advising Rulers involves intense interactions with much broader systems, as already indicated when mentioning relations with departments and with policy analysis and policy thinking capacities dispersed in society. Policy analysis for advising Rulers also produces significant systemic effects and second-order consequences, going beyond direct inputs into Rulers' decisions. Understanding of these interactions and effects is necessary to get a realistic view of policy analysis for advising Rulers and its difficulties; as well as to identify adjustments necessary in policy analysis, to aid Rulers within given environments, while trying to increase beneficial systemic side-effects.

To explore this broad subject, let me move briefly through 7 systematic interactions:

1. Strengthening the equipment of Rulers is not power neutral. Establishing policy analysis for advising Rulers creates a new political reality, usually being decided upon without full recognition of the semi-

constitutional consequences. In particular, such units augment the power of the Ruler by providing him with tools for increasing his quantitative and qualitative influence in and through decision-making. This power-implication is strongly sensed by his colleagues and competitors, who will first try to prevent policy analysis for advising Rulers from taking off; then, they will try to reduce its impacts or/and take it over; and, finally they try to offset its effects by establishing counter-units of their own, to fight policy analysis with policy analysis (which is often all for the better for the quality of decision-making as a whole).

2. Policy analysis can easily be used and misused by Rulers to serve as an alibi and a legitimation device. If this provides an entry for policy analysis into doing substantively useful work, such side uses on a limited scale may be acceptable. Otherwise, they pose very serious professional-ethical problems to the policy analysts.

3. From a systemic point of view, policy analysis for advising Rulers adds competition, multiple advocacy and positive redundancy to decision processes. Departments lose their monopoly; proposals are double-analysed from a different, more comprehensive perspective; Rulers get an additional source for ideas; some devil's advocacy is assured; and so on. This useful redundancy cuts both ways: Rulers' policy analysis units should not try and monopolize inputs to their masters, otherwise a basic rationale for their very existence is undermined.

4. On a broader level, policy analysis for advising Rulers may influence public decision-making as a whole, by provoking adjustive responses, such as encouragement of policy research and policy analysis throughout the system and stimulating changes in style and argumentation of public debates and political controversy. Hence, Rulers' policy analysis units can fulfill useful indirect roles in upgrading the quality of policy development and societal problem-handling capacities, in the broad sense, throughout the system. From an egocentric and short-term perspective, this may reduce the influence of the Rulers' policy analysis unit by breaking its monopoly. From a broader governmental and societal perspective, as well as from a longer-range view of the opportunities and potentials of the Rulers' policy analysis unit itself, diffusion of good policy analysis to many public decision centres constitutes a main benefit.

5. Related to the above, as well as additional, systemic effects is the role of Rulers' policy analysis units in developing highly qualified professionals, with profound knowledge of top level government. Thus, they produce an essential ingredient for advancing policy analysis, as a societal tool as well as a profession-craft discipline.

6. Interesting and novel are the effects of development of an informal

network of policy analysts. This is especially important with the multiplication of policy analysis units. In addition to informal contacts in the machinery of government, policy analysis units for advising Rulers may and will establish relations with similar units outside central government, such as in legislatures, and also with units working for Rulers in other countries. It is too early to evaluate the repercussions of such networks, which may help communication, consensus building and mutual learning. Traditional fears of "technocracy" ignore the much-observed identification of policy-analysis professionals with the organizations and interests for which they work, so that little danger is posed to pluralism by collegial relations between policy analysts dispersed among different societal and governmental organizations. Encouragement of such professional relations is a useful side task of policy analysts working for Rulers, though the sensitivities of their position require restraint in participation in collegial activities.

7. Special problems are posed by relations between policy analysis in government and, especially, on the level of the Ruler, and interparty political processes. Thus, an important question is, whether and how policy analysis for the head of the opposition should be encouraged and supported, to increase the quality of political argumentation and to prepare the potential next Ruler for utilizing policy analysis, if and when he becomes the Rulership incumbent. First steps in such a direction are illustrated by arrangements in New Zealand and Austria to support research staffs for the caucuses and parties respectively, including the opposition, from public funds.

3. Power Ecology

A distinct quality of policy analysis for advising Rulers is its location in a high-power ecology. Positioned in the centre of the antechamber of power and serving as one of the main mindgates to the Ruler, policy analysis for Rulers can easily become power-spoiled. Main pressures exerted on policy analysis by the power ecology include:

Overwhelming by acute and immediate problems, which provide a sense of real impact and of feeling the pulse of history and which, therefore, easily displace longer-range considerations and in-depth analysis.
Interest pressures, external as well as bureaucratic-political, which push and tempt to adjust analysis and transform it into advocacy.
Mass media attention, which beckons with momentary glory and with opportunities to influence decisions by carefully manipulated leaks and by tacit exchange arrangements with media personnel.
Overinvolvement with court politics and bureaucratic infighting, initially as

essential for building up and protecting the position of the unit, but rapidly because of fascination with the various power games.
- Attention and flattery, which result in ego-hypertrophia, with disastrous consequences for analytical quality.
- Oscillations between euphoria on influencing a Ruler and despair at being ignored, ruining the concerned detachment that policy analysis should contribute.
- Pressure-cooker emotional tensions with red-hot cognition easily overcoming clinical detachment and a "cold" look, which should characterize policy analysis and constitute a main contribution to Rulers' decisions.

Some of the presented institutional features serve to contain and handle such pressures. But more is needed. Thus:

1. Policy analysts must learn to move in power mine-fields, without compromising their professional roles.
2. Preserving and building up the power of the policy analysis unit itself must be a concern, but not a main preoccupation. For example, even if technically superfluous thanks to modern communication technology, it is very important to locate the policy analysis unit physically near the Ruler, *inter alia* to demonstrate proximity as a source of influence.
3. Special attention needs to be given to access to information and presence at meetings, not only because of a "need to know", but also because of power implications of such access.

The power environment within which policy analysis for advising Rulers operates is a neglected issue that must be put on the agenda of rethinking the process and nature of policy analysis, even if no simple "solution" is conceivable or possible (Goldwin, 1980; Meltsner, 1976).

POLICY ANALYSIS NEAR AND FOR RULERS

The very definition of policy analysis for advising Rulers, adopted for the pure type treatment of this paper, is "near and for Rulers". This is much more than a definitional postulate, constituting a unique and overwhelming dimension from which many requisites follow, including:

4. Single-Person Focus

A quintessential feature of policy analysis for advising Rulers, shaping all features of that activity, is its single-person focus. There is one clearly defined, very visible and highly personal client – the incumbent of the Rulership, with all his preferences, habits, personality traits and ideosyncrasies. (This also applies, with suitable adjustments, to collegial Ruler-groups.) The pervasive impact of this dominating reality results in hard problems requiring significant rethinking of policy analysis. Representative are the following facets, aspects and issues:

(a) It is the duty of policy analysis for advising Rulers to adjust to their client and serve him loyally. But, it is also the *raison d'être* of policy analysis for advising Rulers to confront their client, demand his attention to their often not welcome findings and studies and to insist on their professional autonomy. This constitutes a major inbuilt antinomy of policy analysis for advising Rulers, with possible mutual dynamic accommodations, but no stable saddlepoints. Especially vexing is the question, where should adjustments to a Ruler's wishes stop, with the ultimate possibility of resignation of the policy analysts if their mission becomes impossible. To try and handle such tensions, a main requisite of successful policy analysis for a Ruler is to study him, so as to take into due account his judgement and to adjust to his needs and preferences. Dangerous are pathologies in two directions, namely manipulation of the Ruler and of his decisions; and overadjustment, in the sense of fitting conclusions and recommendations to the predilections of the Ruler.

(b) Thanks to the present scarcity of policy analysis in governments and politics, few Rulers bring with them any familiarity with it. Neither do usual career patterns of Rulers convey knowledge related to policy analysis. This situation may and should change. But, at present, policy analysis is quite strange if not esoteric to most Rulers, and often also somewhat frightening. Rulers are used to politicians, to civil servants and to mono-disciplinary experts – but not to policy analysts. Disappointments with professional advisers, such as economists, add to Rulers' apprehensions about policy analysis. Such apprehensions are reinforced by the presumptions of policy analysis to engage the Ruler's most important decision functions, with a claim for some professional autonomy. It is up to policy analysts to understand this situation and to market their capacities to the Ruler, without overselling themselves. This is quite a task, for which policy analysis is ill prepared.

(c) Interfaces between policy analysis and Rulers are conditioned by their contrary-cultures, as illustrated by the following antinomies inbuilt into their respective dynamics:

Policy analysis	*Politics*
1. Clinical and semi-detached, with concern	Fighting and deep personal involvement
2. Uncertainty and complexity explicating	Situation simplifying and uncertainty ignoring

3. Searching for more options	Rapidly overloaded and option rejecting
4. Posing need for decision criteria and value choice	Avoiding clear-cut choices, in order to maintain essential consensus
5. Long-term perspective	Pressing troubles are enough
6. Emphasizing interrelations between various problems and decisions	Piecemeal approach dominates
7. Constraints and costs constantly considered	Hopeful thinking and optimistic assumptions preferred; sometimes visionary
8. Doubtful and re-evaluation oriented	Dissonance repressing, biased to see everywhere "successes" and tending to escalate commitment to doubtful decisions

This partial list illustrates unavoidable sharp differences in underlying cultures, inbuilt dynamics and dominating perspectives of policy analysis and Rulers, with resulting inherent tensions and clashes between them. Advanced policy analysis is directed at helping Rulers achieve a higher quality of decision-making, but not at making Rulers feel better. Indeed, policy analysis will often cause pain to the Ruler, who may reasonably hesitate to swallow bitter medicine about the final benefits of which he does not feel too sure. On such contrary-culture tensions, mutual accommodation is possible, but on a temporary and precarious basis only. This is one of the more central issues for rethinking the process of policy analysis.

(d) Policy analysts working near Rulers can easily slide into the role of providing emotional support for the Ruler, thus deviating from their main function, as already mentioned. It is not easy to draw a line between taking correctly into account the Ruler's mood, e.g. by delaying inputs which will upset the Ruler till he has a relaxed day (which may mean quite a long wait); and getting overapprehensive about provoking negative reactions, up to repressing important, but very unwelcome, analyses. These dangers are especially acute the more face-to-face relations develop between the main policy analysts and the Ruler. Direct contact is essential, but the policy analysts can easily become dependent on the Ruler emotionally, waiting for his smile and fearing his frown.

(e) Inputs of policy analysis to Rulers go far beyond specific contributions to discrete decisions. They include broad and often very important functions of educating the Ruler to better comprehension of com-plexity, more correct estimation of reality and less distorted self-evaluation. Careful delineation is necessary between serving as a modernized version of Grey Eminences and Court Priests, not to speak of Court Jesters, which are not appropriate functions of policy analysis; and professional-tutorial activities, which are essential. An additional very important educative function is to stimulate innovation and encourage de-dogmatization, e.g. by devil's advocacy, by inputting of unconventional opinions and by debunking pet opinions of Rulers, functions to be discussed at greater length soon.

Problems of communication between the policy analysis unit and Rulers put into sharp focus, on a less exalted level, some of the special issues of advanced policy analysis.

A basic dilemma is posed by the dependence of useful policy analysis for Rulers on good communication between the senior policy analysts and the Ruler, both orally and in writing, on one hand; and the fact that time and energy are the scarcest of all of Rulers' resources, on the other hand. Give-and-take between the policy analysts and their Ruler-client; involvement of the Ruler-client in the very process of policy analysis, from which Rulers may benefit more than from any policy analysis outputs; bull-sessions, where the policy analysts serve as a reaction group to the Ruler throwing out his intuitive ideas; careful study by the Ruler of policy analysis documents, which do not unduly distort contents by being truncated to fit a "no more than two pages" standing order – these are requisites of effective policy analysis for advising Rulers. But these, also, are near impossibilities: Rulers are much too busy and overloaded to devote more than a fraction of their time to policy analysis, and even then their patience may wear thin rapidly.

Needs for communication go both ways: in addition to communication of policy analysis to the Ruler, the Ruler must communicate his interests, values, perspectives, plans and agendas to the policy analysis unit. Without being privy to the Ruler's thinking, policy analysis cannot effectively help him, neither in timing, nor in contents. This is an additional main reason why the policy analysis unit must be presented at most of the Ruler's policy meetings, as well as at a fair sample of his other activities. But, care must be taken not to become part of the Ruler's entourage, neither physically and, even less so, psychologically.

There is a communication threshold below which policy analysis for advising Rulers is futile: without some direct contact with the Ruler and some of his time for oral briefings, for give-and-take and for study of policy analysis memoranda, it is better to help lesser decision-makers or influence top decisions from some distance. Concomitantly, a number of steps to adjust policy analysis to the realities of Rulers' constraints are necessary and possible. Broadening the concept of Ruler-client and including in it his main personal assistants and intimate advisers may help, though it cannot serve as a substitute for direct contacts with the Ruler. More intrinsic to policy analysis itself is the need to develop novel communication modes for reaching Rulers. Thus, it is necessary to develop multimedia briefing systems for Rulers, where complexity can be conveyed in comprehensible form without undue over-simplification, thanks to utilization of multi-dimensional and dynamic media, with attempts to move towards interactive systems that the Ruler can work with on his own.[3] Subject to avoidance of gadgeteering, this is a neglected potential for policy analysis inputs to Rulers' decisions.

Such problems of Rulers as the main focus of policy analysis are put into even sharper relief by looking at debugging, debunking and iconoclasm as main modi operandi of policy analysis for advising Rulers.

5. Debugging, Debunking and Iconoclasm

Some of the special features of policy analysis for advising Rulers and resulting needs for significant changes in policy analysis itself are sharply brought out by the debugging, debunking and iconoclasm functions. In brief, these complex and sensitive functions and their underlying logic can be described as follows: Rulers, by their very role and position, tend to a number of decision mistakes, with individual differences within a statistical range. A main way to help Rulers improve their decisions is, therefore, "debugging", in the sense of eliminating some of the error-propensities and compensating for them. This also involves some "debunking" and "iconoclasm", in the sense of exposing to the Ruler his own mistake propensities, which is quite a delicate operation but an essential one to render him real help. To fulfil these functions, policy analysis must (a) add to its "optimality" models debugging approaches; and (b) move into a decision-aiding role *vis-à-vis* the Ruler which permits "clinical" help in the sense of decision-psychological remedials.

While mentioned in single publications in a lower-level context (Janis and Mann, 1977; Ripley, 1977), decision-therapeutics is a quite far-reaching proposal, in need of further thinking and experimentation before it is ripe to serve as a full-fledged recommendation for revamping policy analysis for advising Rulers. The debugging function is more operational and less radical, but potentially of very high importance.

Policy analysis, as well as most of operations research, tries in the main to improve decisions by moving, explicitly or implicitly, towards some kind of normative model, either a "rationality" model for decision-making or, more recently and somewhat more ambiguously, some systems model for decision-making (Ackoff, 1981). True, experienced policy analysts are better than their objective knowledge, recognizing the limits of normative decision models as guides for action and overcoming those through reliance on applied skills, often hidden behind the term "common sense". But, as already discussed, practical insights are sporadic and cannot compensate for formal weaknesses of a discipline. Explicit, "optimality"-conditioned policy analysis approaches, as presently developed, are only of limited utility when facing Rulers' decisions. Even when supplemented by theoretic recognition of the importance of extra-rational components in preferable decision-making, which is still more an exception than the rule (Dror, 1983, Part IV), policy analysis models suffer from neglecting the situational dynamics within which Rulers' decisions take place. On the basis of bitter experience, capable policy analysts learn with time to admit this fact, but on superficially pragmatic a level which is not integrated with their professional knowledge.

One of the more serious omissions of contemporary policy analysis is ignorance of decision error propensities inbuilt into the very situation of Rulership and their interaction with the personality of Rulers, with inexorable negative effects on Rulers' decisions, within a range of individual variance. Inputting of "normal" policy analysis into Rulers' decision-making behaviour, without taking into account and counter-acting such negative dynamics, is a mistake in two respects: (a) the policy analysis inputs may be mis-processed, with counterproductive decision results; and (b) the wide possibilities of improving Rulers' decisions through direct efforts to reduce error propensities are not taken up. Advanced policy analysis for advising Rulers should accept as a main task the improvement of Rulers' decisions through reducing inbuilt decision-incapacitators of Rulership. This requires a "debugging" (as well as "debunking") approach, with policy analysis contributing to the quality of Rulers' decision-making by counteracting pitfalls, biases, distortions and errors typically inherent in that very process.

Overloads, strain and stress, information manipulations, court politics, power paraphernalia, deference – these are among the decision-ruining inbuilt features of Rulership. They produce main decision-mistakes, such as: cognitive map distortions; pendulum between delay and hyperdecision-activity; closed positive-feedback loops, insensitive to real results; options and creativity repression and many more (Buchanan, 1978; Janis, 1972; May, 1972). If we add decision-incapacitators inherent in the problems Rulers must deal with such as tragic choice (Calabresi and Bobbitt, 1979), radical uncertainty, and high complexity; and if we take into account the difficulties of all decision-makers in facing stressful problems as multiplied by the special features of Rulership – the inescapable conclusion is, that improvement of Rulers' decisions requires policy analysis to adopt a strong debugging (as well as some debunking and iconoclasm) posture. This necessitates decision-psychological ideas and models (Axelrod, 1976; de Rivera, 1968; Holsti and George, 1975) to be added to the main bases of advanced policy analysis (George, 1980).

POLICY ANALYSIS FOR RULERS AS PROVIDING ESSENTIAL AND UNIQUE HELP

The main purpose of policy analysis for advising Rulers is not to become institutionalized, nor to be located near Rulers and claiming to work for them. The main *raison d'être* of policy analysis for advising Rulers, for which institutionalization and location are but tools, is to provide essential and unique help, such as:

6. Comprehensive and Long-Term Perspectives

A main contribution of advanced policy analysis to Rulers' decisions is to further comprehensive and long-term perspectives, both in respect to background world views and underlying assumptions of Rulers and in respect to discrete decision issues. This is salient for the task of Rulers in assuring inter-departmentality and overall governmental outlook in reviewing and approving proposals coming up from the ministries and, especially, for the growing role of Rulers in giving directions to society as already discussed. Operationally, this function involves a variety of activities, ranging from preparation of alternative comprehensive futures to evaluation options within a broad horizon, in terms of domains and time alike. In more technical terminology: This function involves enlarging the systems perspective of the Ruler and of his main decisions.

Handling of longer-range and more comprehensive perspectives necessarily fuses some aspects of policy analysis for advising Rulers with some aspects of national planning. Examination, clarification and improvement of the relations between these two approaches to decision improvement is, therefore, necessary within the rethinking of policy analysis, both on a theoretic and a professional-applied level.

At present, relations between policy analysis and national planning are quite unclear, in part because policy analysis developed mainly in countries with little national planning, especially the United States. From a sociology of knowledge point-of-view, it may be that the absence of national planning made policy analysis all the more necessary, while in countries which have a lot of national planning, much of the content of policy analysis is covered by part of planning theory. Nevertheless, even when the variety of meanings of "planning" in different worlds of discourse is taken into account (Dill and Popov, 1979; Lompe, 1971; Steiner, 1979; Wilson, 1980), two distinct features seem quite clear:

- Policy analysis tends to concentrate on the improvement of discrete decisions, neglecting interconnected decision sets moving from the present

into a longer-range future. Also, present policy analysis deals mainly with secondary decisions, regarding grand policies and main policy assumption as beyond its domain, though a few grand policy analyses do exist (Kahn and Pepper, 1980). Socio-economic-political conditions are accepted as given, rather than as targets for intervention and directed change through critical decisions, grand policy innovation, societal architecture etc.
- Planning tends in reality, and despite much theory, to concentrate on detailed programming, again neglecting underlying assumptions, guiding decisions and critical choices.

Consequently, a shared omission urgently needs attention, never mind if under the heading of "planning" and/or "policy analysis": These are the planning assumptions, critical choices, policy guidelines, societal architecture principles and similar underlying macro-choices, at present neglected both by most of policy analysis and by most of planning. Hence, the importance of advanced policy analysis, including policy analysis for advising Rulers, as a shared need of more planned and less planned societies alike. Growing needs for innovative societal direction in all highly industrialized countries (and, even more so, in Third World countries), which urgently require supreme quality decisions by Rulers as one of the conditions for success, make advanced policy analysis an especially urgent need, whether as a basis for programming and detailed societal management, or as a basis for other intervention technologies, such as social market mechanisms.[4]

7. Diagnostics

It is amazing that problems of estimating situations are neatly ignored in policy analysis. This omission becomes shocking when one bears in mind that defence intelligence is a governmental endeavour highly endowed with resources – and distinguished by a permanence of dismal failures (Betts, 1980; Hughes, 1976; Jarvis, 1975). When the situation is misread, when fundamentally wrong world perceptions serve as underlying assumptions, when obsolescent frames of reference determine formulation of problems for analysis, then decisions must be dismal; with their initial errors being multiplied and reinforced, rather than corrected, by narrow policy analysis postulated upon misleading foundations.

These dangers waylay in particular Rulers' decisions. Situational pressures, inherent ambiguities, sensitivity to ideological and political pressures and similar typical features of issues reaching Rulers, plus partisan over-simplification of information inputs characterizing much of their in-communication – all these strongly aggravate misdiagnosis of situations and consequent problem-misformulation. To reduce such decision-ruining phenomena, policy analysis must move into diagnostics, including methods for estimating complex and ultra-dynamic situations and for multidimensional and self-corrective problem formulation. This is a critical phase in advanced policy analysis for advising Rulers.

Especially necessary is policy analysis aid in diagnosing overall situations, rather than the decomposed sub-issues. Thus, diagnosing broad issue-areas as either on a downward slope or an upward slope is essential for considering the need for innovative grand policies by Rulers, with search for continuity-breaking decisions being the overriding mission when important societal facets are on a downward slope and incrementalism being appropriate for societal facets that are on an upward slope.[5]

Another illustration of diagnostic requirements is the need to overcome "issue-attention cycles" (Downs, 1972) and identify basic needs and problems *in statu nascendi*, much before they ordinarily reach Rulers via organizational processes, political channels or mass-media. Such looking-forward and looking-outward diagnostic functions are necessary in order to improve the decision agenda of Rulers, which is a prior requirement to improving decisions themselves.

Closely related to diagnostics, while going beyond it, is the already mentioned requirement that the policy analysis unit for advising Rulers enjoys some freedom in choosing subjects to work on. Many subjects will be dictated by circumstances and the will and needs of the Ruler. But, to be able to fulfil its main functions, the unit should initiate study on subjects which it diagnoses as important, though not yet recognized as such by the Ruler and not included in the explicit policy agenda. Sensitizing Rulers to neglected issues and being well prepared when problems suddenly become acute – are important contributions of policy analysis for advising Rulers.

All in all, diagnostics can constitute one of the most important offerings of advanced policy analysis for advising Rulers; but, this presupposes quite a jump in present policy analysis capabilities.

8. Innovation and Unconventionality

Policy analysis for advising Rulers is a professional-craft activity; as such, there are limits to its contributions. Thus, wild futuristic ideas, radical social alternatives, ideological visions and purely symbolic activities are beyond its domains. But marginal improvements and incremental enhancement, while well within the competence of present policy analysis, are of little use for Rulers in a period of turmoil, turbulence and ultra-change. Therefore, innovation and unconventionality are essential contributions to be supplied by policy analysis for advising Rulers, within the limits posed by the fundamental constitution of a professional and rationality-based activity.

Some illustrations will serve to identify a few of the possibilities and impossibilities of advanced policy analysis, in this respect:

(a) It is a relatively easy assignment to serve as "devil's advocate", in the sense of *ad hoc* adoption of assumptions, reality images and predictions contrary to those on which the Ruler's decisions usually are based. If such *Gedankenexperiments* result in definitely impossible constructs, they are dropped. But if, as frequently will be the case, devil's advocacy reasoning looks absurd only to contrary-committed mindsets, without any clear-cut falsification being possible, then the bases of decisions must be broadened accordingly and encompass a more diverse range of assumptions, images, predictions and so on.

(b) It is a difficult question, how far to go in exploring alternatives beyond and contrary to basic ideologies and philosophies of the Ruler and of society as a whole. Probably, such exercises are too speculative as well as threatening to take place in policy analysis for advising Rulers, being better left to units not tied closely into government. But, care must be taken to distinguish between basic ideologies and philosophies, that should be accepted, more or less, as bases for policy analysis for advising Rulers in given situations; and dogmas, fixed ideas and various "holy cows" – the debunking and iconoclastics of which is an essential duty within the closed walls of the Ruler's work habitat.

(c) Psychology and epistimology confirm the findings of the history of ideas (Geertz, 1973, pp. 216–220; Pocock, 1971) that comprehension of events is bound by existing models, concepts and *Weltanschauungen*. This is a constraint limiting even the most outstanding policy analyst and policy-maker (Dickson, 1978). On the other hand, many of the more ominous problems facing societies and their Rules have no solution within contemporarily available policy paradigms, known alternatives being more-or-less equi-final in unsatisfactory results. Therefore, policy analysis for advising Rulers must try to advance at least a little beyond historic boundaries, if not on its own then through drawing upon outstanding thinkers on an *ad hoc* basis, so as to expose analysis to stimulus that can enrich perception and alternatives.

(d) Easier is the task of developing counter-intuitive thinking, through consistent analysis in neutral symbols. Confronting "common sense" with a superior sense of extra-conventional and counter-conventional findings is one of the main contributions of advanced policy analysis, which can help to get Rulers' decisions out of serious *cul-de-sacs*.

(e) Invention of new policy options is a major must of better policy-making, but one which cannot be "programmed". A main task of policy analysis for advising Rulers is to canvas policy inventions wherever they take place, encourage them and inject their results into analysis. In this, as well as other matters discussed above policy analysis for advising Rulers serves as a channel for unconventional, non-bureaucratic and non-partisan-political thinking – to be canvassed, stimulated, distilled and introduced into the analytical work and into Rulers' decisions.

(f) When societies move into crises, as may well be the case for some at least of the highly industrialized countries and perhaps for Western Culture (in the encompassing sense of that term) as a whole, a dominant need may be for new or renewed realistic visions. This is a task beyond even my enlarged vision of advanced policy analysis for advising Rulers. But, advanced policy analysis must consider and partly specify the needs for such visions and contribute to their uses in societal architecture, when semi-utopias must be translated into reality-shaping critical decisions. This requires moving from policy analysis as the craft of achieving the possible effectively, into advanced policy analysis as the craft of helping to make the desirable and necessary approximately possible.

(g) To balance the somewhat over-optimistic tone of the policy analysis tasks considered above, let me conclude the enumeration of innovation and unconventionality contributions of policy analysis for advising Rulers by postulating what should probably be the first and most important assignment. Before one moves into approximating hopes and visions, catastrophe must be avoided. Therefore, work to develop disaster scenarios and to design policies which reduce their probability as much as possible are a must, with creativity and unconventional thinking to be geared to inventing possible distopias and their avoidance. This is an unpopular and thankless job, distasteful to most Rulers. But, it is an important innovative and unconventional contribution of policy analysis for advising Rulers.

To conclude this subject on a more operational note, let me mention the preparation of surprises to be thrown at history as a concrete illustration of innovative and unconventional tasks of policy analysis for advising Rulers (Axelrod, 1979; Dror, 1975; Handel, 1981). When diagnosis identifies some important policy areas as being on a declining curve or when cascading reality produces rapidly disappearing opportunities or suddenly crystallizing grievous dangers, the preferable response may be to try and transmute parts of emerging reality so as to achieve some hopes or to prevent some evils. Shock-interventions with history are risky, but in some situations not attempting them may be much more dangerous. To design suitable surprises to be thrown at history and to develop them into concrete options for Rulers under suitable contingencies – this is a supreme test of the capacities of advanced policy analysis in fulfilling its innovation and unconventionality functions.

The "innovation and unconventionality" function is closely related to the noted requirement of policy analysis units for advising Rulers devoting parts of their resources to broad issues, rather than getting more and more preoccupied with current decision issues. The sensitivity of broad issues looked at in innovative and unconventional modes is all the more a reason to include them within the mandate of policy analysis for advising Rulers, with due care being taken to keep such work protected against harmful leakage. Availability of high-quality Think Tanks to engage in in-depth study of such issues at a distance, in close cooperation with the policy analysis unit but separate from it, may often provide a preferable solution.

9. Policy Learning

Recent literature in policy analysis and some of its practice pays increasing attention to "evaluation", but neglects "policy learning". This is a confusion quite typical of the need for rethinking some basics of policy analysis: Evaluation, after all, is an approach, method and set of techniques aimed at permitting and accelerating policy learning. Developing techniques for a process which itself is left in the air is rather doubtful.

Policy learning is a difficult function of advanced policy analysis and an essential one. It is difficult, because:

- Results of complex policies are diffuse, dispersed and take a long time to become visible.
- Sunk costs, mainly political and psychological ones, reinforce dissonance-reducing tendencies, in the form of regarding all but the most flagrant failures, and sometimes even these, as successes, near-successes, the best possible achievements, or as due to unforeseeable causes.
- Even if policy results are perceived as weak, "learning", in the sense of drawing correct conclusions, is still far off. Typical incorrect lessons of experience are escalating commitment, as if a failing policy is essentially correct, but has not been tried hard enough. Or, in case of calamities, panic-learning with wild results tends to take place.

Valid policy learning is more of an unnatural than a self-sustaining process. This is in particular true of Rulers' decisions, where many screens against presenting failure-information, as well as other distortion processes surrounding Rulers, add to non-learning and mis-learning. When critical decisions are largely "fuzzy bets", then constant learning and re-learning become a main mode of containing costs and improving decisions (Holling, 1980). Under such conditions, the consequences of inadequate policy learning are dire indeed.

Hence, the importance of policy learning as a function of policy analysis for advising Rulers. This requires, *inter alia:*

- Building up an "institutional memory" of Rulers' decisions and their consequences.

- Broadening the basis for learning, through comparative study of relevant episodes in other countries and in other periods, as an integral dimension of advanced policy analysis.
- Initiating evaluation of the results of Rulers' main decisions and transforming findings into explicit policy lessons, to be stored in the institutional memory and used for policy revision, as well as to be presented to the Ruler for his personal learning.
- Applying the above activities in intensified form to the policy analysis unit itself, together with periodic self-evaluation and external review.

It should be noted, that none of the above activities implies that policy analysis for advising Rulers should itself engage in decision implementation control or detailed evaluation studies, which would over-dilute its own missions.

10. Policy Implementation Institutions

Restructuring institutions is a main component of a broad range of policies, ranging from administrative reforms to societal architecture. At present, our concern is with a different kind of engagement of policy analysis for advising Rulers with institutions, namely in the context of implementation and feasibility considerations.

Feasibility of policy options is a main concern of advanced policy analysis. Here, a sharp distinction (even though blurred in reality) should be made between feasibility with present implementation institutions being viewed more-or-less as given, as contrasted with feasibility achieved through revamping and changing implementation institutions. This is especially important because of the quite clear lesson from historic studies that innovative policies have little hope of implementation without far-reaching reforms and nova-designs of implementation institutions (Black, 1975; Findley, 1980; Orlovsky, 1981). Hence, the necessity to include institutional changes as an integral part of innovative policy options, as a precondition of feasibility.

This does not imply that advanced policy analysis for advising Rulers should deal with administrative reforms, implementation management and similar detailed organizational matters. To move into such items cannot but ruin the essence of policy analysis as focusing on policy-making. Policy analysis should consider implementation institutions to gauge option feasibility and propose institution redesign directions when essential for implementation. But not more than that. Thus, when Rulers become active in administrative reforms, as they often must, they should be aided by special outfits separate from their policy analysis unit.

Policy analysis for advising Rulers may have negative self-fulfilling prophecy effects, especially when declaring options as non-feasible. Difficulties in adequately appreciating the strength, for better and worse, of visions, dogmas, ideologies and beliefs in human action constitute a fallacy inbuilt into much of contemporary policy analysis, because of economic models and rationalistic assumptions (Dror, 1980, chapter 1). This bias can lead to serious harm in situations when the nearly impossible must be attempted, or when high aspiration levels might serve as a driving force. When visions are crucial, it is necessary to circumscribe appropriate roles for policy analysis at the Rulers' level, so as to benefit from policy analysis inputs in making vision-approximating decisions, but without too much disenchantment being generated by over-"realistic" analysis; especially when based on narrow methods.

Policy analysis may overwhelm Rulers with uncertainties, complexities, broad perspectives, counter-intuitive findings and all its other blessings. This may result in strain and stress, depressing decision quality; in indecisiveness, which sometimes is a benefit but often a curse, producing stalemate and policy paralysis; in decision procrastination; or in rejection of all of policy analysis, including its many positive contributions.

To such potential dangerous dysfunctional effects must be added the simple, but ominous, possibility of wrong analysis, resulting from the many weaknesses, fallacies, inadequacies and pitfalls of contemporary policy analysis (as discussed, in part, in Majone and Quade, 1980).

Three main conclusions emerge from consideration of such possible dangerous dysfunctional effects of policy analysis for Rulers:

(a) Rulers should be sophisticated about possible benefits and dangers of policy analysis as an aid to their decisions. This can be promoted by suitable, informal and on-the-job tutorials by the policy analysis unit itself, and, sometimes, by providing tailor-made learning opportunities for Rulers or, which is easier, for potential Rulers-to-be.

(b) Policy analysis for Rulers should engage in self-debugging and self-debunking, partly in conjunction with the already mentioned need for self-learning and self-evaluation; partly through institutional arrangements, such as staff rotation; and partly by strict quality control.

(c) Improvement of policy analysis methods is a *sine qua non.*

ADVANCED POLICY ANALYSIS METHODS FOR ADVISING RULERS

The difference between traditional advisers to Rulers and policy analysis for advising Rulers is in the methodological base of the latter, which permits special qualities of contributions to Rulers and their decisions. But, to achieve this distinctive capability, policy analysis must undergo a deep transformation, especially in its methods. I express this verbally with the term "advanced policy analysis".

It is to some illustrations of the latter that I now turn.

14. Methodological Requisites and Possibilities

All policy analysis functions and tasks considered till now converge and add up to a needed transformation of policy analysis methodologies. To provide significant help to Rulers' decisions, policy analysis must enlarge its methodological repertoire and advance to quite different levels of comprehension and sophistication. The real need is for integrative, or at least combinational, methods that can handle problems the main parameters of which cannot be quantified with presently available scales and important parts of which defy conceptualization. In other words, purposeful and semi-structured heurisms must be added as a main content of advanced policy analysis. Some beginnings exist, but the vast majority of present policy analysis literature and large parts of policy analysis practice are of little help to most of the important choices facing Rulers.

Systematic consideration of these needs requires examination of existing methods and their sufficiency and insufficiency for fulfilling the various main functions of policy analysis for advising Rulers, including *inter alia* those discussed already; identification of *lacunae*, and indication of main methodological innovations needed to fill the large empty areas. Here is not the place for such a comprehensive treatment, nor for presenting a compendium of methods of advanced policy analysis. Instead, in order not to leave the central thrust of this chapter completely vague, a partial conspectus of methodological requisites and possibilities of advanced policy analysis for advising Rulers can be summed up as follows:

- Additional languages to conceptualize messy realities, ranging from non-metric measurement scales to processing of impressionistic insights.
- Guides to the utilization of history, anthropology and psychology for evaluating situations, examining problems, gaining perspectives and analysing issues.
- Broad "policiographic" approaches to collect, process and apply policy knowledge and policy experiences from a large range of countries, periods and situations.
- Special approaches to handle what has been called "large-scale policy making" (Schulman, 1980) where issues cannot be decomposed into simpler and easier to analyse problems and where dynamic interrelations between components require comprehensive decisions with high threshold parameters.
- Related to large-scale policy-making, as mentioned above, but not identical

with it: capacities to comprehend and manage intense complexities (La Porte, 1975; Warfield, 1976).

- Methods fitting conditions of ignorance, when important decisions must be viewed as "fuzzy bets" and allocation of subjective probabilities may be in error. Combination between gambling studies and structured learning opportunities indicate some appropriate ways to proceed.

- Value analysis, facing the unavoidability of "tragic choice" with tools from analytical philosophy, value mapping from anthropology, goal clarification from psychoanalysis, concept clarification from some branches of semantics, multi-goal scaling from welfare economics, and value aggregation theory from collective choice logic (Klages and Kmieciak, 1979).

- Designs for handling the speculative, such as schemata for "thinking experiments".

- Approaches to policy alternative invention, with idea canvassing, creativity stimulation and "alternative thinking" exploration. Special attention should also be paid to unusual sources of options, such as technological shortcuts (Etzioni and Remp, 1973).

- Crosscutting and combining some of the above clusters and applying them differently to improving Rulers' decisions: decision error research and experimentation, to debug, debunk, off-set and counter-balance error propensities.

- Broad look-out and prediction methods, able to canvas future possibilities, without covering up inherent indeterminance and irreducible ignorance (Choucri and Robinson, 1978; Whiston, 1979).

- Approaches to macro-organizational analysis, based probably in part on merging components from organization theory with components from political science and political sociology, together with canvassing of historical experiences with the help of modern conceptual tools.

- Evaluation methods, together with social experimentation techniques, transposed to the level of policy-making and based on available experiences and theories (Ferber and Hirsch, 1981).

- Time-compressing quick-response methods, based in part on preset analysis schemata, to permit preferable inputs under intense time pressures.

- Integrated tools for analysing bargaining and negotiation decisions, from theory of games, through psychological profiles, to external-event canvassing and controlling.

- Crisis handling improvement designs, ranging from crisis exercises to stress-containing psycho-tools (Hermann and Hermann, 1975; Smart and Stanbury, 1978).

- Display techniques, to help with the communication of complex analysis to busy Rulers, without spoiling oversimplifications.

- Principles for reasoning, judgement and drawing of conclusions, encompassing also appropriate ideas from aesthetics, jurisprudence, rhetorics (in its correct meaning as the theory of sound argument) and additional branches of purposeful activity (Toulmin, Rieke and Janik, 1979).

– Beginnings of a philosophic underpinning for advanced policy analysis methods, such as: elements of philosophy of knowledge and science; fundamental approaches to the nature of "decisions" and their effects or mis-effects in influencing futures; general systems theory; and fundamental treatment of concepts of "rationality" in their metaphysical, positivistic, sociological and cultural world of discourse (Michalos, 1978).

Progress on the lines mentioned above is essential for applying policy analysis to complex, high level and indeterminate issues. It is an imperative for policy analysis for advising Rulers.

Further insights into needs for methodological advancements are provided by looking at two requisites more distant from the mainstreams of contemporary policy analysis, and operational research in general, namely: social sciences in policy analysis and politics in policy analysis.

15. Social Sciences in Policy Analysis

The needs for rethinking policy analysis and for methodological innovations are well brought out by problems of social sciences in policy analysis. At present, applied social sciences are capable of providing data helpful for policy issues, such as current surveys (Rich, 1981). Applied social sciences are also useful in a number of low-level issues. But, with the exception of economics, social sciences are still of little use in the handling of major policy problems. The difficulties of applied social sciences for high-policy issues are well-illustrated by recent undermining of the reliability of the bastion of successful policy-contributions by a social science discipline, namely economics. This leaves policy analysis for advising Rulers quite lacking, because suitable social science knowledge inputs are essential for handling a growing range of challenges, especially in societal architecture and in transincremental decisions in general. Therefore, there is a necessity to introduce changes in social sciences and in policy analysis, so as to build a basis for improved Rulers' decisions.

The satisfaction of this need meets multiple, strong and mutually supportive barriers, such as:

– Inadequate knowledge by applied social sciences of policy analysis and prescriptive decision approaches in general, with resulting: (a) insufficient and often also incorrect processing of social science knowledge into policy recommendations; (b) inadequate design of social science research so as to meet advanced policy analysis needs. Thus, contemporary applied social sciences eschew historical and comparative studies, which are essential for many policy purposes; and (c) little help to policy analysis in learning to integrate correctly available social science knowledge.

- Misapprehension by policy analysis of social sciences, with inadequate understanding of the potentials and limitations of contemporary social science paradigms. As a result: (a) the social sciences are expected to produce findings fitting policy analysis schemata of quite narrow a format, which ignore the inherent characteristics of the material dealt with by social sciences; (b) policy analysis is often unable to utilize correctly social science knowledge which is available, and frequently does not even reach that material; and (c) policy analysis does not provide helpful guidance to social sciences on those of its needs that could be satisfied by present social science capacities, if correctly applied.

- Behind this mismatch, more fundamental factors may be at work, such as (a) differences in personality type and value profiles between many social scientists and many policy analysts; (b) differences in basic attitudes to working in and for governments and establishments. These, in turn, may be related to differences in actual and desired societal functions, with social scientists in some countries tending more to roles of social critics, and policy analysts more to roles of improvers of policy-making from within governments; and (c) possible differences and also divergence between philosophy of science bases and assumptions of social sciences and policy analysis.

Productive interface between policy analysis and social sciences is not easy to achieve, as evidenced by the scarcity of fruitful mixed activities between highly-qualified social scientists and highly-qualified policy analysts. The absence of successful combined policy analysis and social science teaching programs is also symptomatic, despite the success of combined programs between policy studies on one hand and law, public health and additional subjects on the other.

To this must be added, that despite much insightful literature in applied social sciences (Rein, 1976; Scott and Shore, 1979; Weiss, 1980) the needs for and problems of more convergence between applied social sciences and policy analysis is very seldom taken up and even more seldom perceived correctly.

16. Politics in Policy Analysis

Problems of applied social sciences in policy analysis preview, in part, some of the difficulties of adequately handling politics in policy analysis, though the latter is even more urgent a need and even more difficult a task. After all, Rulers are predominantly political decision-makers, with politics permeating their thinking and behaviour and political considerations necessarily placing a pivotal role in their choices. Therefore, policy analysis for advising Rulers must squarely face the issue of how to take politics into account.

Many of the responses by contemporary policy analysis to the needs of handling politics are inadequate for advanced policy analysis and, in particular, policy analysis for Rulers. It is doubtful to view politics as an "enemy" (Churchman, 1979) to regard politics as ripe for reform by policy analysis, to adopt narrow concepts of "political feasibility testing" as a main mode to accommodate politics in policy analysis, or to regard political constraints as inferior to technological or economical ones.[6]

Adequate treatment of politics in policy analysis for advising Rulers must start with a distinction between various overlapping contents of the term "politics", looked at from the point-of-view of Rulers' decisions: (a) expected responses from targets of his decisions, domestic and external; (b) possibilities for gaining support for various options, each one separately and for a number of them as packages; (c) longer-term impacts of his decisions on domestic and external politics, as a main goal for Rulers' decisions; (d) impacts of his decisions on his own political stature; (e) politics as expressing ideologies and belief systems, which a Ruler may accept as a commitment and base for his decisions.

Policy analysis must clearly consider these and additional dimensions of politics as very salient for Rulers' decisions.

Handling of politics in policy analysis for advising Rulers can either try and do a maximum job in considering politics, within the limits of present and emerging methods, or can prefer to do a minimum job, which still must include quite a lot. Choice between these extremes and in-between positions depends on the political ideology and culture of different countries, as well as different structures of Rulers' units, which may or may not include various types of political advisers other than the policy analysis island.

Maximum handling of politics in policy analysis for advising Rulers includes, in the main: (a) mapping of political fields within which decisions operate and attempts to predict responses and supports as well as oppositions; (b) efforts to generate options more favourable in political responses, including special attention to decision marketing as part of advanced analysis; (c) some consideration of impacts on Rulers' own political power, but subdued and left mainly in the hands of political advisers, in close interaction with them; and (d) basic acceptance of Rulers' ideological position as a frame-of-reference for policy analysis, but with constant struggle for distinction between ideological values and dogmatic fiats and with intense efforts to expose Rulers to alternative perspectives and counter-dogmatic options.

Minimum handling of politics in policy analysis for advising Rulers still requires full understanding of the political dimensions of Rulers' decisions, but accepts a different division of labour with political advisers, leaving to the latter most of the tasks of working out political dimensions. But, unless close communication is maintained between policy analysts and political advisers and unless each understands the other's functions and perspectives, both the quality of policy analysis help for the Ruler and the quality of the political advice help for the Ruler will suffer, with dire consequences for the quality of Rulers' decisions.

Minimum inclusion of politics in policy analysis for advising Rulers does require much rethinking of the process of policy analysis. Movement towards maximum inclusion of politics in policy analysis, which may well be needed in quite a number of situations, probably requires paradigmatic innovations in policy analysis.

It is fitting to conclude our circumnavigation of special features of policy analysis for advising Rulers, which require rethinking the process of policy analysis, with politics in policy analysis. It is the special duality of Rulers as the political heads of their countries and as in charge of the policies of their countries, which causes and conditions the special features of policy analysis for advising Rulers.

IV. REALITY AND PROSPECTS

Let us turn from proposed specifications of advanced policy analysis for advising Rulers to the actual equipment of Rulers with policy analysis or policy-analysis-approximating help. Excluding countries on which I have no material available and basing generalizations mainly on field study and the little available literature, the emerging picture can provisionally be summed up as follows:

- A general trend to build up staff supports for Rulers can be discerned. There is a large disparity in the size of such staffs, ranging from five to ten aides up to Prime Ministerial and Presidential offices with up to two to three hundred professionals, in a few countries.
- Some countries have quite sophisticated set-ups, with special Rulers' research centres and planning units, separate policy and political advisory staffs, integrative policy review units, etc. But, in most countries, such units are *in status nascendi*.
- In most countries, Rulers' units are staffed with regular civil servants. In a few countries, outsiders including professionals are also recruited.
- Only in single countries do Rulers' units partake some of the characteristics of policy analysis staffs, as discussed in the paper. Usually, intuition and experience are relied upon, augmented with some economics and traditional social sciences at the most. Professional policy analysis for advising Rulers is, at present, an anomaly.

However overgeneralized this picture may be, it does pose the question why policy analysis for advising Rulers is distinguished by its absence, despite uneasiness felt by most contemporary Rulers and search on their part for help in confronting overwhelming challenges.

The main factors inhibiting demand for policy analysis to advise Rulers can be illustrated, as follows:

(a) Conflict between Rulership and political dynamics on one hand and policy analysis dynamics on the other hand, as discussed earlier. As a result of such conflict, policy analysis causes obvious pain to Rulers, while benefits may seem quite ephemeral.

(b) Political costs of setting up such units, when the building up of Rulers' equipment is resisted by constitutional norms, political conventions, ideologies, coalition structures and so on.

(c) Personal risks to the Ruler of putting his trust in a professional island of excellence, not bound to him by traditionally proven chains of trust. Instances of indiscretion in a number of countries strengthen such apprehensions about policy analysis professionals.

(d) Bureaucratic resistance to the introduction of novel methods into government, which break civil service monopolies and discount experience and traditional skills and knowledge.

(e) Pragmatism as an ideology, with deep doubts about any claims in the name of "scientific" approaches. Disappointment with economics strongly reinforces nowadays such pragmatic reactions, with Rulers and their counsellors being very sceptical, if not cynical, about the potential contributions of policy analysis and any similar approaches.

(f) Inability of policy analysis to deliver the goods, assuming such units for Rulers are set up. This, as a result both of the underdevelopment of policy analysis, as discussed in this paper; and the scarcity of highly qualified analysts, who might do a good job thanks to their subjective knowledge. The absence of necessary infra-structures, such as Think Tanks and public policy schools, in most countries further aggravates this barrier.

(g) Assuming policy analysis units for Rulers were set up, they probably would fail unless Rulers themselves know something about the main features of policy analysis and give a helping hand to accelerate maturation of their policy analysis unit. But this is to demand quite a lot.

As against these doubts about the chances of advanced policy analysis for advising Rulers, some hopeful signs become increasingly visible, such as:

– An actual tendency, in a small but growing number of countries, to build up integrated professional advisory units for Rulers. While not yet policy analysis based, such units do search for a professional foundation and serve as a potential opening for policy analysis for advising Rulers. The successful contributions of some such units to Rulers' decisions and their survival of changes in Rulers are important antecedents for institutionalization of advanced policy analysis for advising Rulers, on lines discussed in this paper.

- Increasing awareness in more and more countries, including among top decision-makers, that contemporary governmental equipments are unequal to the challenges and are becoming rapidly obsolescent.
- In policy analysis itself, in conjunction with embracing disciplines such as operational research and policy sciences, a recognition of insufficiency in the face of societal and global problems, with readiness for rethinking – as evidenced by this volume, too.

Therefore, opportunities for setting up policy analysis for advising Rulers do exist and can be expected to multiply, either as the result of systematic endeavours to redesign governments better to meet challenges, or thanks to innovative Rulers, or as the result of avalanching crises that crack open systems to new experimentation. To search for such opportunities and to be ready to fulfil the tasks of advanced policy analysis for advising Rulers – this is a heavy responsibility lying upon the professionals of policy analysis itself. Rulers derive their legitimation from the political processes which bring them to their fateful positions. The only justification for policy analysts to enter the chambers of powers is their professional capability to make a substantive contribution to high-level decisions.

It follows, that the-state-of-the-craft of policy analysis must be rapidly upgraded, on lines such as discussed here or on better ones, to be identified after further search. This is an assignment mainly for the informal international college of high-quality policy analysts and related professionals. Professional associations, university departments and policy research organizations, such as IIASA, can do a lot to help such activities.

To try and help progress in that direction, let me conclude with three operational proposals for preparing policy analysis to move into advanced policy analysis for advising Rulers, as well as for helping with major societal problems and global issues at a variety of decision loci.

1. Specific work focused on policy analysis for advising Rulers, in conjunction with endeavours to advance policy analysis as a whole should be organized. Thus, mixed workshops with actual advisors of Rulers and policy analysis professionals can serve to specify needs and possibilities of policy analysis for advising Rulers. Shared study projects with decision psychologists can deal with operationalization of debugging and debunking functions of policy analysis for Rulers. Mixed projects with social scientists provide hope for introducing applied social sciences into advanced policy analysis. And a variety of activities with practising politicians, political correspondents and other persons

knowledgeable in politics, including some political scientists, are essential starting points for upgrading the handling of politics in advanced policy analysis.

2. The infrastructure for upgrading policy analysis must be further developed and diffused. Thus, appropriate professional training programs in advanced policy analysis should be established in more countries, and on a cross-national basis, based in part on the experiences, for better and for worse, of the United States public policy schools. Institutional settings for research on policy analysis methods need also strengthening, with special attention to merging applied experience with theoretic work.

3. Rulers, as well as other main decision-makers, must be sensitized to the potentials as well as the limits of policy analysis as an aid to their society-steering roles. This may require unconventional activities, such as workshops and treatizes specially designed for Rulers, ruler-candidates, and ruler-producing cadres, and also for other Ruler-influencing advisers.[7]

Let us bear in mind that policy analysis for advising Rulers, as treated in this chapter, is not only a subject very important by itself, but also serves as a pure type tool for exploring broader needs of rethinking the processes of policy analysis. Advanced policy analysis can become an important augmentation of hard-pressed human capacities consciously to influence collective futures through deliberate choice and action. Therefore, progress towards advanced policy analysis, including but not exclusively in the form of policy analysis for advising Rulers, is a most urgent task.

FOOTNOTES

1. This chapter is indebted for encouragement and support from a number of institutions, including: IIASA; Samuel Neaman Institute for Advanced Studies in Science and Technology, The Technion – Israel Institute of Technology; Russell Sage Foundation, New York; Woodrow Wilson International Center for Scholars, Washington, DC; and Institute for Advanced Study Berlin.

I am also grateful for helpful comments by colleagues, especially: Rolfe Tomlinson, John M. Ashworth, Gene Fisher, Sir Frank Holmes, Shlomit Keren, Robert A. Levine, J. du Plessis, William Plowden, Max Singer, H. Verwayen, Warren Walker and Michael Wearne.

2. I hope to expand this chapter into a book-length version, with more adequate treatment of main issues and problems. Readers are invited to help in this endeavour by letting me benefit from their comments and observations.

The expanded version will provide extensive bibliographic guidance and discussion of relevant literature. In this paper I limit myself to a few references, as illustrations and samples from a rather large list of publications processed as part of my study.

3. It is amazing how little work has been done on designing multi-dimensional briefing arrangements for top decision-makers. Military briefing is often highly developed, but tends towards serious oversimplifications, such as in handling uncertainty. Good graphic display systems, such as at the Department of Commerce, Washington DC and the National Council of

Science and Technology in Mexico City, provide some starting points, as does some work on data supports to decision-making and some experience with data processing for Rulers' offices (Fick and Sprague, Jr. 1981; Grigg, 1980; Harden, 1980).

Some Rulers have situation rooms, but those few I have seen are overstatic, simplistic, underused and sometimes gadget-prone. Few try to move from simple data series presentation to issue-mapping and policy analysis presentation. (Some attempts are described in Beer, 1975; Beer, 1981, "The Course of History"; and Szanton, 1981, pp. 98 ff.) This is a neglected area, urgently in need of intense work. I think development of well-designed problem-presentation multi-media setups for Rulers is both feasible and useful. Such equipment, if correctly used, can be of real help in making advanced policy analysis serve improvement of Rulers' decisions.

It is interesting to speculate on the impact on future Rulers of getting used from an early age to interactive games and home computers. This serves to illustrate the implications of broader cultural-technological developments for policy analysis possibilities. Speeding up development of homecomputer software inculcating decision sophistication, such as in facing uncertainty, illustrates even wider possibilities to influence decision culture as a whole. The scarcity of such programs despite significant market potentials raises interesting questions, beyond the scope of this chapter.

4. The term "policy analysis" may well be too narrow to fully express needs, the combined verbal symbol "policy planning and policy analysis" being perhaps preferable – especially, in order to convey the contents of what I discuss in this paper under the term "advanced policy analysis".

5. A fascinating illustration is provided by a historic analysis of France between the First and the Second World War (Young, 1978). The basic thesis is, that most French foreign policy and defence decisions during the studied period were incrementally correct. But as France was on a history-produced downwards slope, disjointed "cost effective" decisions could not help. To optimize on a sinking curve – this is worse than useless; but, this is all that most of contemporary policy analysis can do, in the absence of situational diagnostics and advanced prescriptive methodologies. Also worth pondering in this context is Gelb and Betts, 1979.

6. Typical is the following statement, made while discussing the design of desirable futures and after specifying that technological feasibility should be accepted as a constraint: "All other types of externally imposed constraint – for example, economic, political and legal – should be disregarded". (Ackoff, 1978, p. 72.)

With due respect to the distinguished author, assuming *a priori* that human nature, on which politics is based, can be changed produces fiction, just as unrealistic technological assumptions would do. Why outstanding systems scientists tend towards wishful thinking when human variables are concerned – this is a question deserving much thought. Whatever the answer may be, here is a main root for the narrow utility of large parts of policy analysis.

7. Some experimentation with a *Workshop in Policy Planning and Policy Analysis* which I run with such persons in a number of countries leads me to the tentative impression, that lack of suitable offering are a contributing cause of underequipment of Rulers.

Similarly symptomatic is the absence of books written for Rulers and adjusted to their special needs, despite the long tradition of "Mirrors for Rulers" at other periods. I try to take up parts of this challenge in a forthcoming *Thinkbook for Rulers*.

REFERENCES

Ackoff, Russell L. (1978) *The Art of Problem Solving*. Wiley, New York.
Ackoff, Russell L. (1981) *Creating the Corporate Future*. Wiley, New York.
Axelrod, Robert, ed. (1976) Structure of Decision. Princeton University Press, Princeton.
Axelrod, Robert (1979) Rational Timing of Surprise. *World Politics*, pp. 230–246.
Beer Stafford (1975) *Platform for Change*. Wiley, New York.
Beer Stafford (1981) *Brain of the Firm*. Wiley, New York. 2nd ed.
Berman, Larry (1979) *The Office of Management and Budget and the Presidency, 1921–1979*. Princeton University Press, Princeton.
Betts, Richard K. (1980) Intelligence for Policymaking. *The Washington Quarterly*, **3**, No. 3 (Summer), pp. 118–129.

Black, Cyril E. *et al.* (1975) *The Modernization of Japan and Russia: A Comparative Study.* Free Press, New York.

Boston, Jonathan G. (1980) *High Level Advisory Groups in Central Government: A Comparative Study of the Origins, Structure and Activities of the Australian Priorities Review Staff and the New Zealand Prime Minister's Advisory Group.* Masters Thesis. University of Canterbury, Christchurch, NZ.

Buchanan, Bruce (1978) *The Presidential Experience: What the Office Does to the Man.* Prentice-Hall, Englewood Cliffs, NJ.

Bunce, Valeria (1981) *Do New Leaders Make a Difference?* Princeton University Press, Princeton.

Calabresi, Guido and Phillip Bobbitt (1979) *Tragic Choice.* Norton, New York.

Choucri, Nazli and Thomas W. Robinson, eds (1978) *Forecasting in International Relations.* Freeman, San Francisco.

Churchman, West C. (1979) *The Systems Approach and Its Enemies.* Basic Books, New York.

Cohen, Samy (1980) *Les Conseillers du President: De Charles de Gaulle à Valéry Giscard d'Estaing.* Presses Universitaires de France, Paris.

De Rivera, Joseph (1980) *The Psychological Dimensions of Foreign Policy.* Charles E. Merrill, Columbus, Ohio.

Dickson, Peter W. (1978) *Kissinger and the Meaning of History.* Cambridge University Press, Cambridge.

Dill, W. R. and G. Kh. Popov, eds (1979) *Organization for Forecasting and Planning: Experience in the Soviet Union and the United States.* Wiley, New York, IIASA Series.

Downs, Anthony (1972) Up and Down with Ecology – the "Issue-Attention Cycle". *The Public Interest,* **28** (Summer), pp. 38–50.

Dror, Yehezkel (1971) *Design for Policy Sciences.* American Elsevier, New York.

Dror, Yehezkel (1975) *How to Spring Surprises on History.* Paper prepared for Leonard Davis Institute for International Relations, Hebrew University of Jerusalem, Symposium on When Patterns Change: Turning Points in International Politics. April 7 to 9.

Dror, Yehezkel (1980) *Crazy States: A Counterconventional Strategic Problem.* Kraus Reprints, Milwood, NY. Updated editions.

Dror, Yehezkel (1983) *Public Policymaking Reexamined.* (2nd Edition). Transaction Books, New Brunswick, NJ.

Elster, Jon (1979) *Ulysses and The Sirens: Studies in Rationality and Irrationality.* Cambridge University Press, Cambridge.

Erikson, Erik H. (1975) *Life History and the Historical Moment: Diverse Presentations.* Norton, New York.

Etzioni, Amitai and Richard Remp (1973) *Technological Shortcuts to Social Change.* Russell Sage Foundation, New York.

Ferber, Robert and Werner Z. Hirsch (1981) *Social Experimentation and Economic Policy.* Cambridge University Press, Cambridge.

Fick, G. and R. H. Sprague, Jr, eds (1981) *Decision Support Systems: Issues and Challenges.* Pergamon Press, Oxford, IIASA Volume.

Findley, Carter V. (1980) *Bureaucratic Reform in the Ottoman Empire: The Sublime Porte, 1789-1922.* Princeton University Press, Princeton.

Geertz, Clifford (1973) *The Interpretation of Cultures: Selected Essays.* Basic Books, New York.

Gelb, Leslie H. with Richard K. Betts (1979) *The Irony of Vietnam: The System Worked.* The Brookings Institution, Washington, DC.

George, L. Alexander (1980) *Presidential Decisionmaking in Foreign Policy: The Effective Use of Information and Advice.* Westview Press, Boulder, Colorado.

Goldhamer, Herbert (1978) *The Adviser.* Elsevier, New York.

Goldwin, Robert A., ed. (1980) *Bureaucrats, Policy Analysts, Stateman: Who Leads?* American Enterprise Institute, Washington, DC.

Grigg, Carolyn (1980) *The Information Efficient Support Staff.* Executive Office of the President, Washington, DC.

Häfele, Wolf (1981) *Energy in a Finite World: Paths to a Sustainable Future.* Ballington Pub., Cambridge, Mass. IIASA Volume.

Handel, Michael I. (1981) *The Diplomacy of Surprise: Hitler, Nixon, Sadat.* Harvard University Center for International Affairs, Cambridge, Mass.

Harden, Richard M. (1980) *The Information Efficient Presidential Adviser*. Executive Office of the President, Washington, DC.

Herman, Margaret G. and Charles F. Hermann (1975) *Maintaining the Quality of Decision Making in Foreign Policy Crisis: A Proposal*. Paper presented at the International Conference on Psychological Stress and Adjustment in Time of War and Peace. Tel Aviv, Israel, January 6 10.

Holling, C. S., ed. (1980) *Adaptive Environmental Assessment and Management*. Wiley, New York. IIASA Volume.

Holsti, Ole E. and Alexander L. George (1975) The Effects of Stress on the Performance of Foreign Policy-Makers. *Political Science Annual*, **6**, pp. 255 319.

Hughes, Thomas L. (1976) *The Fate of Facts in a World of Men Foreign Policy and Intelligence-Making*. Foreign Policy Association, New York.

Janis, Irving L. (1982) *Groupthink: Psychological Studies of Policy Decisions and Fiascoes*. Houghton Mifflin, Boston. Revised ed.

Janis, Irving L. and Leon Mann (1977) *Decision Making: A Psychological Analysis of Conflict, Choice, and Commitment*. Free Press, New York.

Jarvis, R. (1975) *Perception and Misperception in International Relations*. Princeton University Press, Princeton.

Kahn, Herman and Thomas Pepper (1980) *Will She Be Rights? The Future of Australia*. University of Queensland Press, St. Lucia, Queensland.

Klages, Helmut and Peter Kmieciak, Hg. (1979) *Wertwandel und Gesellschaftlicher Wandel*. Campus, Frankfurt.

La Porte, R. Todd, ed. (1975) *Organized Social Complexity: Challenge to Politics and Policy*. Princeton University Press, Princeton.

Lompe, Klaus (1971) *Gesellschaftspolitik und Planung: Probleme Politischer Planung in der Sozialstaat lichen Demokratie*. Rombach, Freiburg.

Majone, Giandomenico and Edward S. Quade, eds (1980) *Pitfalls of Analysis*. Wiley, New York, IIASA Volume.

May, Ernst R. (1972) *Lessons of the Past: The Uses and Misuses of History in American Foreign Policy*. Oxford University Press, NY.

Michalos, Alex C. (1978) *Foundations of Decision-Making*. Canadian Library of Philosophy, Ottawa.

Meltsner, Arnold J. (1976) *Policy Analysis in the Bureaucracy*. University of California Press, Berkeley.

Michalos, Alex C. (1978) *Foundations of Decision-Making*. Canadian Library of Philosophy, Ottawa.

Netherlands Scientific Council for Government Policy (1980) *Place and Future of Industry in The Netherlands*. Wetenschappelijke Raad voor her Regeringsbeleig, The Hague.

OECD (1981) *The Welfare State in Crisis*. OECD, Paris.

Orlovsky, Daniel T. (1981) *The Limits of Reform: The Ministry of Internal Affairs in Imperial Russia, 1802 1881*. Harvard University Press, Cambridge, Mass.

Pocock, J. G. A. (1971) *Politics, Language and Time: Essays on Political Thought and History*. Atheneum, New York.

Preisl, Anton and Armin Mohler, Hrsg. (1979) *Der Ernstfall*. Propylan Verlag, Frankfurt.

Privy Council Office (1981) *The Policy and Expenditure Management System*. Privy Council Office, Ottawa.

Rein, Martin (1976) *Social Science and Public Policy*. Penguin, Harmondsworth.

Rich, Robert F. (1981) *The Power of Social Science Information and Public Policymaking: The Case of the Continuous National Survey*. Jossey-Bass, San Francisco.

Ripley, Randell B. (1977) *Policy Research and the Clinical Relationship*. Mershon Center Position Papers in the Policy Sciences, No. One, Columbus, Ohio.

Schulman, Paul R. (1980) *Large-Scale Policy Making*. Elsevier, New York.

Scharpf, Fritz W. (1981) *The Political Economy of Inflation and Unemployment in Western Europe: An Outline*. International Institute of Management, Wissenschaftszentrum Berlin, Berlin.

Scott, Robert A. and Arnold R. Shore (1979) *Why Sociology Does Not Apply? A Study of the Use of Sociology in Public Policy*. Elsevier, New York.

Smart, C. F. and W. T. Stanbury, eds (1978) *Studies in Crisis Management.* Institute for Research on Public Policy Volume, Butterworth, Toronto.

Steiner, George A. (1979) *Strategic Planning.* Free Press, New York.

Szanton, Peter (1981) *Not Well Advised.* Russell Sage Foundation, New York.

Toulmin, Stephen, Richard Rieke and Allan Janik (1979) *An Introduction to Reasoning.* Collier Macmillan, London.

Tucker, Robert C. (1981) *Politics as Leadership.* University of Missouri Press, Columbia, MI.

Tufte, Edward R. (1978) *Political Control of the Economy.* Princeton University Press, Princeton.

Warfield, N. Johan (1976) *Societal Systems: Planning, Policy and Complexity.* Wiley, New York.

Weiss, H. Carol (1980) *Social Science Research in Decision-Making.* Columbia University Press, New York.

Whiston, Tom, ed. (1979) *The Uses and Abuses of Forecasting.* Macmillan, London, Science Policy Research Unit, Sussex, Book.

Wilson, David E. (1980) *The National Planning Idea in U.S. Public Policy: Five Alternative Approaches.* Westview Press, Boulding, Col.

Young, Robert J. (1978) *In Command of France: French Foreign Policy and Military Planning, 1933–1940.* Harvard University Press, Cambridge, Mass.

Ziman, J. M. (1968) *Public Knowledge: An Essay Concerning the Social Dimensions of Science.* Cambridge University Press, Cambridge.

7

Change in the Paradigms of Systems Analysis*

DR. JÁNOS FARKAS

> As a matter of fact, when we have a closer look at this issue, and investigate the structure of exact sciences more thoroughly, we at once notice that the whole edifice has a dangerously weak point this one being its base itself.
>
> Max Planck

The same thing has happened to system analysis and the system modelling relying on it as it has to several other scientific disciplines: its spectacular and swift rise has come to a halt: it did not prove to be efficient enough, and strong reservations and anxiety have appeared as the first signs of attempts to find a way out of the problem. Thomas Kuhn has already given a general outline of this process as well as concrete examples concerned with physics.[1] Researchers conduct their activities on the basis of assuming "paradigms". The *normal* development stage of science comes, however, to an end when the old paradigm proves to be too narrow to mould the new results and experiences into a theoretical and methodological framework. The "rebels" of the discipline concerned discard the old paradigm and replace it with a new one. This is the *revolutionary* stage of the development of science.

Therefore, in the case of systems theory, too, the crisis phenomena do not indicate anything else but the fact that the old (positivistic) paradigm seems to be exhausted and a theoretical renewal will soon get under way. The present chapter itself poses the task of contributing to this change in paradigms.

The main theses are the following: we have to negate certain lacking or erroneous presuppositions of systems analysis. We have to introduce new presuppositions; namely a type of modern anthropology which corresponds to modern social theory. It is a case of *lacking presuppositions* when scholars of systems theory conceive of social products as phenomena of nature, and specific socio-human factors are not reckoned with. It is a case of *erroneous*

---

* This paper is an abbreviated, modified version of my paper entitled The Hidden, Lacking or Erroneous Presuppositions of Systems Analysis. IIASA Symposium. Laxenburg, Aug. 1980.

presuppositions when the concept of society and the individual is in existence, yet it is obsolete. By *"hidden" presuppositions* I mean that the number of theses can always be augmented and no system has an optimal and final solution.

1. The first question can be formulated as follows: Is it true or is it wrong to state that today systems theory is in the state of *changing paradigms*? My answer to the question is an unequivocal yes. Namely, classical systems theory was based on the *positivist model* of science.

As a matter of fact, the participants of the seminar agreed that the positivist model of SA has to be replaced by a more adequate model. It was Checkland who outlined the differences between the two types of paradigms most vividly.[2] In addition, Churchman and Mitroff not only at the seminar but in earlier writings expressly suggested "dialectic" as a new method.[3]

This method has the characteristic that it conducts research into phenomena examined by natural sciences through quantitative measures which of necessity do not cover the world of consciousness, subjectivity and socio-human characteristics. In spite of this, the methodology was applied to social systems, too. This methodology being reductionist, it was only able to depict social phenomena by such simplified models that they necessarily failed when put into social practice. Thus, the problem identified by Susman–Evered arose: the failures of systems theory are to be ascribed to the epistemological crises brought about by the positivist model of science.[4] In a discussion paper I have made an attempt to transcend this view in some respects. I state that the rise, flourishing and failure of both the positivist method and all methodologies can be traced back to social causes. Production carried out in manufactures has its corresponding link in the Descartes' type of thinking based on logical rules; the positivist methodology corresponds to machine-factory production; and the anti-positivist methodology corresponds to production carried out in the form of scientific-technical revolution. The direction of the inter-relationship is that the given type of production cannot be derived from the logic of cognition, but the other way round.

Not only at the seminar but earlier in the technical literature there were many signs that indicated the negation of the positivist methodology. For example, Majone urged for an SA oriented not at result but rather at the *process.*[5] Checkland, too, emphasized that according to the new paradigm SA is a *process* and not a product.[6] All those who have become aware of the process-like structure of being have practically adopted dialectic. However, the debate could be continued on some philosophical issues. Checkland, for example, has suggested giving preference to the outlook of phenomenology, as against positivism.[7] I could challenge his view, since the phenomenologist is, as a matter of fact, a consequent positivist. This is the only consequent method since it does not aim at examining the given state of affairs in a selective way. It does not examine whether the thing that is given for him, that appears in front of him is, as a phenomenon of his consciousness, derived from experience or from elsewhere. How could he know what is really valid, what is a really reliable experience? Is it a phenomenological analysis to describe that which is given for him and not to transcend this level? Yet, does this lead anywhere?

Naturally, I recognize that it was phenomenology which got closest to the description of the basic structures of everyday life and behaviour. This trend raises a real problem, yet its "solutions" are not fully adequate epistemologically. At the same time, Marxism is at present regrettably not yet capable of giving a description to be operationalized on the facts of every-day life and behaviour. It was perhaps György Lukács who offered the most in this respect in his works *Die Eigenart des Aesthetischen* and *Zur Ontologie des gesellschaftlichen Seins.*

I also have some doubts in connection with the thesis put forward, mainly by Churchman and Checkland, according to which the methodology of SA could be constructed through the help of Kantian and Hegelian dialectic.[8] For example, Kant has described the antinomic structures, because he thought over the bourgeois tendencies of rationalism. The oppositional systems based on the separation of human abilities necessarily lead to irrational solutions. Kant, too, was tempted by this possibility when he thought that *intuition* could be a solution which reconciled contradictions. I regard the idea of the Renaissance emphasizing the possibility of individual unity and manysidedness as much more fruitful; Marxism is the sole continuation of this idea. To be sure, I do not state that idealist types of dialectic cannot be made use of in SA – yet, personally, I see more possibilities in the application of materialist dialectic. Regrettably, the scholars of this latter trend still have to make great efforts to render this dialectic operational.

2. However, by a mere registration of the phenomena of crisis in systems theory which appear of necessity because of methodological limits, the basic problem is not yet solved: can we construct systems models that adequately reflect the nature of complex social phenomena? The second question, too, is answered by an affirmative *yes*. If we succeed in theoretically reflecting such phenomena – characteristic of social quality – as interest, need, value, property, power and the conflicting forms thereof, then the new methodology, too, can be constructed. This, in turn, will cause a *change of paradigms* in systems theory. Before that, some erroneous presupposition of classical systems theory have to be discarded. First of all I discuss the concepts of *rationality* and *optimality* and point out that behind these key concepts an erroneous abstract *image of man and society* lacking social determination is hidden. According to the character of social production, earlier thinking divided the individual into isolated sections: *homo economicus, homo politicus, homo eticus.* Under circumstances of contemporary production, however all essential features of man merge into a unity and the *homo universalis* takes shape. A principal change is also necessary in anthropology, too. Society,

however cannot be deduced from anthropology. The characteristics and behaviour of the individual are socially determined by social existence, by the totality of social circumstances. Thus we must have such a concept of society from which anthropology itself can be deduced.

The idea according to which anthropology as a concept of man is only secondary as compared with the concept of society could be set forth in the following: society is not only a *cluster of individuals* connected by individual relationships, but it is a system of *objective relationships*. Individuals enter various groups as the carriers of these latter relationships and not as "pure individuals". Society consists not of individuals, but it expresses the total of those aspects and relationships which link the individuals with one another.

The "secret" of the methodological drawbacks of some anthropological group researches is that the individual is regarded as the object of research "by itself" and is deprived of its "social determinateness". The individual is not regarded as the carrier of objective social relationships. However, it is also true that the above-mentioned principle of methodology is not easy to assert in researches, its conceptualization is hindered by many obstacles.

When I say that the *relationships of determination* exert their influence on small groups and individuals starting out from the circumstances and facts that determine the character of society as a totality (ownership relations, distribution of labour, economic mechanism, political structure, etc.), I by no means state that here we face a determination of "pure", total and direct character that can be pointed out in each *individual* case *directly*. It is just this lack of total and direct macro-structural determination that creates a scope for the activity of groups and individuals. Yet, the vast theoretical problem hasn't been solved yet that the ecological and other peculiarities of the social medium, i.e. the social system in a broader sense be introduced into the study and interpretation of the formation of interpersonal relationships. Kurt Lewin's significant considerations related to "psychological ecology" are hardly elaborated by others. Instead, it is formal research into the communication structures that started to flourish which hinders the elaboration of the social determinateness – taken in a broader sense – of anthropology.

The self-movement of social totality independent of consciousness cannot be merely regarded as the *subsequent synthesis* of individual target-settings, because it is at the same time also their precondition. If this were not the case, then all the decisions made by individuals would be made in a void. The scope provided by society in which individuals move and make decisions does not merely consist of the "surroundings" but it is the sum total of the life conditions of the individuals. These conditions are shaped into the individual's essence from childhood: the individual is exposed to external influences, then he enters the process of reproduction and he occupies his place in the technical and economic structure of work activities which have arisen in the course of history. According to this, he gets a certain proportion of the gross social product. The *possibilities* of the satisfaction of given material and intellectual needs which are determined socially and historically depend on the mode and extent of the acquisition of the social product i.e. in the last resort on the relationship to the means of production. These possibilities determine the *values* and *objective interests* of the individuals. The individual becomes interested in the reproduction or change of certain circumstances. The individual is, therefore, the externalized, subjective form of objective impersonal external relationships. The activities which turn the assimilated society into something external are directed by individual consciousness: objective life circumstances can assert their decisive influence only through its medium. Needs and interests exert their influence not directly, but through their personal reflections, i.e. through the practical and theoretical hierarchy that manifests itself in the personal system of interests and norms. In a direct way, therefore, consciousness determines the action based on its subjective standards, i.e. dependent upon the ideology and capacity of cognition shown by the individual.

The study and knowledge of anthropology is important, because the *general* social life conditions and their most important elements, i.e. the relationships of ownership, cannot unequivocally determine factors which are *individual*, and *accidental* compared to them. *Therefore, determination has different levels.* The general life conditions determine the *structure of society*, but that of the historical situation only partly. They determine the *transformation of society* and the *main content of its ideological and economic development*, but they do not determine the concrete form of transformation or daily events. The lower the level of generalization is, the closer it is to the individual, the greater is the number of accidental factors. In this case, however, it is not the level of determinateness that increases, but determinateness prevails on other planes. Therefore, *anthropological necessities* account for accidental phenomena from the point of view of the general outlook of social theory. Thus, the duality of social theory and anthropology as a concept of society and a concept of the individual serves the simultaneous understanding of general and concrete aspects.

3. In our day, systems theory moves of necessity in the direction of the change of paradigms. Several signs of those manifest themselves. Majone speaks of "pitfalls"; Churchman of "enemies"; Tomlinson of "semi-truths". Mitroff uses the term "re-interpretation"; Sadowsky–Blauberg sees "paradoxons" in the theory. Some authors expound the necessity of introducing into systems theory the "dialectic" method as a positive programme. Therefore, the *paradigm is dialectic*.[9] The declarative statement thereof is, however, not sufficient.

In our discussions the SA method was called "behaviour dialectic" by Mitroff and "procedure dialectic" by Majone.[10] The essence is that dialectic has to be conceived of as a concrete methodology. In my opinion, the difficulty is caused by the fact that it is always easier to move from the concrete to the abstract, than the other way round. Therefore, at present, Marxist dialectic is still difficult to operationalize, since the *system of mediations* filling the vacuum between the abstract and the concrete is missing. In the abstract thinking that has detached itself from reality, mediations are often ignored. Therefore, all proposals serving the concrete operationalization of dialectic, contribute to the overcoming of dogmatic rationalism.

Blauberg differentiates between the *philosophical, methodological* and *applied* levels of dialectic[11] and thereby, in my opinion, he has made a useful contribution to the study of the system of mediations. To be sure, dialectic has to be applied also for the present-day objectionalized systems, but the finding of the mediations between individuals and greater groups of individuals is also really important. Though with a limited validity, it was Freud and existentialism which gave the best picture of the individual's psychological frustration. To be sure, Freud's phenomenological description starts out primarily from the psychology of the Vienna petit bourgeoisie. Its validity is relevant for bourgeois consciousness, and not for the human psyche in general. Therefore, all efforts aimed at discovering the more general dialectic structure of behaviour have to be welcomed.

Before starting operationalization, we have to assess on two planes theoretically: what does dialectic mean from the aspect of the *logic of cognition* and what does it mean from the aspect of the *ontological movement of society.* What is more important, the *relationship* of subjective and objective dialectic and logic has to be clarified. Classical German philosophy – in the first place Hegel – really offered a rich heritage of dialectic. However, we must not stop at Hegel, because with him the various objectivations – among them the social ones – are to be deduced from the self-realizing process of the spirit. Therefore, from Hegel's idealistic dialectic we have to move towards dialectic, according to which the dialectic of the social existence elicits the peculiarities of a dialectic nature of the mental sphere.

4. I have devoted a separate section in this chapter to *logical presuppositions.* The insight into scientific cognition becomes so gradually prevalent that the prohibition of contradiction is not equal to the measure of truth; indeed the most important relationship is the contradiction. By this insight, the essence of logic becomes the dialectic. In pre-Kantian logic the contradiction was evaluated as a "mistake", as an unhealthy state of the intellect, as a sophism. I present several examples which indicate that in traditional formal logic, and the scientific methodology based on it, prohibition of contradiction is but one rule of thinking, created by man and set before thinking. The principle of contradiction, however, is an inherent law of the nature of objectively existing thinking. Traditional logic, therefore, must be renewed – which would also mean a change of paradigms – it must be made capable of expressing the contradiction in thinking. Therefore, the principle

according to which if we find a contradiction we have to do our utmost to eliminate it – two statements cannot be true at the same time – has to be discarded from systems theory.

5. Besides the subjective dialectic of cognition, I have suggested the inclusion of the *objective dialectic of society* as presuppositions of systems theory. Naturally, I think here of basic theses, for example how social existence determines the superstructure and what a dialectic relationship exists between the development of the forces of production and the relations of production, etc. Other theses belonging here are: What kind of differing – and in most cases antagonistic – relations of distribution and property come into existence owing to the given order of production?

How is power structure based on material relationships? How do class relations develop and corresponding to that – mainly in the satisfaction of demands – how do interests and their collisions and conflicts take shape? If we do not strive to clarify the objective dialectic of society before drawing up the model, then the introduction in systems theory of aspects of *value-orientation* is in vain.[12] (Classical systems analysis completely neglected this and today's striving for reform tries to include the problem of value in order to scrutinize decision-making.)

In SA the interests of at least three groups of people have to be distinguished; namely the analysers of the system, the decision-makers and the interests of those persons who are directly affected by the consequences of the realization of the systems model. The interests of these three groups of people are generally conflicting, and conflict resolution is possible only by arriving at a compromise among values. Dror has called attention to one of these three groups – the decision-makers – who have to be educated for the reception of SA.[13]

If the scholars of systems theory do not clarify the social process of the emergence of values, then only new failures can be expected. Social transformations cannot be understood from a change in the system of values but this also applies to dynamics and intensity of needs. The empiric sociology of value, conceiving of values as a "subjective factor", cannot and will not comment on those social processes in which values, i.e. these "stable factors of inter-subjective preference", take shape and from which – according to the needs of various social strata – common and contradictory values can be understood and from which these values acquire their power of normative guidance over individuals. If we omit from the scrutiny of values history social needs and interests, i.e. all kinds of determination from the aspect of content, then the system of values – in accordance with the teachings of neopositivism – is totally ungrounded.

Also changes in value can become totally accidental and therefore not to be grasped. In saying this I wish to point out that it is not sufficient by itself to refer to dialectic. It has to be decided whether it is a case of materialist or idealist dialectic. Therefore, in itself the inclusion of goals, values, norms, behaviours and other human-subjective values into systems theoretical analysis is not sufficient. It is important to decide whether they are ultimately decisive factors or determined by the material life conditions of society. To regard the problem from the side of logic, it is decisive how we conceive of the relationship between subjective and objective dialectic. If we consider these as complementing one another or if we regard the latter as a function of the former we bring into systems theory erroneous presuppositions.

6. Finally, I should like to summarize my thoughts on *epistemological* presuppositions. On the one hand, we witness the crisis of both traditional rationalism and traditional empiricism. This manifests itself in various terms used by the authors in this book (paradoxes, pitfalls, etc.). In my view, a *new kind of rationalism* may be necessary in the light of which it would become clear that in most cases it is only from the aspect of traditional rational cognition that things seem to be irrational, or have become a pitfall. Therefore, this calls for a methodical change in paradigms. On the other hand, it has to be recognized that objective social reality can pave the way to irrational behaviour and social paradoxes, etc. These objective irrationalities stem from existing totality, and the basic contradictions of the socio-economic structure of societies split by conflicting interests. This contradiction is also reflected in the relations of countries and groups of countries. Therefore, the scholars of systems analysis have to discard their idyllic views of society if they want to draw up models that work in reality, too.

The question is whether social reality is willing to obey our desires or not. We therefore return to my important point, that the scholars of systems analysis – if they want to be successful – have to free themselves of their erroneous ideological presuppositions be they covert or overt.

Therefore, in my view, the new – dialectic – paradigm of systems analysis is already in the making, but because of socially conditioned ideological barriers it is to be expected that many obstacles will arise to its acceptance and application.

As for me, I am optimistic, and hope that the renewal of SA on a dialectic basis will contribute to the alleviation and solution of the basic problems of individuals, nations and the whole of mankind. To be sure, Churchman's scepticism is not totally without foundation.[14] All of us are aware of the truth put in poetic form by Sophocles in his *Antigone*: "If someone knows something which is wonderful and wise he can make use of it for good and evil purposes." If, however, the need so often voiced to develop SA as a "community" enterprise is fulfilled, then it may, in all probability, become the means through which scholars of SA will aim for the good, and not the evil.

REFERENCES

1. Kuhn, T. S. *The Structure of Scientific Revolutions.* Second edition, Enlarged, **II**, No. 2. University of Chicago Press, 1970.
2. See Checkland, P. B. In-Process response at Seminar "Rethinking the Process of Systems Analysis". M. S. Laxenburg, Aug. 1980.
3. See Churchman, C. W. The Design of Inquiring Systems. Basic Books, New York, 1971. Mitroff, I. I. and Kilmann, R. H. On Integrating Behavioral and Philosophical Systems: Towards a Unified Theory of Problem Solving. Annual Series in the Sociology, Vol. 1 (to appear).
   These authors proposed a special problem solving technique known as the Dialectic. Essentially the Dialectic is an adversarial problem *forming* methodology which is especially suited to treating intensely ill-structured, i.e., difficult-to-define issues.
   In: Mitroff, I. I. – Emshoff, J. R. – Kilmann, R. H.: Assumptional Analysis: A Methodology for Strategic Problems Solving. *Management Science*, **25**, No. 6. June, 1979. 583 pp.
4. Susman, G. I. and Evered, R. D. "An assessment of the scientific merits of action research". *Administrative Science Quarterly*, **23**, Dec., 1978.
5. See Pitfalls of Analysis. Ed. by Giandomenico Majone and Edward S. Quade. IIASA, 1980. John Wiley and Sons, Chichester–New York–Brisbane–Toronto.
6. See Checkland, P. B. Systems methodology in problem-solving: some notes from experience. In: Progress in Cybernetics and Systems Research. Vol. V. Hemisphere Publications, 1979.
7. He writes: By Thursday teatime much of what is being said can be seen as proposing a paradigm of systems analysis as *process not product*. The vision is of a phenomenological rather than a positivist SA. See Checkland, P. B.: reference No. 2. See above.
8. This point was raised by them during the discussion. Besides see Churchman, C. W.: Chapter V. Dialectic. In: The Systems Approach and Its Enemies. Basic Books, Inc., New York, 1979. pp. 108–116.
9. See Majone, G. and Quade, E. S. (eds.): Pitfalls of Analysis. International Series on Applied Systems Analysis. John Wiley and Sons. 1980; Churchman, C. W.: The Systems Approach and its Enemies. Basic Books, New York. 1979.; Tomlinson, R.: Doing Something about the Future. J. Opl. Res. Soc. Vol. 31. pp. 467–476. 1980.; Blauberg, I. V., Sadowsky, V. V. and Yudin, E. G.: Systems Theory – Philosophical and Methodological Problems. Progress Publ., Moscow, 1977, etc. The signs indicating a change in paradigms are perhaps summarized in the most systematic way by Kindler and Kiss in Future Methodology Based on Past Assumptions?
10. Additionally these authors have discussed these terms in their writings. See Mitroff, I. I. and Emshoff, J.: On Strategic Assumption-Making: A Dialectical Approach to Policy and Planning. Academy of Management Review, Vol. 4. (1979.) pp. 1–12. Resp. reference to No. 2, see above. Majone means by the term "procedure dialectic" the term "action programmes". He writes: In such a case following Hylton Boothroyd, we speak of *action programmes*, the policy equivalent of Lakatos' scientific research programmes. In: Majone, G.: Policies as Theories, IIASA, RR-80-17. April 1980. p. 157.
    Resp. Boothroyd, H.: On the Theory of Operational Research. Report No. 51. Centre for Industrial Economic and Business Research. University of Warwick, Coventry, UK. 1974.
11. Besides Blauberg, I., Mirsky, E. and Sadovsky, V. Systems Approach to Systems Analysis. See in this issue.
12. The participants of the Laxenburg seminar unanimously agreed on the great role of the values played in SA. It was especially Ratoosh, Levien, Mitroff, Moscarola and Miser who emphasized the importance of an approach based on values. Boothroyd analysed the interrelationship between the system of values of the individual and the social environment. Tomlinson, too, called the study and description of the values represented by the individuals participating in SA an interactive process. Churchman's idea, according to which the model is a representation of reality, could be complemented by my view according to which reality, too, contains values.
13. See Dror, Y.: Applied Systems Analysis of Grand-Policy Issues. Outline of a Pointillistic Presentation at IIASA Task Force Meeting on Rethinking the Process of Systems Analysis. 25–29 Aug. 1980. MS.

14. He quoted a part from Shakespeare's The Tragedy of King Richard the Second ending with these words: Cover your heads, and mock not flesh and blood /With solemn reverence: throw away respect/, Tradition, form, and ceremonious duty, (For you have but mistook me all this while: I live with bread like you, feel want,/ Taste grief, need friends: subjected thus,/ How can you say to me I am a king?) Shakespeare. Complete Works. Oxford University Press, London, p. 396.

8

Current Methodological Problems of Systems Analysis and Its Application

O. I. LARICHEV (USSR)

1. HISTORICAL BACKGROUND OF SYSTEMS ANALYSIS

Part of the basic thesis of the workshop sponsors is that the smooth stage of systems analysis development is over and there are signs of current difficulties in its application to practical problems.

To better understand the current state-of-the-art of systems analysis methodology one has to trace the history of its origins and development.

Undoubtedly, systems analysis originated as a means of handling certain military and engineering problems as described in the well-known book *Analysis for Military Decision* by E. S. Quade.[1] The majority of these problems resembled those in operational research. The objective description of the core of the problems was considered quite possible. The methodological features of the operational research approach may be easily traced using the example of the well-known "cost-efficiency" method, considered by many as an integral part of systems analysis. Originally cost-efficiency models were developed just like models in operational research (transportation problems, assignment problems and the like). It was supposed that a researcher was able to define objectively the existing features of a problem and to reflect them in the model, and that the studied phenomena lacked "behavioural freedom". The difference in the approach to synthesizing the cost and efficiency estimates boiled down to the consideration of the decision-maker's opinion. Complex as they may be, the problems first subjected to systems analysis were, in our opinion, at the interface of well- and ill-structured ones. These problems, however, required an independent methodology of systems analysis comprising the known stages of the systems approach, i.e. to define goals; find alternative ways of achieving them; develop a model integrating the goals, means and parameters of the system; find the rules to select the best alternative[2] as well as a cost-effective method for comparing alternative methods of accomplishing the

135

goals. It is worth pointing out that Quade distinguished quantitative differences rather than qualitative ones between operational research and systems analysis.

2. New applications

Great difficulties were encountered in extending the methodology to ill-structured problems wherein the qualitative, poorly-defined, aspects tend to dominate. In our opinion, the major features of these systems are as follows:

The impossibility of constructing objective models of the investigated system.

In fact, the majority of ill-structured problems lack an objective, scientifically based model integrating the system parameters in a unified whole. Consider, for example, the problem of R & D project estimation. Here we find that the quality of the project depends on such factors as the scientific skill of researchers, the value of the end result of the completed scientific tasks, cost of the project etc. However, one cannot say there is only one correct mathematical relationship between these factors which defines the general utility of the project. There can be many relationships, as well as factors, and the choice is made by the decision-maker according to his experience, intuition and world outlook. Another decision-maker may prefer some other model. It is noteworthy that the factors included in the model are very difficult to measure quantitatively.

Thus, we are now in the world of subjective models. The lack of objective, scientifically valid, relationships make us regard the system's parameters as criteria for evaluation of alternative solutions. The problems acquire a multi-attribute nature.

H. Rittel and M. M. Webber in their interesting paper[3] write about "wicked" problems with many possible approaches to their definition, where the goals are influenced by the method of approval adopted. There is a great variety of such problems, e.g. development of tourism in a country or region, allocation of resources for basic research, selection of manuscripts for publishing in a publishing house. One could say that all strategic problems have features of wicked ill-structured problems. It is quite understandable that the original methodology of systems analysis was not fully able to cope with the peculiarities of such ill-structured problems; giving rise to many new problems which are exemplified in the application of the PPB system to civil problems. I. R. Hoos in the excellent book "Systems Analysis in Public Policy; a critique"[4] writes about unsuccessful attempts to use quantitative indicators and to construct "cost-effective" models.

Systems analysis in its primary form implied from the beginning that there would be a sequential analysis of the problem, from the goals to the means. Experience shows that this systems approach is not a universal solution to all problems. As a constructive tool for comparing alternatives, systems analysis implies using the "cost-efficiency" method. Now it is clear that the construction of "cost efficiency" models for many problems is characterized by a great degree of subjectiveness and can be done in various ways.

It is also clear that the methods used in comparing alternatives greatly influences the entire systems analysis methodology with respect to its applicability.

3. Modern key methodological problems: practical view

Systems analysis in the 1970s differs undoubtedly from that in the 1960s; the problem analysis is more flexible, improved multicriteria methods are applied to compare the alternatives.

In modern systems analysis one can distinguish three directions. The first one is not connected directly with decision making. It is directed at the investigation of the entire problem or its parts in order to establish a basis for decision-making.

Although such projects are mostly undertaken on the instructions of the decision-maker, his policy preferences are hardly, if at all, taken into account in the course of investigation. Such applications of systems analysis can be called system studies. System studies of ill-structured problems may include detailed verbal descriptions of all the system attributes identified, of all possible decision estimation criteria, of forecasts with respect to the system and to changes in the environment, and so on. Some problems may be approached with mathematical models.

The second direction of systems analysis relates to decision-making situations, where no decision-maker or a group of decision-makers can be identified; for example, where it is necessary to solve a social problem, touching upon the interests of a large group of people, but where there is no organization responsible for handling this problem. Thus, there is a decision-making problem but no decision-maker whose preferences could serve as a basis for a decision rule.

The third direction concerns the estimation of the decision alternatives and the selection of the best alternative.

Since the decision in ill-structured problems should be developed on the basis of the decision-makers preferences, research is carried out not only on the decision-makers instructions but also with his direct participation. In such cases systems analysis can be viewed as a synthesis of the systems approach, methods of multi-criteria alternative estimation and decision-maker's experience, preferences, intuition. In applying systems analysis in its present state to practical problems one encounters, in our opinion, the following major main methodological problems:

1. The difficulty of measuring the qualitative concepts characteristic of ill-structured systems.

Today, the qualitative concepts are mostly brought in line with numerical, quantitative scales. A lot of methods used for measuring the decision-maker and expert preferences employ lotteries, number scales etc. Such measurements can often distort the actual human preferences. At present there are no techniques for quantitative measurement of many subjective criteria of decision estimation such as, for example, scientific quality, organizational prestige, and so on. It is well-known, however, that ordinal scales had been used for many physical variables (heat, length) until quantitative scales were developed. Nevertheless, at present we lack any reliable method for quantitative measurement of variables in ill-structured problems. Consequently, ordinal scales with verbal labels of quality degrees must be used. These scales make it possible to get equivalent descriptions of ill-structured problems in natural language.[5]

Great skill must be used in employing natural language in this way so as to preserve pithy and qualitative descriptions at every stage of decision-making.

2. Development of decision rules in ill-structured problems.

Since the alternative estimation models have to account for the decision-maker's preferences, one must be able to identify these preferences and utilize them in decision rule construction. In this case the main problems are connected with the psychology of decision-making.

Recent investigations[6] show, that a number of limitations inherent in the human cognitive apparatus sharply reduce its possibility to cope with information and the reliability of this information. For example, we know, that due to the limited capacity of short-term memory people have to resort to a number of heuristic methods for the analysis of multidimensional information.

The major techniques are:

(i)   dropping of a number of criteria;
(ii) neglect of small differences in the estimations by one criterion;
(iii) successive consideration of the criteria.

These devices are very important for the human being since they help him to cope with complex problems. On the other hand, however, the same methods lead to contradictions and errors.[7]

One of the major current problems of systems analysis methodology is how to enhance and extend human capacity so as to process multidimensional information in a reliable and non-controversial manner.

We are trying in our investigations to develop special decision making techniques[5] which would take into account the data processing capabilities of a man and extend them.

3. The problem of applying the systems approach to the analysis of ill-structured systems.

The application of the systems approach to real life complex situations of decision-making is only possible by an interactive approval, examining many ways of moving from changing goals to changing means in order to find a single (or several) "solvable" representation of the problem for a decision-maker.

4. Current trends in systems analysis

The current state-of-the-art of systems analysis makes a complex picture. Problems continue to be studied (and sometimes successfully) with objective cost-effectiveness models, similar to the approaches used in the earliest applications of systems analysis. As the boundaries between various types of problems are fuzzy, there are continuing attempts to build objective models for problems where inadequate, objective information must be supplemented through subjective judgement. Very often, due to the lack of any data source, the consulting analyst "patches the holes" on the basis of his own knowledge of relationships between the system parameters. In complex models this "patching" affects the final results in an unpredictable manner. The developed models to a great extent reflect the belief of their creators that the world is arranged in that way, and not some other way.

Sometimes the qualitative dependences between model parameters are quite explicit but it is difficult (or impossible) to determine the exact strength of these dependences. By filling the gap the consultant also strongly affects the result.

The resulting pseudo-objective models are unacceptable for decision-makers as they are not based on the executives' experience, intuition, preferences. As a result the model builders often do not exert any influence on decision-making.

Though the well-known and popular definitions of systems analysis emphasize its direct orientation towards decision-making, the same term (systems analysis) has often been associated in recent years with the development of mathematical models with a view toward creating "banks" of models with potential use in decision-making. A realization of the fact that the application of systems analysis represents a combination of "art" and scientific analysis, was used actually as an excuse for the "separation" of the analytical aid from the "art" and its further study. This approach has resulted in the emergence of a great number of mathematical models; but there is little evidence relating to their practical application. We believe that practical problems possess characteristic features which can be reflected only by a model built specially for the problem. Many models (e.g. so-called global models) contain a lot of assumptions and premises of their creators, intermixed with certain objective dependences. Hence, application of such models in decision-making is simply dangerous.

The experience gained from unsuccessful applications of systems analysis to problems with a subjective structure brought about two directions of research. The first one "policy analysis" is concerned with solution of public policy problems. The research conducted along these lines place a strong emphasis on the art of problem analysis, problems of organizational mechanism of decision implementation, etc. As an example of interesting research conducted in this field, we shall mention the article by H. Rittel and M. M. Webber.[3]

The second direction is connected with systematization of the experience of applying systems analysis, identifying standard mistakes and miscalculations. It is worth mentioning E. S. Quade and G. Majone's book *Pitfalls of Analysis*[8] recently published by the International Institute for Applied Systems Analysis. The book attempts to systematize the unsuccessful approaches to problem analysis, model formulation, consultant-decision-maker interrelationships, etc.

For all this, extremely little attention has been paid to improving the methods and procedures for the analytical comparison of alternative decisions. As usual, one encounters in the literature, descriptions of cases of applying the "cost-effectiveness" techniques to such problems as storage of radioactive waste, construction of atomic power stations, though these problems undoubtedly involve various subjective and objective factors. An impression is gained that the authors of these papers have overlooked popular critical articles and books.[4, 9] Actually, major research in the methods of comparing complex decision alternatives are conducted at present by specialist decision analysts and not by systems analysts.

5. On the crises in systems analysis

One symptom of a crisis in systems analysis is doubt as to its capability to solve complex practical problems. This doubt follows from several causes. One cause arises from unsuccessful attempts to evaluate decision alternatives using pseudo-objective models. Another cause follows from attempts to use the systems approach as a universal and constructive method for solving ill-structured problems. In addition the abundance of useless mathematical models (developed in the name of systems analysis) does not at all increase the attraction of systems analysis.

All these causes are linked to a considerable extent with the aspiration (sometimes subconscious) to convert systems analysis to an "exact science" like operations research. The main potential value of systems analysis arises

---

*"Operations Research" is used here in the narrow sense of mathematical model building. (Ed.)

just from the differences which distinguish systems analysis from operations research.*

From our point of view the most valuable thing that system analysis has introduced into the methodology of complex problem solving consists in the understanding of the fact that subjective judgement must be accompanied by deep analysis. The methods of this analysis can, and must, change and improve. We have defined above the three major directions of improvement of these methods.

It must always be remembered that the application of systems analysis is a combination of art and science, where art prevails. The logical analysis of a problem is an art; the search of the ways to construct alternative estimation rules is an art. As this art improves new techniques and methods emerge that can be scientifically proved and their application area mapped. The methodology of systems analysis should not be regarded as something rigid but as a tool for the analysis of complex problems changing both under the influence of the researcher-analysts. Let us hope that these changes will take us to new and perfect methods.

REFERENCES

1. Quade, E. S. (Ed.) Analysis for military decisions. Rand McNally, Chicago, 1967.
2. Optner, S. L. System analysis for business and industrial problem solving. Prentice-Hall, Inc., Englewood Cliffs, New Jersey, 1965.
3. Rittel, H. and Webber, M. M. Dilemmas in a general theory of planning. *Policy Sciences*, **4**, 1972.
4. Hoos, I. R. Systems analysis in public policy: a critique. Univ. of California Press, 1972.
5. Larichev, O. I. Science and Art of Decision Making (in Russian). Nauka, Moscow, 1979.
6. Slovic, P., Fischhoff, B. and Lichtenstein, S. Behavioral decision theory. *Ann. Psychol. Review*, **28**, 1977.
7. Tversky, A. Intransitivity of preferences. *Psychological Review*, **76**, No. 1, 1969.
8. Majone, G. and Quade, E. S. (Eds) Pitfalls of Analysis. J. Wiley and Sons, New York, 1980.
9. Hoos, I. Can Systems Analysis Solve Social Problems. *Datamation*, June, 1974, pp. 82–92.

9

The Craft of Applied Systems Analysis

GIANDOMENICO MAJONE

1. HOW SCIENTIFIC IS APPLIED SYSTEMS ANALYSIS?

Like the legendary phoenix, the question: How scientific is systems analysis? (or operational research, or management science) keeps rising alive from the ashes of past methodological debates and official definitions. For instance, more than 20 years ago, the Operational Research Society of Britain adopted a definition of OR in which the word "science" or "scientific" occurred three times. Operational research was proclaimed to be the application of the methods of science to complex problems, a discipline whose distinctive approach is the development of a scientific model of the system being analysed, and whose purpose is to help management determine its policy and actions scientifically.

Similarly, Quade[1] observes that "It is easy to find statements in the literature of operations research which imply that analysis to aid any decision-maker is really nothing more than the 'scientific method' extended to problems outside the realm of pure science," where "scientific method" is interpreted to mean that analysis advances through the successive steps of formulation, search, explanation, interpretation and, hopefully, verification. And according to Olaf Helmer, "in comparing operations research with an exact science, it is with regard to exactness that operations research falls short, but not necessarily with regard to the scientific character for its methods".[2]

Can anything of value be learned from these methodological discussions, anything, that is, that is useful to applied systems analysis (ASA) as it is practised today? In this section I shall try to show that questions about the "scientific character" of ASA are, today, rather irrelevant, when not positively misleading, if taken literally; but, also, that they can be reformulated in a way that makes them highly meaningful for the practising analyst.

One problem with the older methodological discussions about the scientific nature of ASA is that, when the meaning of "scientific method" has not remained implicit (and hence open to a variety of different and often

143

contrasting interpretations), it has been construed in terms which contemporary epistemology finds unacceptable, or at least in need of substantial
revisions. Few scientists and philosophers of science still believe that scientific
knowledge is, or can be, proven knowledge. If there is one point on which all
major schools of thought agree today, it is that scientific knowledge is always
tentative and open to refutation. And while the older history of science was
little more than a chronicle of the irresistible advance of the different sciences,
the contemporary historian tries to understand "how such sciences can
succeed in fulfilling their actual explanatory missions, despite the fact that, at
any chosen moment in time, their intellectual contents are marked by logical
gaps, incoherences, and contradictions".[3]

However, the conceptual revolution that has taken place in the philosophy
and history of science in the last three decades – a revolution commonly
associated with the names of Popper, Kuhn, and Lakatos – is having its
impact on systems analysis and closely-related disciplines, as shown by some
recent contributions to the literature.[4] But even these methodologically more
sophisticated and updated discussions often fail to explain what lies behind
the persistent preoccupation with the scientific status of ASA.

It is, of course, no secret that the claim to scientific status has in the past
served an important ideological function by increasing the collective confidence of a group of new disciplines striving for academic and social
recognition. But today science (or, rather, folk-science) has lost much of its
ideological appeal, and it would be difficult to explain the scientific aspirations
of the ASA profession on such grounds. Also, fallibilism – the currently
accepted doctrine that scientific arguments are never conclusive and always
perfectible – seems to be a poor principle from which to derive mechanical
rules of method. Finally, traditional claims to scientific status for ASA have
always been faced by what appears to be an insoluble contradiction: if ASA is
scientific, its task is not to prescribe or suggest a course of action, but to
provide scientific explanations and predictions; if, on the other hand, ASA
aspires to guide action, it must be prescriptive (and, I shall argue, persuasive as
well), and hence cannot be scientific – not, at any rate, according to the
received view of scientific method. Some writers have attempted to solve the
dilemma by arguing that ASA offers "scientifically based" advice. But such an
argument is logically unsound and runs immediately against the Humean
impossibility of deriving "ought" from "is".

So the question about the scientific status of ASA does indeed seem to lead
nowhere, except into a thicket of conceptual obscurities and logical dilemmas.
But then, why do methodologically conscious analysts keep raising it? The
reason, I suggest, is that behind this question loom two issues which people
rightly feel to be of crucial importance, even if they are unable to clearly
articulate them. First: what is the language of ASA, i.e. what is the logical
status of the different propositions which an analyst produces in the course of

his work? Second: which standards of quality and rules of methodological criticism are applicable to the different kinds of propositions?

2, THE SEARCH FOR STANDARDS OF QUALITY

Even if we interpret "science" in the broadest possible sense of an organized body of knowledge (the sense suggested, for example, by the German term "Wissenschaft"), the existence of generally recognized rules of evaluation and criticism is a necessary precondition for any reasonable claim to scientific status. Only in immature fields of inquiry, as Ravetz has pointed out, criteria of quality or adequacy cannot be taken for granted.

The dilemmas facing the leaders of an immature field of inquiry have been shrewdly analysed by Ravetz:

> The present social institutions of science, and of learning in general, impose such constraints that the growth and even the survival of an immature field would be endangered by the simple honesty of public announcement of its condition. For these institutions were developed around mature or rapidly maturing fields in the nineteenth century. If the representatives of a discipline announce that they do not fit in with such a system, they can be simply excluded from it, to the benefit of their competitors for the perennially limited resources. The field would be relegated to amateur status, and thereby pushed over to the very margin of the world of learning; it would be deprived of funds and prestige.[5]

He continues:

> An immature field, in chaos internally, experiences the additional strains of hypertrophy; its leaders and practitioners are exposed to the temptations of being accepted as consultants and experts for the rapid solution of urgent practical problems. The field can soon become identical in outward appearance to an established physical technology, but in reality be a gigantic confidence-game . . . To thread one's way through these pitfalls, making a genuine contribution both to scientific knowledge and to the welfare of society, requires a combination of knowledge and understanding in so many different areas of experience, that its only correct title is wisdom.[6]

What, then, does the "wisdom" of ASA include (assuming, as I think we must, that it is a still-maturing field)? ASA is concerned with theorizing (at different levels of generality), choosing, and acting. Hence its three-fold character: descriptive (scientific), prescriptive (advisory), and persuasive (argumentative-interactive). In fact, if we look at the fine structure of an analytic argument we usually discover a complex blend of factual statements, methodological choices, evaluations, recommendations, and persuasive definitions and communication acts. An even more complex structure would became apparent if we were to include (as we should, in a complete treatment) the interactions taking place between analysts and their audience of clients, sponsors, policy-makers, and interested publics. Moreover, descriptive propositions, prescriptions, and persuasion are intertwined in a way that rules out the possibility of applying a unique set of evaluative criteria, let alone conclusively proving or refuting an argument. Whatever testing can be done must rely on a variety of disciplinary standards, corresponding to the different techniques and methods used in the study, on the plausibility and robustness of the results, on the quality criteria of the clients, and even on such hard-to-formalize qualities as style and persuasiveness. For this reason, the historical pattern of development of ASA can be seen as "the slow business of getting to grips with the problems of devising patterns of criticism, of constructing critical methodologies, for those areas not readily dealt with by the methods built up over so long a period in the natural sciences".[7]

But why has the analytic profession been so slow in recognizing the importance and the necessary complexity of a relevant body of criteria and mechanisms of quality control? The reasons are, to a large extent, historical. The pioneers of systems analysis and operational research were natural scientists, many of them of outstanding ability, with a long experience in the actual conduct of empirical research. Their most important contributions to the new fields of inquiry were not advanced theoretical insights or sophisticated research tools, but active minds, and a set of superb craft skills in recording, analysing, and evaluating data, in establishing quantitative relationships, and in setting up testable hypotheses. Their main goal, as they saw it, was "to find a scientific explanation of the facts". For, as C. H. Waddington writes, "[o]nly when this is done can the two main objects of operational research be attained. These are the prediction of the effects of new weapons and of new tactics."[8]

Given this paradigm, the relevant standards of criticism were, of course, those of natural science. Indeed, the situations investigated by operational researchers during World War 2 were particularly well-suited for this approach. Typically, military operations could be regarded, without distortion, as representative of a class of repetitive situations "where theories built up in response to earlier examples of the situation could be checked out against later examples, monitored while proposals for improved action were in use, and used to detect their own dwindling validity as the situations changed".[9] In the years immediately following the War, industrial applications of OR, exemplified by L. C. Edie's classic study "Traffic delays at toll booths",[10] still followed the standard pattern, and explicitly appealed to the established criteria of evaluation and criticism.

But soon the situation began to change. While people like Blackett and Waddington were returning to their laboratories and research institutes, a new generation of analysts was entering the scene – people primarily interested in the more formal aspects of scientific research, and often lacking the craft skills and the maturity of critical judgement of the old masters. At the same time, the problems claiming the attention of the analysts were becoming increasingly abstract and complex. Direct empirical verification of the conclusion was often impossible (as in the case of the strategic studies done at Rand), and the very notion of solution, except in the simplest situations, tended to become a matter of methodological agreement. In sum, as allegiance to the traditional standards of criticism were weakened by changes in the disciplinary background of the profession, the standards themselves were becoming increasingly irrelevant to current professional practice.

3. SYSTEMS ANALYSIS AND PROBLEM SOLVING

And yet, the pioneers of OR were correct in asserting the existence of a strong similarity between operational and scientific research. Their mistake, from our present viewpoint, consisted in thinking that the similarity was to be found in the *outcome* ("scientific explanation of the facts", "prediction of the effects of new weapons and of new tactics"), rather than in the *process*, that is to say, in the basic craft aspects common to all types of disciplined intellectual inquiry. Shifting our perspective from outcome to process, the following points become almost obvious:[11]

1. Like scientific research, ASA is essentially a craft activity, or, as some authors prefer to put it, an "art";[11a]
2. However, the objects to which analytic work is applied are not physical things and phenomena, as in the case of traditional arts and crafts, but intellectual constructs studied through the investigation of policy problems;
3. The work of the systems analyst (and of the scientist as well) is guided and controlled by criteria which are mainly informal and tacit, rather than public and explicit. It is the task of a methodology of ASA to make these criteria as explicit as possible, as a precondition for a critical discussion of their validity;
4. The standards and criteria of quality used in evaluating analytic work must reflect the threefold nature of ASA: descriptive, prescriptive, and argumentative. These standards are partly technical (reflecting the best practice in the field), and partly social (since their effectiveness depends on the existence of professional organizations and other institutional arrangements).

In the discussion of these theses, the notion of "problem" plays a central role. In fact, ASA can be described as problem solving on intellectually constructed objects; and the different stages of analytic work roughly correspond to the phases of problem solving, from formulation to proposed solution. Thus, the craft character of the work is seen most clearly in the early stages, where the analyst interacts with the external world (collection of data, assessment of their reliability and transformation into information, modelling of the system under investigation, etc.); the social character is exhibited in the methodological choices and judgments which guide and control the analyst's work; the abstractness of the objects of inquiry is most obvious when we consider what is involved in "solving" a policy problem; while the influence of social processes is evident in the transformation of analytical recommendations into actual decisions and institutional changes. Perhaps the first thing to be noted in our characterization of ASA as problem solving is the difficulty of finding explicit criteria by which scientific problems may be distinguished from policy problems. Consider, for instance, the characterization of scientific problems that has been proposed by Ravetz:[12] a major part of the work is the formulation of the question itself; the question changes as the work progresses; there is no simple rule for distinguishing a "correct" answer for "incorrect" ones; and there is no guarantee that the question, as originally set or later developed, can be answered at all. Only a moment's reflection is needed to see that policy problems exhibit the same characteristics; and if supporting evidence is wanted, this can be easily found in the literature of systems analysis. Thus, according to Quade, "the 'typical' systems analysis problem is often first: What is the problem?"; "The problem itself does not remain stationary. Interplay between a growing understanding of the problem and of possible developments will refine the problem itself"; "There is frequently no way to verify the conclusions of the study."[13] Again: "The problems an analyst can be asked to tackle in the public sector are particularly frustrating. Usually they are urgent and ill-defined. Often they are complicated, and sometimes *they change radically during the investigation.*"[14]

Or see what Eilon has to say about solving decision problems under uncertainty (which is, of course, the natural condition in any policy problem): "In all decisions under uncertainty ... actual results often deviate substantially from predicted 'expected' results (based on subjective probabilities). To say that the decision is still valid because one should compare the expected results not with the actual results but with their mean value (had the 'one-off' reality been repeated many times) is of little help, since the statement is not testable."[15]

That policy problems may have no solution under the economic, political, and institutional constraints existing at a given moment in a given country should be obvious to anyone familiar with its administrative and legislative history. Indeed, it can be argued that the proper role of the analyst consists in establishing the conditions of feasibility of a proposed course of action, rather than in accumulating evidence in favour of a pet solution. As I have written elsewhere, "Too often we take it for granted that any social problem can be solved, if only sufficient resources are available. But the manageability of a social task cannot be rationally discussed until we have specified the acceptable means of collective action, as well as the limitations imposed by the availability of resources, knowledge, and organizational skills."[16]

Thus, Ravetz's criteria do not allow one to separate policy problems sharply from scientific problems. The similarity is further emphasized by the shared abstract quality of the objects of both scientific and analytic inquiry. In this respect, systems analysis is actually more "theoretical" than many natural sciences. For, if it is true that even basic concepts, like "substance" in chemistry, or "force", "particle", and "field" in physics, are purely intellectual constructs, the more descriptive natural sciences operate largely with concepts whose concrete correspondents are fairly obvious.[17] On the other hand, because of the abstract character of social and economic relations, all concepts appearing in the formulation or solution of a policy problem are necessarily the product of convention and definition. This is obvious in the case of terms like "price", "cost", "GNP", "efficiency", "need", "urbanization", "pollution", but is equally true for concepts like "poverty", "health", "unemployment", "crime", which acquire operational meaning only when expressed in terms of legal or administrative definitions. Indeed, as Alan Coddington has observed "economic statistics are extremely abstract things", the product of "arbitrariness" and "convention".[18]

The same holds true, *a fortiori*, of the social data (but even of most technical data) which represent such a large part of the numerical input of analytic studies.

Although I have spoken, so far, only of problems, creative analysis usually begins with something less than a problem; we may call it a "problem situation". This is an awareness that things are not as they should be, but there is no clear conception, as yet, of how they might be put right. An important part of the problem situation is the historical background and the "issue context" in which the policy debate takes place. It is obviously important for the analyst "to know as much as possible about the background of the problem – where it came from, why it is important, and what decision it is going to assist".[19]

But notice that, although the problem situation is in a less specified state than the problem to which it may give rise, it is already a very artificial thing. The very existence of a problem situation presupposes a matrix of technical materials: existing information, tools, and a body of methods including criteria of adequacy and value.

4. APPLIED SYSTEMS ANALYSIS AS CRAFT WORK

Although craft aspects are evident in every phase of the analyst's work, I shall discuss them here with reference to the categories of data, information, tools, and pitfalls.

Data. Data are the results of the first working up of the materials relevant to the investigation of a problem. In ASA data are often "found" rather than "manufactured", i.e. they are produced by observation rather than by experiment. This requires craft skills that are rather different, and in many respects more difficult to acquire, than those needed for the analysis of experimental data. For instance, the sampling process through which the data are obtained is very much influenced by the methods used, the skill of the samplers, and a host of other factors which may lead to results quite unrepresentative of the general situation. Also, data are collected according to categorical descriptions which never fit perfectly the objects of the inquiry at hand.

Data pertaining to preference and probability assessments are notorious for their subjectivity and unreliability.

Even when data can be obtained from experimentation, as in the case of some recent large-scale social experiments, there is no guarantee that the best experimental design offers sufficient protection against dangers and pitfalls, of which the "Hawthorne effect" is only one of the best-known examples.

Since perfection of data is impossible, the standards of acceptance will have to be based on a common judgment of what is good enough for the functions which the data perform in the problem treated by the analyst. This judgment depends in turn on the criteria of adequacy generally accepted for the solution of such problems. Thus, the simple judgment of soundness of data is a microcosmos of the personal judgments and accumulated social experience which go into analytic work.[20]

Information. At least in quantitative terms, an excess, rather than a scarcity, of data is the usual situation in ASA. Hence the need to reduce the mass of data, to refine them into a more useful and more reliable form. Data transformation involves a new set of craft skills, with the application of new tools (often of a statistical or mathematical nature), and the making of a new set of judgments. This new phase of the analyst's work, the production of information, can be illustrated by a number of examples: the calculation of averages and other statistical parameters, the fitting of a curve to a set of points, the reduction of data through some multivariate statistical technique. The operations performed on the original data may be involved or quite simple, but they always represent a crucial step. Through these operations, the raw data have been transformed into a new sort of material, and from this point on the analysis is carried out only in terms of these new entities.

This transformation of data into information involves three basic judgments, which all present the risk of serious pitfalls. The first is that the advantages achieved through data reduction compensate for the probable loss of information; generally speaking, the existence of "sufficient statistics", i.e. of summaries of the data which contain exactly the same amount of information as the original sample, is the exception rather than the rule. The second is a judgment of the goodness of fit of the model to the original data. The third is that this particular model, among the infinitely many possible ones, is the significant one for the problem under examination. All the operations and judgments involved in data reduction, transformation, and testing are, of course, craft operations.

Tools. Analytic tools may be roughly classified in terms of data production, manipulation, and interpretation.

The category of interpretive tools, which is of special importance here, includes "tool disciplines", i.e. other fields of natural or social science which must be mastered to some extent in order that competent analytic work may be done.

Each set of tools has its characteristic pitfalls, and, if major blunders are to be avoided, the user must develop a craftsman's knowledge of their properties. For instance, the dangers inherent in the use (and abuse) of statistical tools have been often pointed out, although serious fallacies can still be detected even in standard applications.

These dangers are made particularly acute by the prevailing metaphysics, according to which a field becomes more genuinely "scientific" as it more closely resembles theoretical physics in its mathematical formalization. Thus, in an attempt to give a more scientific appearance to his conclusions, the analyst is often induced to use formal tools that exceed the limits of his mathematical or statistical sophistication, and whose range of meaningful applicability he is therefore unable to assess. The consequences have been well-illustrated by the mathematician Jacob Schwartz:

> Mathematics must deal with well-defined situations. Thus, in its relations with science mathematics depends on an intellectual effort outside of mathematics for the crucial specification of the approximation which mathematics is to take literally. Give a mathematician a situation which is the least bit ill-defined – he will first of all make it well-defined. Perhaps appropriately, but perhaps also inappropriately. . . . The mathematician turns the scientist's theoretical assumptions, i.e. convenient points of analytical emphasis, into axioms, and then takes axioms literally. This brings with it the danger that he may also persuade the scientist to take these axioms literally. The question, central to the scientific investigation but intensely disturbing in the mathematical context – what happens to all this if the axioms are relaxed? – is thereby put into shadow. . . . That form of wisdom which is the opposite of single-mindedness, the ability to keep many threads in hand, to draw for an argument from many disparate sources, is quite foreign to mathematics. This inability accounts for much of the difficulty which mathematics experiences in attempting to penetrate the social sciences.[21]

It is important to realize that the influence of tools on a field is more subtle than a mere opening up of possibilities. The extensive use of a tool involves shaping the work around its distinctive strengths and limitations; one can rarely apply a new tool to an ongoing stream of research without modifying it strongly. In the best case, as new tools come into being and are judged appropriate and valuable by people in the field, they alter the direction of work in the field, and the conception of the field itself. In the worst case, we assist the phenomenon of "new toolism", a disease to which operational researchers and systems analysts seem particularly predisposed.

Those affected by this disease "come possessed of and by new tools (various forms of mathematical programming, vast air-battle simulation machine models, queuing models and the like), and they look earnestly for a problem to which one of these tools might conceivably apply".[22]

Pitfalls. The craft character of systems analysis can be seen most clearly in the concept of "pitfall". A pitfall is the sort of error that destroys the solution of a problem and nullifies the validity of a policy recommendation. Perhaps the most reliable way of assessing the maturity of a practical or theoretical discipline is by the degree to which the ways around its common pitfalls are well-charted, and those encountered in the applications of the discipline to new fields of inquiry can be sensed in advance. Hence, the increasing realization of the many pitfalls which can be encountered in the application of systems analysis to policy problems is a sign of increasing maturity, rather than an admission of weakness.

Quade[23] distinguishes two categories of pitfalls in applied systems analysis. Those internal to the analysis itself, and those concerned with getting it used. Internal pitfalls are further subdivided into those that are inherent in all analysis, and those introduced by the analyst himself. Most important among the internal pitfalls of the first type are those associated with misconceptions in the treatment of uncertainty and of the time element, with the selection of inappropriate criteria of choice or measures of cost and effectiveness, with an incomplete analysis of feasibility conditions (e.g. the disregard of political and administrative constraints) and of the distributional consequences of the proposed policy.

Of the pitfalls introduced by the analyst, the most serious is probably that of personal bias, both in the form of preconceived notions concerning the nature of the problem, and of inflexible commitments to a given solution. Another common pitfall is a misplaced pragmatism which suggests "getting started" with the analysis, before the problem has been sufficiently understood.

Examples of external pitfalls are many kinds of errors arising in the process of communicating the conclusions of analysis; for instance, the arguments supporting a conclusion may be unsuited to the type of audience to which the analyst is addressing himself. A particular form of this pitfall is what Quade calls the "myth of a unique decision-maker":

> Analyses are ordinarily designed and carried out, although perhaps not always deliberately, as if they were to assist a solitary decision-maker who had full authority over acceptance and implementation. This may sometimes be the case but it is not the usual situation, even in the military, and almost never when broad social issues are involved. Even when there is a single decision-maker his staff at a minimum supplies the details of any policy that is set. . . . Influencing organizational behavior can be quite different from influencing the behavior of an individual and, since we understand so little about it, can constitute a pitfall for policy analysis.[24]

In mature disciplines, the avoidance of pitfalls is accomplished primarily in two ways: by the charting of standard paths, through a body of standard techniques which can be safely applied as a routine, which skirt them; and by each researcher becoming sensitive to the clues which indicate the presence of special sorts of pitfalls he is likely to encounter in his work.[25] Systems analysts have up to now followed the second approach, but as experience in the conduct of analytic studies accumulates, we can expect that standard procedures for the avoidance of the most serious pitfalls will be systematically developed.

5. THE COMPONENTS OF ANALYSIS

Having described the activity of the applied systems analyst as craftsman's work applied to the solution of problems involving intellectual constructs, it is now appropriate to examine the constituents making up a solution or policy proposal. As it turns out, the basic categories introduced by Aristotle in his analysis of the craftsman's task can be adapted to our present purposes.[26] Aristotle examines a task in terms of four categories or "causes": material, efficient, formal, and final. These four causes correspond, respectively, to the physical substance which is worked on; the activity of the agent in shaping it; the shape which the object finally assumes; and the purpose of the activity, or the functions of the object itself.

In adapting the Aristotelian scheme, the crucial difference to be kept in mind is that the purpose ("final cause") of the analyst's activity is not the production of a material object satisfying certain requirements but the analysis of a complex situation and the presentation of proposals. The "form" of the analysis is an argument in which evidence is cited and from which a conclusion is drawn. In turn, the evidence will contain a more or less explicit description of the "efficient cause": the tools, techniques, and models that have been used, and perhaps, difficulties and pitfalls encountered and overcome. Finally, the intellectual constructs and the data in whose terms the policy problem is formulated are the "material" component of the analyst's task.

In the preceding section, I have discussed the significance of the abstract character of the objects of analytic inquiry, and the connection between the tools and the personal craft judgments of the analyst. Here I shall concentrate on the other two constituents of analysis: the argument (with the important related category of evidence), and the conclusion.

The Argument. The argument represents the link between the material and efficient components of the analysis and the conclusion. In spite of its crucial importance, surprisingly little has been written on this topic by methodologists of systems analysis. The three-fold nature of the language of ASA (descriptive, prescriptive, argumentative) is reflected in the complex structure of an analytic argument, which will typically include mathematical and logical deductions, statistical, empirical, and analogical inferences, as well as evaluations and recommendations. This unavoidable complexity of the argument prevents any direct testing of its adequacy as can be done, for instance, in the case of a mathematical proof or a simple syllogism. Rather, the testing is done by applying, often implicitly, the criteria of adequacy that are accepted in a particular field, or by the particular audience to which the argument is directed.

The adequacy of an analytic argument only in part can be judged according to scientific or professional standards; in fact, the nature of the testing process is more social than logical. This can be seen from the fact that the argument is never addressed to an abstract, "universal" audience, as in the case of purely deductive proofs, but to a particular one (client, decision-maker, special interest group, etc.) whose characteristics the analyst must keep constantly in mind if his argument is to carry conviction and affect the course of events. In discussing external pitfalls, I have already mentioned the fallacy of assuming a monolithic decision-maker, but the relation between the analyst and his audience(s) is more complicated than is suggested by this single consideration. For, while the analyst must adapt his argument to the audience (and this requires a careful selection of data, methods, and techniques of communication), it is also true that the audience is, to some extent, the creation of the analyst:[27] the structure of the argument and the style of presentation will largely determine the type of audience that can be reached and influenced by the conclusion.

It is interesting to note that two rather typical procedures of systems analysis, the so-called *a fortiori* and break-even analyses, are essentially techniques of argumentation. The argumentative purpose is, in fact, indicated very clearly in the following quotation:

> More than any other single thing, the skilled use of *a fortiori* and break-even analyses separates the professionals from the amateurs. Most analyses should (conceptually) be done in two stages: a first stage to find out what one wants to recommend, and a second stage that *makes the recommendations convincing even to a hostile and disbelieving, but intelligent audience.*[28]

In the construction of an argument, evidence occupies a central position. Although the terms "facts" and "evidence" are often treated as synonymous in common parlance and also in some methodological discussions, a useful distinction can be made in terms of the relevant audience. "Facts" are pieces of (supposedly objective) information presented to an audience of persons who are experts in a given field. Evidence, on the other hand, is information embedded in an argument, for the purpose not so much of *proving* an assertion, but rather of *convincing* the audience of the reasonableness or convenience of a proposal. The contemporary fashion for using mathematical formalism at every possible point of an argument tends to blur this distinction, as it induces a tendency to accept statistical and other kinds of information as facts, rather than evidence.

The category of evidence is most easily recognized in fields where problems involve both complex arguments and large masses of information, and where the reliability and relevance of the information cannot be easily assessed by standard methods. This is a common situation in ASA but also in other fields like law, where there is a highly developed "law of evidence" for the presentation and testing of information offered as evidence in court cases. In the natural sciences, on the other hand, one usually has either a large mass of information with a relatively simple argument, or a complex theoretical argument needing evidence at only a few points. Hence, neither descriptive nor theoretical natural sciences generally require highly developed skills in testing evidence beyond the standard tests for reliability and relevance already involved in producing information.[29]

The assessment of the strength and fit of the evidence is considerably more complicated than judgements about the validity and reliability of data. For this reason, there often arise disputes about the adequacy of a proposed solution of a policy problem which cannot be settled either by an examination of the data and information, nor by an appeal to accepted criteria of adequacy. Such situations seem to justify a certain scepticism of the ability of systems analysis to provide concrete help to the decision-maker. It should be noted, however, that even in the field of "pure" science this aspect of the objectivity of scientific knowledge, which is really a result of a successful social tradition of producing and testing the materials of that knowledge, breaks down more often than the outside observer usually assumes.

The Conclusion. The conclusion of a policy study is not concerned with "things themselves", but with the intellectually constructed concepts and categories that can serve as the objects of an argument. The contact with the external world of economic, social, and political phenomena is always indirect. Of course, the analyst tries to probe as deeply as possible into the part of social reality with which he is concerned; but his assessment of the problem situation can only serve as the basis for evidence which is embedded in an argument whose objective validity can never be formally established. A different conceptualization of that reality, different tools, a few different personal judgments made at crucial points of the analysis, can always lead to radically different conclusions. This is unavoidable in any form of intellectual inquiry, including that of the natural scientist. Moreover, it is usually impossible to verify whether or not the decision-maker made a right decision based on the analysis. One cannot be judged by what actually happens, for there are always circumstances beyond his control. Even when social experiments can be carried out, which is seldom, definite conclusions can hardly be expected. Not only because of the possibility that the experiment may not be properly designed or analysed but, more significantly, because a policy embodies a large number of hypotheses; a negative result will constitute evidence against some of them, and it is usually very difficult to determine exactly which hypotheses are being contradicted by the experience.

In sum, we are faced here with a situation that arises in many contexts in which some form of evaluation takes place. The natural tendency is to evaluate an activity by the results it produces. This is not only an intuitively appealing, but also a reasonable approach – *provided* that reasonably objective criteria of evaluation exist. In such a case knowledge of the process producing the outcomes to be evaluated is largely immaterial – only results count. A car buyer is not usually concerned about the internal organization of the producing firm. But when the factual and value premises of the evaluation are moot, when no objective criterion for what is a correct decision or a good outcome exists, then the process or procedure by which the results are obtained acquires special significance. This is the basic reason why procedural questions become so important in legislative and judicial decision-making.[31]

For the reasons stated above, the conclusions of an analytic study can seldom be validated or refuted unambiguously. Hence, evaluation by results is either impossible or unfair (as when the quality of an analytic study is evaluated exclusively in terms of the actual success or failure of its conclusions and recommendations – too many factors outside the analyst's control determine the success or failure of a policy). Evaluation by process becomes unavoidable, and in this context the notion of craft and craft skills plays a crucial role.

REFERENCES

1. E. S. Quade, "Methods and Procedures" in E. S. Quade, ed. *Analysis For Military Decisions*, North-Holland Publishing Company, London, Amsterdam, 1970, p. 156.
2. O. Helmer, *The Systematic Use of Expert Judgment in Operations Research*, The Rand Corporation. Santa Monica, Calif., P-2795, September, 1963.
3. S. Toulmin, "The Structure of Scientific Theories" in *The Structure of Scientific Theories* (ed. F. Suppe), University of Illinois Press, Urbana, Illinois, 1974, p. 605.
4. See, for example, S. Eilon, How Scientific is O.R.? *Omega*, vol. 3, no. 1, 1975, pp. 1–8; R. G. Bevan, The Language of Operational Research, *Operational Research Quarterly*, vol. 27, no. 2, 1976, pp. 305–313; T. W. Hutchison, *Knowledge and Ignorance in Economics*, Basil Blackwell. Oxford, 1977; G. Majone, Policies as Theories, *Omega*, vol. 8, 1980, pp. 151–162; and especially H. Boothroyd, *Articulate Intervention*, Taylor and Francis, London, 1978.
5. J. R. Ravetz, *Scientific Knowledge and its Social Problems*, Penguin Books, Harmondsworth, 1971, p. 378.
6. *Ibid.*, p. 400.
7. Boothroyd, *op. cit.*, p. 115.
8. C. H. Waddington, *O.R. in World War 2*, ELEK Science Ltd., London, 1973, p. 26.
9. Boothroyd, *cit.*, p. 113.
10. L. C. Edie, Traffic Delays at Toll Booths, *Operations Research*, 2, 1954, pp. 107–138.
11. See J. R. Ravetz, *Scientific Knowledge and its Social Problems*, cit., p. 71 and following. The significance of the craft element in scientific work has been pointed out by M. Polanyi, *Personal Knowledge*, The University of Chicago Press, Chicago, 1958, and further elaborated in Ravetz's important contribution to the philosophy of science. It should be noted that although my discussion owes much to Ravetz's ideas, it differs at a number of important points from his; for instance, in the characterization of policy problems ("practical problems" in his terminology).
11a. Thus the question: Is systems analysis an art or a science? can be seen to rest on a mistaken view of science, since scientific research is also an art, i.e. an activity conducted according to personal and largely tacit rules.
12. J. R. Ravetz, *Scientific Knowledge and its Social Problems*, cit., p. 72.

13. E. S. Quade, "Methods and Procedures", in E. S. Quade, ed. *Analysis For Military Decisions*, *cit.*, pp. 151, 154, 157.
14. E. S. Quade, *Analysis for Public Decisions*, American Elsevier, New York, 1975, p. 298. Italics mine.
15. S. Eilon, How Scientific is OR? *cit.*, p. 8.
16. G. Majone, The Role of Constraints In Policy Analysis, *Quantity and Quality*, **8**, 1974, pp. 65–76; see also The Feasibility of Social Policies, *Policy Sciences*, **6**, 1975, pp. 49–69.
17. On the intellectual character of the objects of scientific research, see, for instance, J. R. Ravetz, *Scientific Knowledge and its Social Problems*, *cit.*, especially ch. 4, and M. Deutsch, "Evidence and Inference in Nuclear Research", in D. Lerner, ed., *Evidence and Inference*, The Free Press, Glencoe, Ill., 1959, pp. 96–106. Deutsch gives several examples of the abstract nature of the basic data of high-energy physics.
18. A. Coddington, Are Statistics Vital? *The Listener*, 11 December, 1969, pp. 822–823.
19. E. S. Quade, *Analysis for Public Decisions*, *cit.*, p. 306.
20. J. R. Ravetz, *op. cit.*, p. 1.
21. J. Schwartz, "The Pernicious Influence of Mathematics On Science" in P. Suppes, ed., *Symposium On Logic, Mathematics and Methodology*, Stanford University Press, Palo Alto, Calif., 1960, pp. 356–360.
22. A. Wohlstetter, "Analysis and Design of Conflict Systems", in E. S. Quade, ed., *Analysis For Military Decisions*, *cit.*, p. 106. The expression "new toolism" is attributed by Wohlstetter to the late mathematical statistician L. J. Savage.
23. E. S. Quade, *Analysis for Public Decisions*, *cit.*, pp. 300–317. For an extensive discussion of this topic, see G. Majone and E. S. Quade, editors, *Pitfalls of Analysis*, Wiley, London, 1980.
24. E. S. Quade, *Analysis for Public Decisions*, *cit.*, pp. 314–315.
25. See J. R. Ravetz, *Scientific Knowledge and its Social Problems*, *cit.*, p. 97.
26. Aristotle, *Ethica Nicomachea*, Book VI. The Aristotelian scheme has been used by Ravetz to study the activity of scientific inquiry, and by the Polish praxiological school to analyse the general category of "efficient action". On the praxiological approach see, in particular, T. Kotarbinski, *Praxiology*, Pergamon Press, London, 1965.
27. On this point, see C. Perelman and L. Olbrechts-Tyteca, *Traité de l'Argumentation. La Nouvelle Rhetorique*, Presses Universitaires de France, Paris, 1958, Part I, sec. 5.
28. H. Kahn and I. Mann, *Techniques of Systems Analysis*, The Rand Corporation, Santa Monica, Calif., RM-1829, December, 1956. Italics mine.
29. J. R. Ravetz, *Scientific Knowledge and its Social Problems*, *cit.*, ch. 4.
30. *Ibid.*
31. E. Barker, *Reflections on Government*. Oxford University Press, New York, 1958; N. Luhmann, *Legitimation durch Verfahren*, Luchterhand, Neuwied, 1975.

10

If Applied Systems Analysis is "True", must it also be "Bad" and "Ugly"? A note on the emerging methodology of Systems Analysis

IAIN MITROFF

INTRODUCTION

If the success of an endeavour be measured by the mix of emotions it stirs, then I would judge this seminar to have been an important success. Most such occasions fail to generate little if any emotion, save that of incredible boredom, but I felt myself alternating between excitement, hope, and optimism, on the one hand, and despair on the other. I felt excitement and optimism because for all our differences in culture, educational background, and language, there was a clear convergence in our thinking. It was abundantly clear that despite our differences in terms, a number of us had converged on the same general methodology for applied systems analysis. It was further clear that our methods were not abstract in the sense that they had been developed in the context of working on real problems.

My despair resulted from the comments of West Churchman, who throughout the seminar raised the greatest challenge of all to applied systems analysis. Churchman's challenge was not that we would be unable to develop a methodology and that this methodology would be ineffective. Rather, if I interpret him correctly, the danger is that we are developing something that indeed works, but that it works in perverse ways. In a word, we are in danger of developing but another example of an unaesthetic methodology of social science.[2] To the extent that we are unaesthetic, we distort once again the true needs and spirit of those we pretend to aid. Worst of all, we distort our own needs and spirit as participants in a social system.[7]

Since I am naturally optimistic, the despair I felt needs to be clarified. It was not despair in the fatal or cynical sense. Rather, it was despair in the heroic mood.[7] The challenge posed by Churchman was not intended to stop us in our efforts to develop applied systems analysis, but rather to spur us on to develop a richer concept of inquiry.[1, 2]

The plan of this chapter is essentially twofold. First, I describe the component parts of a general method of applied systems analysis. Although the component parts were called different things and lumped together differently by the different participants, there seemed to be general agreement on the necessity of certain critical functions. Second, I describe the problems of this methodology in the sense of the special challenge raised by Churchman.[2] I also show that, given the current state of our social technology and political systems, there may be no simple or easy way of overcoming these difficulties. The outcome, I hope, is a better assessment of the current "truth", "beauty", and "goodness" of applied systems analysis.

AN OVERVIEW OF A GENERAL METHODOLOGY FOR ASA

As regards current knowledge and thinking, Table 1 shows the *necessary* steps in a generalized methodology of applied systems analysis (ASA). That is, given current knowledge, each of the steps accomplishes a necessary function. Needless to say, at this time we do not know the full set of sufficient conditions. In fact we may never arrive at such a set for social systems do not admit of this kind of strict determinancy. Indeed, it is of critical importance to realize at the outset that ASA deals with a special type of knowledge claims or set of problems.

ASA deals with problems which are basically ill-structured. Well-structured problems constitute the bulk of "normal" academic science.[7] For these problems, the statement or formulation of an issue is itself relatively unproblematic. In contradistinction, the statement of a problem is itself at issue for ill-structured problems. Different analysts and/or actors in a social system will tend to have very different perceptions of a problem, let alone its resolution.[5] As a result, a fundamentally different type of problem-solving procedure and an associated set of criteria for judging success is called for in ASA.[4, 7] One of the most common fallacies is that of using criteria that were historically developed and appropriate for well-structured problems to the treatment of ill-structured problems.[1] If there was any serious failing of our seminar, it was that this confusion still seems to reign in our minds from time to time.

Each of the steps in Table 1 has been described in extensive detail elsewhere.[4, 6] My purpose is thus merely to illustrate their nature and resulting importance for ASA. One of the first things that is apparent from Table 1 is that a great variety of different traditional and nontraditional academic disciplines are involved in the creation of a methodology of ASA. The reason for this is the great variety of levels and types of systems and their associated functions that must be dealt with in ASA. I comment briefly on each of the steps in Table 1.

TABLE 1

Steps in a general methodology of applied systems analysis

Step	Type of system involved	Activity(ies)	Purpose	Disciplines involved
1.	Participant/social	Partitioning of larger social group into small group, team building	Effective functioning, interaction, conditions for participation, explicit generation of different views	Multivariate statistics, personality theory, organizational development
2.	Social	Stakeholder identification/ generation	Identification of vested interest groups/actors affecting a social policy	Social systems science
3.	Epistemic	Assumption generation/ identification	Identification of premises that must be posited to derive competing social policies	Social systems science
4.	Epistemic	Prioritization of assumptions and structured dialectical debate	Determination of the epistemic status of key knowledge claims	Management science, small group processes
5.	Epistemic	Argumentation analysis	Determination of the relationship between assumptions and social policies	Symbolic logic, concepts of argumentation
6.	Participant/social, epistemic	Knowledge synthesis, group synthesis	Group integration, knowledge integration	Organization development, symbolic logic, social systems science

Step 1. Group Formation

There was general agreement among the conference participants that because of its potentially widespread social impacts ASA must involve a broader conception of an expert. This means that those who are affected by a problem must be included, if only potentially, as members of an ASA team.

The issue of participation, in short, is critical. Participation cannot be confined to traditional conceptions of the expert. This is not only ruled out on ethical considerations, but on epistemic grounds as well. On grounds of equity, it is unethical not to involve in some significant manner those who are the supposed beneficiaries of ASA. On epistemic grounds, it is an illusion to think one can know the true needs of a community, society, or culture without some meaningful form of their participation. To paraphrase, an expert is not a special kind of person, but each person is a special kind of expert, especially when it comes to each person's problems, or more generally, troubles.

The issue of participation also arises from the fundamental epistemic consideration that the more complex the problem, the wider the set of expert skills that are required to define the problem, let alone cope with it. That is, when it comes to ill-structured as opposed to well-structured problems, no one single expert or discipline possesses the requisite knowledge to grapple with the problem. Further, since complex problems require for their effective management, the cooperation of diverse individuals and social institutions, no one person, no matter how powerful that person is, can command successful implementation of a policy. Time and again, the social science literature shows that for successful implementation of a policy to occur, people must be involved in the formulation of that policy.[4]

The social science literature also shows that small problem-solving groups of two to eight persons generally outperform large groups.[4] The reason is that small groups, *properly trained* in team-building methods, are better in communicating and sharing ideas. The same literature, however, is also split on the issue as to whether homogeneous versus heterogeneous groups do better in creative problem solving. We have tried to combine the advantages of both factors by forming small groups which are as homogeneous *within* and as heterogeneous *between* one another as possible. The homogeneity within a small group allows it to deal more effectively with the *task* of problem solving. Needed energy does not have to be diverted into dealing with interpersonal *process* issues such as conflict over styles, etc. On the other hand, by deliberately constructing small groups which are as different from one another as possible we have not left to chance the opportunity to witness and to debate different perceptions of a problem.[3] We thereby hope through such a process to minimize the chance of solving the "wrong" version of a problem precisely.[4]

There exist enumerable methods by which to form small groups from a larger one. Since they have been described elsewhere,[4, 6] we shall not mention them here. At the end of this paper, we will, however, comment from the standpoint of aesthetics what all these methods share in common.

Steps 2 and 3. Stakeholder and Assumption Specification

Assumptions are the epistemic cornerstone of ill-structured problems.[4]

Fundamentally different assumptions about the nature of man, social systems, and social science govern the production of different formulations of a problem.[7] Also, since very few assumptions can actually be verified prior or even subsequent to action, they must remain problematic. In short, they must remain uncertain; that is, they must remain assumptions. Indeed, facts and assumptions bear a symbiotic relationship to one another.

A fact is an assumption about which we feel confident, i.e. relatively certain. Conversely, an assumption is a potential but doubtful (i.e. problematic) fact. The point is that there is always a potential movement back and forth between the class of assumptions and that of facts. What is regarded as a fact by one social group at one point in time may be regarded by another group at another point in time as an assumption, and vice versa.[7]

Assumptions thereby become the basic ground of social reality. For this reason, the uncovering, analysis, and challenging of assumptions is of fundamental importance to ASA. Unfortunately, the surfacing of assumptions is not something which in general cannot be done directly.

Most people are as unaware of their assumptions as they are of their unconscious. Asking a person to produce his or her assumptions about reality is equivalent to asking a person to produce a map of their conscious and unconscious mind and the interaction between them – no simple task! Thus, from a behavioural standpoint, the injunction to "State your assumptions!" is virtually meaningless.

Fortunately, there is an indirect way of getting at assumptions which is both meaningful and simple to do. Assumptions are in effect the properties of the stakeholders which comprise a complex social system. That is, complex social systems are comprised of multiple actors, vested interest groups, in short, stakeholders. Stakeholders are called such because they represent those persons, groups, and institutions which have a "stake" in a social policy. Every social policy depends upon, or affects, and in turn is affected by certain stakeholders. The nature of the relationship between policies and stakeholders depends on the properties of the stakeholders which are posited. Various methods for identifying different kinds and classes of stakeholders can be found in Mason and Mitroff.[4]

Step 4. The Epistemic Status of Assumptions

Typically, a group feels more confident about the certainty or truth of some assumptions than that of others. Additionally, some assumptions are felt to be more important to the success of a policy than others. Plotting the assumptions identified relative to one another on two dimensions of perceived importance and certainty accomplishes three important functions. One, it gives groups, often for the first time, a concrete, externalized image or map of their internal belief system. Two, it allows for a concrete comparison between different belief systems. Three, it allows for a more effective dialectical debate between belief systems.

The importance of these functions cannot be overstressed. So much of social debate is unproductive because it is designed to accomplish precisely this purpose. That is, the conditions are set up, often intentionally, but just as often unintentionally, for the irresolution of differences. Our point is that the visualization of differences in the form of a clear and concrete map is essential and prior to the resolution of such differences. Again, every step of the process of ASA needs careful design and management from a behavioural standpoint.

Step 5. Argumentation Analysis

Recently, Richard Mason and I[4] have married Stephen Toulmin's[9] interesting framework for argumentation analyses to Nicholas Rescher's[8] provocative notions regarding plausibility. The result is an expanded framework for capturing the structure and dynamics of complex policy arguments.

More specifically, assumptions play the role of premises in the body of a policy argument. The framework thus allows one to locate more precisely how, why, when, and where assumptions enter into the structure of a policy. Also, since plausibility analysis was designed to allow one to deal with explicit logical contradictions in an argument, the expanded framework allows one to deal with strong (i.e. dialectical) challenges to a policy. The result is a mechanism for tracking the structure and shifting credibility of a policy over time. Also as the plausibility of the assumptions upon which a policy depends varies, the variability in the plausibility of the resultant policy can also be studied or charted.

Since this part of the methodology was the subject of some critical discussion during the conference, it deserves further clarification. I am not contending that the expanded framework is *the* framework for capturing the structure of complex policy arguments. This is not the point. The point is that *some* mechanism for tracking arguments will be implicit in a general methodology of ASA. The reason is that, à la Kant, the analysis of arguments is an *a priori* necessity for the possibility of ASA's existence.

It is likewise not a fundamental criticism of Toulmin to point out that different persons and/or groups will structure a policy argument differently. This again shows a basic misunderstanding of the differences between well-structured and ill-structured problems. In the methodology we have been outlining for ASA, we wish *deliberately* to set up the *behavioural* conditions so that groups can first of all witness why they view a situation differently and then secondly explore their differences. *It is not a fatal flaw to point out that different groups do not agree in their use of a tool when this is one of the fundamental purposes of the tool, i.e. to allow differences to emerge and be examined in a systematic way.* One of the reasons for setting up different groups is to allow each group to *negotiate for itself* the structure of *its* reality. This is one of its most important tasks in ASA.

Step 6. Knowledge Synthesis Through Group Synthesis

If groups are initially set up to be as different from one another as possible in order to do everything in our power to encourage systematic differences – the nature of important problems is too important to go unchallenged – then new groups are composed later in an attempt to synthesize important differences. The point is that synthesis is as much a social psychological process as it is a logical one.[4, 7] Hence, once again, we have to do everything we can to set up the appropriate *behavioural* conditions that will favour the emergence of a synthesis, if one is possible. This entails the setting up of new groups to work around the win-lose, competitive psychology that is the basis of the initial groupings. Whereas such win-lose competition is appropriate to the earlier phases of the methodology, it is inappropriate to the later phases. Again, the actual accomplishment of this is beyond the scope of this discussion.[4]

On the Aesthetics of ASA

The philosophical mood that has governed this paper thus far has been that of dialectical pragmatism. That is, the roots of the methodology we have been describing are grounded in a blending of two distinct traditions of philosophy, pragmatism and dialectics.[1] The methodology is dialectical in that it stresses the continual need for sharply contrasting points of view throughout the entire process of ASA. It is pragmatic in that the sequence of steps in Table 1 suggests an operational procedure for actually applying the methodology and in judging its success. In short, the "truth" status of the methodology described here is grounded in dialectical pragmatism. Whereas rationalism and empiricism have been historically appropriate for well-structured problems,[1] I have argued that the form of dialectical pragmatism discussed here is appropriate for ill-structured problems.[4, 7]

When it comes to assessing the aesthetic mood of ASA, the situation is not as promising. The dominant aesthetic mood which pervades the entire methodology is that of "cold reason", or, in Jungian terms, that of thinking.[7] For instance, consider the first step in the methodology, that of partitioning a larger group down into a number of small groups. Now there is nothing wrong or evil *per se* in breaking down a large group in order to facilitate discussion, although the very term "partitioning", when it comes to people, is offensive for some. What is at issue is the means, and the mood underlying it, by which the partitioning is accomplished.

In the methodology described, the partitioning is accomplished by categorizing people in to various personality, job, or functional "types". Thus, a person is described by virtue of membership in some abstract class, i.e. the properties the person *shares in common* with other members of a class or group.

It is precisely here where aesthetics comes squarely to the centre. If there is anything that seems to lie at the centre of one of the most important concepts of aesthetics, it is uniqueness. Simply stated, no two people are ever alike in all their characteristics.[2,7] Even stronger, all of us resist the notion that two people *should* ever be alike even in principle. This means that one of the most central aspects of an individual's *psyche* is that of uniqueness, that every individual has a unique side or aspect of style. It is this unique aspect of *style* that defines a very different aesthetic than that of the aesthetic of class similarity.

To put the matter directly, we know how to partition a group based on concepts of class similarity, but how do we form small *groups* of people based on the notion of each person's *uniqueness*? Or, how do we preserve each person's uniqueness in the process of partitioning? Little wonder that one could begin to conclude that splitting a group of people is more difficult than splitting an atom!

There are other aspects of the methodology which are equally unaesthetic from other concepts of aesthetics. Consider as another example the notion of stakeholders. Again, there is nothing wrong or evil with the concept stakeholders *per se*. Complex social systems are certainly composed of many actors. This much is nothing but a tautology although a potentially important one to realize.

What is at issue (stake!) is how the stakeholders are displayed pictorially. It is one thing to label people and institutions with abstract names. It is quite another to convey by means of colour and more sophisticated representation the complex of emotions that humans are capable of experiencing about archetypes.

In this sense, our science is still woefully underdeveloped in its appreciation and use of the various modes of conveying human expression.[7] There is no fundamental reason, save that of prejudice and outmoded custom, for the continuation of this state of affairs. Are we willing to apply our own newly emerging methodology to ourselves? Are we willing to challenge our own assumptions?

REFERENCES

1. Churchman, C. West, *The Design of Inquiring Systems*, Basic Books, New York, 1971.
2. Churchman, C. West, *The Systems Approach and Its Enemies*, Basic Books, New York, 1979.
3. Mason, Richard, O. A Dialectical Approach to Strategic Planning. *Management Science*, **15** (1969), pp. B-403 B-414.

4. Mason, Richard O. and Mitroff, Iain I. *Challenging Strategic Planning Assumptions*, John Wiley, New York, in press, 1981.
5. Mintzberg, Henry, *et al.* The Structure of "Unstructured" Decision Processes. *Administrative Science Quarterly*, **21** (1976), pp. 246–275.
6. Mitroff, Iain I., Emshoff, James R. and Kilman, Ralph H. Assumptional Analysis: A Methodology for Strategic Problem Solving. *Management Science*, **25**, No. 6 (June, 1979), pp. 583–593.
7. Mitroff, Iain I. and Kilmann, Ralph, *Methodological Approaches to Social Sciences*, Jossey-Bass, San Francisco, 1978.
8. Rescher, Nicholas and Manor, Ruth, On Inference from Inconsistent Premises. *Theory and Decision*, **1** (1970), pp. 179–217.
9. Toulmin, Stephen, *et al. An Introduction to Reasoning*, Macmillan, New York, 1979.

11

Organizational Decision Process and ORASA Intervention

JEAN MOSCAROLA

INTRODUCTION

Rethinking the process of system analysis. This research programme is induced by some difficulties, pitfalls and failures with which system analysts or OR men are faced. It implies an attempt to describe the process in which we intervene – *the decision-making process* – as well as the *study process*.

Most of the very numerous methodological studies familiar to the ORASA Community are exclusively devoted to the *study process*, more precisely to the model building and problem solving techniques. Less attention is paid to the way these techniques are used in concrete situations, and to all *the other skills involved in any study process*. The decision process also is paid little attention by ORASA literature. It is generally assumed to fit to the model of *normative decision theory*, for which decision-making is the activity of a decision-maker who chooses out of a set of alternatives the best one with regard to his objective. Thus in the scientific community the rationale of problem solving disguises the organizational, social or political processes through which action is taken. The *interaction* of the *decision process* with the *study process* is, with few exceptions,[10] hardly taken into account. As far as the specialized literature is concerned, it is dominated by the belief that problem solving techniques are the right and only way to answer problems which have to be solved.

To rethink the process of system analysis we firstly have to be able to *describe* in a concrete and realistic way the study process, the decision process, and their interactions. That is a condition to look for a *better control* of the scientist's intervention.

The research team I have been involved in for 3 years partly contributes to this programme and is mainly devoted to the study of decision processes, and ORASA intervention.

I shall firstly present the research project which is an attempt to bring together observations of concrete decision processes and development of intervention methods. This will lead us to focus on the manifold complexities of decision processes. Finally I shall conclude with some implications regarding ORASA intervention.

The subject is quite large, and given the shortage of space, I have to be brief. So the reader is referred to the bibliography at the end of the chapter.

1. A RESEARCH PROGRAM: TO OBSERVE THE CONCRETE DECISION PROCESS IN ORDER TO MASTER INTERVENTION

Analysts are concerned with "real world problems", with questions raised within firms, government, international agencies. Among these, applied system analysis is mainly directed towards complex actions involving several organizational elements, which may be more or less well identified – a "mess", following R. Ackoff. Let us call it the *perceived world*.

We introduce this notion rather than the notion of reality to point out that the context, the mess, with which the analyst is faced is perceived and interpreted through a cognitive grid made of knowledge, theories, belief. Some of them belong to *common sense experience* involving common languages and theories learnt through action. Others are called scientific. They involve more precise concepts and theories and fit the criteria of scientific knowledge.

Decision theory is certainly the favourite cognitive grid of most scientists. It is a rigorous, axiomatically developed theory. It implies mathematics, allows calculations to be made and has close links with the economic theory of rational behaviour. It benefits from the prestige of hard science. Furthermore it formally lays the foundations of most problem solving techniques used by OR men and applied system analysts. But its own foundations are a set of axioms.

Organization theory provides us with concepts and theories from the soft sciences. Psychology, psychoanalysis, sociology (applied both to individual and collective human behaviour) – allow deep insight and understanding of the functioning of organizational and decision processes. A wide range of literature in social, administrative, and policy sciences covers this field and provides interesting results based on empirical studies, reflecting as much as possible the phenomena of the perceived world.

If we want to examine the cognitive grid through which system analysts perceive the situations in which they intervene, the following main features appear:

Common sense experience, although shared by everyone, is largely ignored or censored, at least when scientists express themselves in publications on communications within the scientific community.

Organization theory is badly known by people whose educational training emphasizes mathematics and the hard sciences.

– Decision theory seems to be their main and most familiar reference by which to interpret and understand situations in terms of alternatives in relation to the decision-makers objectives and choice. Recourse to these concepts is reinforced by lack of adequate knowledge of organizational theory and by a censor mechanism against common sense experience. Last but not the least, an understanding of the situation in the light of decision theory is the best way to justify the use of the common optimizing problem-solving techniques.

Our main research thesis follows from this analysis: Operational Research and Applied System Analysis are founded on a much too simple, abstract, and naive representation of problem situations and decision processes. Some of the difficulties it faces in particularly complex situations come from this weakness.

To improve ORASA intervention we have thus to develop a more accurate representation of action and decision, taking into account learning from organization theory as well as from common sense experience. Therefore we have to observe concrete decision processes in their social and/or organizational context.

More precisely, the purpose of our research has been to develop a set of concepts, drawing on organizational theory, common sense experience, and decision theory, which can be used to:

– describe in as a concrete manner as possible the perceived world, and speak about it,
– conceive formal tools and techniques relevant to practice, and apply them in concrete/decision situations and processes.

To achieve the previous research objectives the following programme has been developed:

1.1. Theory building

In order to build up a set of concepts and propositions suitable for representing decision processes which can lead to the construction of decision-making tools, we began from the following ground base:

– the familiar concepts of decision theory and notions used in the ORASA Community,
– a wide survey of its literature on the social political and administrative sciences (see bibliography)
– the lessons from our own experience of decision-making and ORASA interventions.

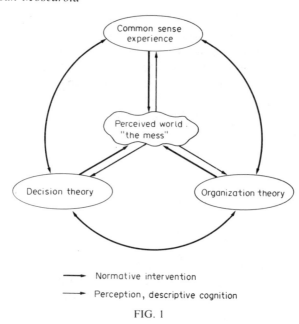

FIG. 1

A quite important theoretical contribution has been thus developed by members of the team (E. Jacquet Lagreze, G. Hirsch, J. Moscarola, B. Roy) and by other French researchers (E. Heurgon, J. Lessourne, J. Lemoigne, B. Walliser, J. C. Moisdon and others).

1.2. Testing the empirical relevance of theories

Do the concepts and propositions used to represent decision processes have any empirical content, do they fit concrete phenomena? As an attempt to answer this question the following tasks have been carried out:

– *Literature survey* of empirical studies devoted to decision processes.[30] The English language literature is the most important and the best known, but the German one has also provided very many interesting things.[46, 31]
– *Case studies.*[28, 17, 32, 12]

The purpose of these clinical studies was to test the usefulness of concepts and theories which describe and explain a decision process, and thus to discover whether theoretical assumptions are compatible with actual behaviour.

Clinical observation of past ORASA interventions (E. Jacquet Lagreze,[14] J. Moscarola[29] and J. Siskos[33]). These more original case studies are particularly intended to test and analyse concepts regarding the linking of decision and analytical processes, and the usefulness, effectiveness or success of ORASA interventions. Therefore researchers look at a decision process, for which a procedure or a model has been implemented by other members of the team, a year or more previously. These investigations are made under stringent conditions so as to guarantee as little bias as possible in the results.

1.3. Developing tools and techniques suitable for intervention which will provide better controls and efficiency in the investigational process.

The main theme of the work is thus to improve decision-making models and procedures for a clearer understanding of the complexity of decision processes and of the needs of their actors, rather than by increasing the technical complexity of existing problem solving techniques.

The development of multicriteria and multi-actor decision-making procedures[37, 38, 16] is an example of the impact of such an empirical research on normative techniques. This point will be developed in part 4 of this chapter, but let us first present the main lessons learnt from our attempt to construct an empirical theory of decision processes.

2. WHAT IS DECISION? THE MANIFOLD COMPLEXITIES OF CONCRETE DECISION PROCESS

Literature surveys, case studies, and clinical observations of past intervention have led us to a general conclusion: Decision theory, which is a normative theory does not allow us to describe what occurs when decisions are taken in organizations. Therefore we need what can be called following the München school,[45, 46] an *empirical theory of decision process*: a descriptive theory. It introduces us to the description of the concrete behaviour and process with which intervention is faced. We are going to focus on their complexity and their dynamic within the organization context. This will lead us to some interrogations regarding the reality of what is called decision.

2.4. The gap between normative theory and descriptive theory

The following propositions sum up the main results of our research:

Most concepts of decision theory which have led to formalized procedures or models used in common ORASA *have no empirical content*, i.e. they are not relevant to a realistic description of decision processes.

The most *useful concepts for describing concrete phenomena* proceed from social sciences or common sense experience, and *can hardly – if at all – be formalized* using usual mathematical language or modelling techniques.

For example the concepts of objective, or optimizing criteria are some of the main elements out of which decision models are built, but these concepts appear as irrelevant to a description of the operation of many decision processes, or to the behaviour of decision-makers. On the contrary, the concepts of *influence* or *satisficing* are much more useful in proving an accurate description, even though they cannot be formalized with usual techniques.

These striking results must not be interpreted as an argument for rejecting decision theory. In fact decision theory has never been developed as a descriptive theory. It represents the norm of individual rational behaviour, according to a set of axioms. This is sometimes forgotten or overlooked by analysts. Our general conclusions thus *emphasize the gap existing between the theoretical norm and real-life situations.* No wonder that the former differs from the latter. We shall not be able to interpret and perceive concrete situations through the cognitive grid derived from the norm.

On the contrary, in order to move with efficiency towards more rational decisions and a better control of operations, we need to get as realistic as possible a picture as we can of the true decision-making environment. That should be the contribution of an empirical theory of decision process.

Let us now introduce more precisely our main findings.

2.2. Discovering complexity again

The classical picture of decision-making (the problem-solving activity of a free and well-informed decision-maker who chooses from a set of alternatives, the one that is best with regard to his objective) does not reflect the complexity that is revealed by empirical studies. This complexity is manifold. There are many factors which differentiate each particular decision process but also the classical assumptions made on the decision-maker, the objectives and information have to be revised in the light of empirical studies.

(a) variety of factors

The generality of those concepts of classical decision-making must be replaced to take account of the variety of quite separate elements in the decision process, including the following:

Degree of structure. The action to be taken, as well as the activities of problem solving, may be more or less clearly defined and complex. The concepts of action and problem-solving activity are spread over the continuum from well-structured processes to ill-structured processes.

Degree of standardization. Some decision processes occur very often and follow familiar patterns, others are novel and are supported by no previous experience.

- *Level.* Individual and collective decision processes are distinguishable. Among collective ones some are at an organizational or department level, others are interorganizational processes involving several organizations without any particular unique institution being in charge of the overall process.
- *Importance.* Strategic and tactical decision process are distinguishable regarding the consequences and the degree of reversibility in the action to be taken.
- *Structure, standardization and level* are neither independent nor objective characteristics of a decision-making process. The level largely depends on the analyst's choice: for example an investment process can be studied on the individual level of the financial director as well as on the collective level of the firm.

The degree of structuring and standardization may depend on the level chosen for analysis. For example a disinvestment decision to be taken at the level of a particular firm is a new and rather ill-structured decision, but may be regarded as a routine and more structured decision from the point of view of a holding company.

(b) multiple actors

Even at the level of an individual, empirical studies show that the decision-maker is submitted to many influences from other people intervening in his/her own decision. Thus, empirical studies have led to a major concept substitution, the decision-maker disappears within the concert of *actors.*

There are many ways in which different actors may intervene directly: for example, the institutional decision-maker has the official power to ratify a decision, the initiators and *promotors*[46] are able to initiate and progress the process, the *opponents*, the *mediator*, the *adviser* the *analyst* . . .[15] Others do not actively intervene, but have an influence, whether the directly intervening actors take into account their preferences for fear they become active, as opponents for example, or may even tacitly appeal for their opinion or support. General De Gaulle is a good example of such a *ghost actor* dominating political decision in France.

The actors analysis enables us also to destroy one of the most pregnant myths in ORASA literature: the singular "decision-maker" and "scientist". Not only does the decision-maker give place to multiple actors: the *client* who pays for the study, the *institutional* decision-maker, the *promotors*, the *affected persons* (those who are going to be affected by the decision), but the concept of *"scientist"* or *"consultant" very often also encompasses a chain of several actors.* It puts into context the idea of the ORASA scientist dealing with models and problem-solving techniques and the client actors only interested in the results of the study. We must think of intermediary advisers, involved to differing degrees with the study process proper, but whose activity is interpreting, sorting, transmitting information produced by the ORASA specialist. This is particularly true for very large studies involving complex government actions without clearly defined institutional decision-makers, where politicians, public opinion, people in various positions of authority are the most influential actors, and the ordinary citizen is an affected person. In that kind of process the "single" decision-maker is obviously a myth and the direct users or interlocutors are other advisers or scientists, if not ghost actors!

(c) Objectives

The assumptions made by decision theory regarding the objective concept do not stand up to empirical examination. This has been particularly well demonstrated by a German study of the initial decision of a firm to buy a computer.[9, 31]

Objectives are not given and cannot always be empirically discovered. Quite often actors express official objectives, or give publicity to them, only at the end of the decision process – or at least after a first selection of alternatives. It does not really mean that they did not previously have objectives. For example, there may be reasons for keeping them secret. But the real objectives may also be unconscious. The situation may even be exacerbated by the scientist who may project his own objectives. *Stated objectives* may even be deliberately misleading.

This variety of actual behaviour is obviously an important barrier when ORASA is supposed to be based on a modelling of objectives.

Objectives are multiple and alternatives have to be evaluated throughout several dimensions. The postulated aggregation of objectives or criteria along a utility function does not appear to fit concrete behaviour. On the contrary, objectives are examined sequentially according to procedures rather than to a balanced analysis. The picture of an overall rationality at a level at which inconsistencies may be removed, gives room to partial rationalities bounded to some objectives or actors interests. The over-lapping between partial rationalities and groups of actors turns inconsistent objectives into a conflict between actors. The problem of rational choice between multiple objectives is then changed into conflict solving and negotiation procedures.

Concrete decision processes are moved by an examination of the first satisfactory alternative rather than by the idealized concept of optimization. Specification and stepwise improvement (or incrementalism) are the more usual approaches to be found in empirical studies.

Specification consists of the study of an action satisfying some chosen characteristics or aspiration levels. Alternatives are sequentially taken into consideration, but not compared to each other. There is no choice proper, alternatives are looked for so long as one fits the specifications.

Progressive improvement[21] consists in a partial comparison of those alternatives which only differ on some point – a proximity comparison.

The properties of such a problematique, compared to the optimization one, is to put the emphasis on a search for, and evaluation of, particular alternatives, rather than on their ordering and selection. This appears as one of the important lessons from empirical studies which greatly reduces the important lessons attributed to objectives.

(d) Incomplete fuzzy and paradoxical information

Information seldom exists on the surface, it has to be sought – this is the first experience of any ORASA analyst. But furthermore, although important theoretical developments have taken place in the literature concerning decision-making under uncertainty, some striking properties of information and behaviour about information have been revealed through empirical studies. Although information is always lacking in some degree, the need for information is more common than the disposal of excess data. In most decision-processes, certainly the ill-structured ones, both conditions lack of information and information pollution – may apply; at the same time actors may look for information and be blinded by data.

Qualitative, fuzzy, ambiguous, imprecise information plays a very important role in the improvement of complex decision-making,[25] inconsistent objectives and conflicting actors. Despite this, actors and organizations demand hard and detailed figures, and look for certitudes. The whole decision process may be side-tracked by the controversy about some unique and quasi-magic figure.[27]

This very brief survey of the results from empirical studies shows that in spite of the too poor image given by classical conceptions on decision-making, we have to deal with the set of concrete actors and their different roles, with the complexity of their objectives and with the very problematic nature of information. This is a first step towards an empirical theory of decision process. It has to be extended by a deeper examination of the dynamics of the process within its organization context.

2.3. The dynamics of the decision processes within the organizational context

(a) Time as a production factor

If we forget the picture which relates the decision to an event taken out of time, the very moment of choice, we find that decision-making appears to be a genuine productive process involving a lot of activities, resources and organization. Time is in this process more than a bench mark, it is a productive factor essential to the development of the decision. This development is not a progressive on-going and regular maturation, but is made up of cycles with feedback, trial and error. It does not obey the postulated rational succession of steps. On the contrary a nesting of phases ("cycles within cycles") are to be observed. The progression of the decision process is chaotic, some periods of low activity are broken by periods of intensive activity (highlights) allowing sudden progression towards a culmination of the process.[4, 14, 26]

(b) Interaction between organizational context and decision

The evolution of the process cannot be regarded as entirely context dependent. On the contrary, decision processes generate evolution in the context and organizational change.

Decision theory assumes that, given a decision-maker, his objectives, and information about alternatives (i.e. the contextual elements which structure the problem) the selected alternative follows. Empirical studies show however that these elements are changing during the course of decision.

- *actors are changing*, some appear, others disappear. The system of relations and influences between them is also liable to change for example in case of negotiation. Thus the decision process contributes to the structuring of human relations within an organization.
- *objectives are not objective.* They are not stated at the outset but are discovered and modified throughout the process. For example, the examination of a new alternative can unveil new objectives. The decision process is thus an important element in organizational goal setting.
- *information is also produced* throughout the decision process. It is produced and processed. Actors do not only need information in order to make decisions, they also have to decide what information they need, which information has to be taken into account, which information is to be communicated, to be calculated, etc.[19] The decision process helps determine organizational information systems.

Thus, being regarded as a production process, decision-making appears as being itself the convergence of a lot of decisions taken by the actors (among them, all the decisions taken by the analyst relating to the conduct of the investigation). Decisions are taken about the decision. Thus the decision process affects what happens in the immediate environment, not only by the action it initiates, but also through all the activities, actions and decisions that have to take place in that environment.

2.4. What about the reality and effectiveness of decision process?

(a) What is the reality of the decision process?

The overlapping in organizations and society of decision processes with different objects at different levels, which accidentally, as well as on purpose, come into relationship, may give us the image of a *garbage can model*[25] which seems to have nothing to do with any kind of obvious rationality.

Likewise, the boundaries of the decision process appear as very difficult to define. In fact, to speak of the start or the end of a decision process is rather artificial: it is preceded by an initiative process which may or may not lead to the examination of the problem set by the initiators.[40] On the other hand, after the decision has been taken a number of events may modify it and thus lengthen the decision process proper.

Thus a particular decision process is neither clearly standing out against other on-going decision, nor does it correspond to a well-identified period of time.

In the face of such confusing observations, the main conclusion is that decision processes are not "hard facts" belonging to any kind of objective reality enjoining and allowing only one unambiguous description. *On the contrary a decision process is a model, an image*, a narration, a relation of events built up by actors, and which help them either to structure and guide their own actions, or to understand their surrounding world. This image is constructed on purpose – action, or analysis – and is an attempt to sketch some order out of the mess of organizational or social life. To this attempt some fundamental rationale, assumptions, skeleton, or paradigm is required. That is the very use and utility of theories. Thus empirical theory of decision process opens out to more realistic and pragmatic narrations or images of the decision process. It also introduces some new points of view.

(b) What is the necessity and utility of a decision process?

This question has to be interpreted within the framework of the preceding remarks. Given a particular rationale, skeleton or theory, projected on the perceived world in order to describe it in terms of a decision process, what are the values referred to, and which criterion is used to select the elements and phenomena which will take into account, evaluate the usefulness, and justify the existence of decision processes.

Roughly speaking the lessons from the empirical studies lead us to a paradigm shift:

Normative decision theory focuses on the *properties of the results*: the decision action which has to be taken. These properties are evaluated at the level of *organization* conceived as an entity (the firm is like the entrepreneur) and using *efficiency criteria* (ratio output/input) related to economic means and rationality.

On the way to an empirical theory of decision process we are led to focus our description on the events of the process (the programmes followed) and the behavioural habits (evaluated at the level of particular actors on the basis of legitimacy criteria). They are an evaluation of the conformity of behaviour and action with past experience, routine programmes and work patterns, pressure from social norms, and of their contribution to the safeguarding of actors and organization identity.[13] It is a move towards concepts largely influenced by cybernetic models and the social sciences.

This is only a brief overview of recent developments and discussion about decision and system analysis.[13, 6, 34, 11] These developments have led to a shift of paradigm symbolized as follows:

Properties of results→Events of the process
Organization→Actors
Economic efficiency→Social legitimacy

A change relating to our understanding of decision analysis may be a necessary condition for new development, and for progress regarding description as well as intervention.

But as a major conclusion let this remind us that if a decision can be certainly thought as an attempt towards a rational and progressist mastering of action, it is also and always a social ritual. To forget this aspect of decision is a recipe for disaster, experienced at least once by most analysts.

3. IMPLICATIONS FOR ORASA INTERVENTIONS

At the same time that we were looking for an empirical theory of decision processes, we were engaged in methodological research and practice regarding ways to improve ORASA intervention.

Thus in addition to an ongoing effort towards new modelling techniques we have been looking for a methodology of decisional audit or organizational diagnosis. More recently we made some attempts towards a methodology for post-evaluation of ORASA intervention. Thus we hope to learn how the organizational context of decision reacts to intervention mode and tools

3.1. Decisional audit another manner to help decision-making in organizations

To be able to give an accurate description of the process in which the scientist has to intervene, it is certainly necessary for him to find the right method and tools. But a simple description of the decision process can also be regarded as a first step to help the actors involved.

Therefore we have developed a methodology that helps the analyst to describe the situation he is involved in. This method[13] is based upon the analysis and description of five systems that structure the context of decision: The systems of *actors*, of *actions*, of *values*, of *information*, of *procedures*. In addition to the concepts useful to such a description, the following principle is assessed: Several descriptions of the same situation may at the same time be relevant as far as different actors are concerned.

– Such an attempt to outline a coherent structure which provides a relevant description of the "mess", provides actors with significant help. Starting from better intelligence and understanding, founded on the description of their perception of the situation and of the on-going process, actors are thus able to improve their own motivation towards a satisfactory conclusion and to better structure their own actions and strategies. This is particularly useful when they have a tendency to oversimplify or overrationalize their perception of the situation.
– With regard to the specific strategy of the scientist, such an approach makes it possible to reverse the proposition "the methods and models enable the definition of the problem i.e. models are looking for problems" (which is all too often a rather good description of current practice). We now say "The contextual analysis and decisional audit direct the choice of methods and models". To which audience must the study be devoted? Which arguments, or rationale have to be developed to perform a persuasive intervention? The answers to questions of that kind depend on knowledge of the context, and direct us towards such or such a method, model and style of intervention.

3.2. Developments in decision-making models and techniques

We have been faced in the field of multicriteria methods with the difficulties raised by objectives and preference assessments. These difficulties experienced by all analysts appear, within the framework of an empirical theory of the decision process, as the result of the gap between the norm (action should be directed by objectives) and actual behaviour (objectives are fuzzy and discovered when action takes place).

To take this gap into account we have developed two types of novel modelling techniques and procedures.

(a) An alternative axiom for preference modelling

Given two actions a and a' it is generally assumed that with regard to the decision-maker's preferences, objectives, or criteria one of the actions is preferred to the other, and when not, they are indifferent.

This preference axiom has been one of the basic assumptions made by scientists. It allows the construction of powerful algorithms, but also postulates that the knowledge of what is preferred or indifferent is clear for everyone, or at least that the actors concerned by the decision are able to express their own preference. However, empirical studies and our own practice of multicriteria methods have convinced us of the impossibility in many situations of assessing whether a is preferred to a' or a' preferred to a or a is indifferent to a'.

In such situations we have to introduce a new relation which takes into account the fact that for such and such a reason the analyst cannot assess and model a preference or an indifference between two actions. This relation is called the incomparability relation.

We come thus to a new axiom: given two actions, a and a', one and only one of the following relations may exist:

Classical axiom	Alternative axiom
a is preferred to a' a' is preferred to a a is indifferent to a' (reflexive)	a is preferred to a' a' is preferred to a a is indifferent to a' a is incomparable to a'

B. Roy and his team have developed in France several methods using incomparability relations. They make it possible to:

- look for some satisfying actions (ELECTRE I)
- rank actions (ELECTRE II and III)
- sort out well-known actions (either good or bad) from less known actions (TRICHON)

(b) Reverse preference analysis

When objectives are imperfectly understood it is often much easier to ask actors about their preferences with regard to some concrete actions that they know well rather than asking them to tell what in general their criteria are. They will be able to rank a few actions according to their feeling but will not be able to assess which is the relative importance of each criteria to take into account.

In order to help them in this task the basic idea of reverse preference analysis is to compute the relative importance of a set of criteria out of an ordered list of actions, previously ranked by the actor. This is the reverse way of usual decision-making techniques that from the criteria compute the ranking of actions.

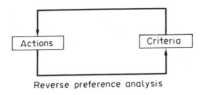

Reverse preference analysis

FIG. 2

Using a linear programming code, UTA,[13, 33, 41] is a method that allows us to assess an additive utility function that aggregates in criteria according to the holistic preference given by the actor. This method can then be used in an interactive way which involves the analyst and his client in a learning process of the preference structures inherent in the problem.

(c) These methods share with other recent developments in ORASA the following features that particularly fit in with empirical evidence

They are not problem-solving techniques but only represent an attempt to assist actors by the way of simulation, partial ordering of alternatives, or simply trial and error.

The methodologies do not imply strong assumptions regarding objective preferences or utility, so as to allow a complete modelling of preferences of actors.

These methods are *actors or audience oriented*, thus taking into account the plurality of actors shown by empirical studies, and giving room to some new concepts. According to this, ORASA has to be concerned with *persuasion or argumentation* about alternatives.

3.3. Post evaluation of ORASA intervention

Recently we have been engaged in a new research direction toward a methodology for the evaluation of ORASA intervention. The idea is to look 6 months or a year after the conclusion of a study on its impact with regard to the decision process. This evaluation raises theoretical difficulties[32, 33] but may really be useful. As far as we have experienced it, it shows that the interaction between the study process and the decision process is very fuzzy and ambiguous. Quite often what is regarded as very important by the analyst is completely overlooked by the decision-makers who on the contrary may find a great help in activities in which the analyst has been less interested.

The major conclusions that we may draw at the moment are that:

— Within the organizational context, information processing is perhaps more important than concern about the rationality of choices

– Short and flexible studies are capable of adapting to the changing nature of actors' perceptions and they may be more effective than in depth, too specialized and long studies

These are for us the major challenges for further technique development in ORASA.

4. COMING BACK NOW TO THINKING ABOUT ORASA IN ORGANIZATIONS

Rethinking the process of ORASA within an organizational and social context also implies paying more attention to identifying and legitimizing phenomena rather than to means and analysis and the search for efficiency. The scientist is thus faced with a double challenge:

– to accept and recognize the limits of pure rational analysis and abstract scientific calculations, which are neither sufficient nor necessary to lead to sound action. The intellectual search for the one best way has been a dream, if not a dangerous mystification. On the contrary – ambiguous time-wasting, compromising, unconscious mechanisms are the incentives to action which have as their aspirations that they should be satisfactory, feasible or not too bad. The earlier ORASA enthusiasm has thus to be tempered and changed into a self-awareness of our real abilities and contributions.
– to develop other modes of intervention and skills if we, nevertheless, still wish to bring in some more rationality and contribute to help mastering action. These skills are those of the organizer, the communicator, the negotiator. They are essential to ensure an impact from the work of the analyst using hard science.

Thus we return to the origins of OR. At that point in time, its promoters claimed the necessity for multidisciplinary teams or multidisciplinary training. They had already experienced the problem of controlling their approach in the light of practical experience. Thirty-five years later, the empirical theory of decision process reminds us of those lessons. If we bring together common sense experience, decision theory and organization theory, we may hope that we can make real progress in the effectiveness of ORASA intervention.

BIBLIOGRAPHY

(Does not pretend to give a thorough insight)
1. AFCET ADSG. L'avenir de la recherche opérationnelle, pratiques et controverses. Colloque de Cerisy, Hommes et techniques, 1979.
2. H. Boothroyd. Articulated Intervention, Taylor and Francis, London, 1978.
3. J. C. Courbon, J. Grajew and J. Tolovi. Conception et mise en oeuvre des systèmes interactifs d'aid à la décision par une approche évolutive. Informatique et gestion, Mars, 1979.
4. M. Crozier and A. Friedberg. L'acteur et le système, Seuil, Paris, 1977.
5. R. M. Cyert and J. C. March. A behavioural Theory of the firm, Prentice Hall, 1963.

6. M. R. Dando and R. G. Sharp. Operational Research in the UK in 1977. The causes and consequences of a Myth? Journal of Operational Research Society, Vol. 29, 1978.
7. Despontin, J. Spronk and J. Moscarola. A user-oriented listing of Multicriteria decision methods. Cahier de LAMSADE Université, Paris IX, 1981.
8. G. Eden, S. Jones and D. Sims. Thinking in organizations, Macmillan Press Ltd, 1979.
9. J. Hauschildt. Entscheidungsziele, JCB Mohr (P. Siebeck) Tübingen, 1977.
10. E. Heurgon. OR intervention: Study Process and Decision Making Process matching, Euro IV Forth European Congress on OR, Cambridge, 1980.
11. E. Heurgon. Penser autrement la recherche opérationnelle, Congrès Euro III, 1979.
12. G. Hirsch, E. Jacquet Lagrèze and J. C. Marchet. Description d'un processus de décision II Illustration Le cas de la raffinerie de Brest, Juillet, 1978.
13. P. Huard. Rationalité et identité, vers une alternative à la théorie de la décision dans les organisations, Revenue Economique no. 3, Mai, 1980.
14. E. Jacquet Lagrèze. Système de décision et acteurs multiples. Contribution à une théorie de l'action. Thèse d'Etat Paris IX, 1981.
15. E. Jacquet Lagrèze, G. Hirsch, J. Moscarola and B. Roy. Description d'un processus de décision. Cahier du LAMSADE, Février, 1978.
16. E. Jacquet Lagrèze and B. Roy. Aide à la décision multicritère et systèmes relationnels préférences in Montjardet, Batteau, Jacquet Lagrèze (eds). Analyse et Agrégation des Préférences Economica, 1980.
17. E. Jacquet Lagrèze and J. C. Marchet. Description d'un processus de décision: extension d'une station d'épuration d'eaux usées. Cahier du LAMSADE, Oct., 1978.
18. J. C. Lemoigne. Système de décision dans les organisations PUF, 1973.
19. J. C. Lemoigne. Informer la décision ou décider de l'information. Economie et société, Vol. XIII, Juin, 1979.
20. J. Lessourne. A theory of the individual for economic analysis. North Holland Publishing Company, 1977.
21. C. E. Lindblom. The science of Muddling through Public administration Review, 1959.
22. G. Majone. The Craft of applied systems analysis working Paper IIASA, Vienne, 1980.
23. G. Majone and E. S. Quade. Pitfalls of Analysis IIASA Report. Wiley, Chichester, UK, 1980.
24. J. C. March and H. A. Simon. Organizations J. Wiley, N 4, 1958.
25. J. C. March and J. P. Oosen. Ambiguity and choice in organizations, Bergen, 1976.
26. H. Mintzberg, D. Raisighani and A. Theoret. "The structure of unstructured decision processes". Administrative Science Anaterly, June, 1976.
27. J. C. Moisdon. L'itinéraire du Centre de Gestion Scientifique de l'Ecole des Mines de Paris. L'avenir de la Recherche Opérationnel Edition Hommes et Techniques, 1979.
28. W. Major and J. Moscarola. Analyse d'un processus de décision. Quelques conclusions à partir d'une étude de cas sur ia sélection de projets d'expériences en physique nucléaire. Cahier du LAMSADE, Mai, 1979.
29. J. Moscarola. Stratégie d'insertion dans un processus de décision. L'avenir de la recherche opérationnelle, Hommes et Techniques, 1979.
30. J. Moscarola. Les tendances actuelles des travaux sur les processus de décision dans les organisations. Enseignement et gestion Automne, 1980.
31. J. Moscarola. La contribution des travaux empiriques allemands à la théorie du processus de décision. Document du LAMSADE no. 10, Juin, 1980. Université Paris IX.
32. J. Moscarola. Elaboration de l'accord d'établissement d'une petite société appartenant à un grand groupe. Congrès AFCET, Petits Groupes, Grands Systemes, Edition Hommes et Techniques, Paris, 1979.
33. J. Moscarola and J. Siskos. Analyse à posteriori d'une intervention d'aide à la décision, Note LAMSADE, 1981.
34. J. Moscarola. The efficiency of decision, how to assist decision making in the organization. Proceeding of IFORS, Congres, Hamburg, 1981.
35. A. Newell and H. A. Simon. Human Problem Solving, Englewood Cliffs, 1972.
36. H. Raiffa. Decision analysis, Addison Wesley, London, 1970.
37. B. Roy. Vers une méthodologie générale d'aide à la décision, Revue Metra, 1975.
38. B. Roy. L'aide à la décision Critères Multiples et optimisation pour choisir, trier, ranger. Livre à paraître.
39. B. Saint Sernin. Le décideur, Gallimard, 1979.

40. D. H. Schultz. Die Initiative zu Entscheidungen, TC. B. Hohr Tübingen, 1977.
41. H. A. Simon. The new science of Management Decision, Prentice Hall, Englewood Cliffs, N. 5, 1977.
42. J. Siskos. Comment modeliser les préférences au moyen de fonctions d'utilité additive RAZRO, Vol. 14, no. 1 Février, 1980.
43. L. Sfez. Critique de la décision, A. Colin, Paris, 1973.
44. H. Teznas du Montcel. L'utilité de la décision. La décision. Colloque de Cérisy, 1980.
45. B. Walliser. Le modèle rationnel et le modèle cybernétique de décision individuelle, 1980.
46. E. Witte. Entscheidungsprozesse in Handwörterbuch der Organisation. E. Grochla, Editor, C. E. Poeschel Verlag, Stuttgart, 1980.
47. E. Witte. Pathology of decision making. French–German Conference on Empirische Entscheidungstheorie, München, 1978.

12

Analysis of Systems Support –
Some ideas on improving
Systems Analysis

GERARD DE ZEEUW

INTRODUCTION

Systems analysis is relatively young as an identified set of activities: only some 20 to 30 years of age. These years have brought some successes, recognition, and some degree of establishment. But also two difficult problems have appeared, concomitant to this development. One is of course that one has come to expect something from systems analysis. It turns out not to be easy to satisfy all these expectations. The other type of problem is that one starts to run into various peculiar difficulties, when one wants to improve the activity of systems analysis itself, in order to be able to satisfy better such expectations.

In this chapter I shall be especially concerned with the latter type of problem, covering something that we may call difficulties of the second order, or difficulties on a meta-level. What can we do about these difficulties or problems, how can we "rethink" systems analysis to raise the level of satisfied and satisfiable expectations? Or, conversely, what are the stumbling blocks to be overcome? I will try to describe one possibly useful answer to the latter.

There are still many different ways of characterizing systems analysis, in terms of the activities it covers. But at least one can already do more than just enumerate those activities! The following may be a reasonable characteristic, to be entertained in the sequel. Systems analysis stands for two main activities: *constructing* combinations of various systems – be the latter identifiable activities, languages, artifacts, people, concrete organizations, advice or objects – such that new possibilities for improved action (of users, participants, clients) are generated; and at the same time trying to *justify* that the combinations are necessary and adequate for the latter purpose (e.g. see Quade and Miser, 1980). This defining characteristic implies systems analysis to be an activity to answer at least two types of frequently asked and important questions: (a) I want X, but cannot get it; you indicate how to get it in an acceptable way; (b) I want Y so people can get X′ via Y, if they want it. In both (a) and (b) the "I" usually is a more or less powerful decision-maker or actor and the "you" is someone who does systems analysis – and should construct something like X, X′ and Y (systematically and justifiably). The "I" and "you" may of course overlap.

It will be clear that this characterization still allows for many different activities to be called systems analysis. Some of these have established themselves in their own right, like innovation management, technological problem-solving, action-research, decision-making, urban development. As suggested however, they have some important common element, allowing them to be subsumed here under systems analysis – albeit with different interpretations for X, X′ or Y – or for what was called "new possibilities for improved action". In what follows I will mainly confine myself however to the systems analysts' activity of "change and improvement in human affairs". This is the field where my main interest lies (Jungermann and De Zeeuw, 1977; Groen *et al.*, 1980). It also seems to be one of the fields where the meta-level difficulties mentioned earlier turn up most frequently. Indeed here some subsystems not only can be observed and talked about, but can do such talking themselves – being apparently level-switchers more or less by nature (De Zeeuw, 1981a). People in fact are quite different in this respect from non-talking systems like iron, electricity, etc. Activities not dealing mainly with such talking or so called I-saying systems (De Zeeuw, 1981b) will only be dealt with here by implication.

SIGNALS TO RETHINKING

Would everybody agree that there are meta-difficulties to systems analysis? Presumably not. Hence it seems fair, as a first step, to list at least some of these difficulties, as I see them. They must be distinguished of course quite clearly from what may be called the difficulties of the first order. The latter encompass (direct) questions such as: what to advise as energy-saving policies; what to do about the world (or local) food situation; how not to further unbalance government budgets with social security outlays, while not decreasing such security support; etc. These are difficulties of the first order, for systems analysis. In answering each of these, as a systems analyst, one tries to avoid the so called environmental fallacy (Churchman, 1980). Let us point out some difficulties of the second order.

A. Policy-makers do not listen (often) enough to what systems analysts advise. Feasibility studies go unheeded; alternatives that are preferable according to systems analysts are rejected – and all this much too often, and not due to any apparent lack of quality on their part.

B. In most cases the relation between X and X′ (see above) remains unclear

– i.e. between what decision-makers or a decision-maker wants, and what people more generally may want, or need or want to need. Is an improved airfield an improvement? Is heeding environmentalists an improvement? Does professionalization in psychotherapy imply improvement?

C. What type of knowledge is acquired in the process of systems analysis? Is it something standard? Is it about regularities in a world where the desired combinations of systems are not yet available? How would these regularities change when the latter are introduced, and how would that influence what is desired? Or is it about regularities in or created by the new combinations? Or even about something else – e.g. the experience of the systems analysts themselves?

D. Evading the environmental fallacy implies looking for approaches to a problem, precisely at those places where that problem is not being felt as a problem. This means that one has to enlarge on what is taken as the (relevant) context to the problem – but how far? To what scale should one do so? What should be modelled? How much of the environment should one leave alone, to solve its own problems, thereby however helping to overcome the difficulties of the problem one started out with? What environmental fallacy does evading environmental fallacies introduce?

E. Any advice of a systems analyst presumably may help improve the quality of life in a society – when it is heeded. But to what extent is this only possible by not changing that part of society which makes that heeding possible? How much support for the established structure of society is implied; and will any revolutionary power be generated? Would the fact that people other than the decision-maker know about the advice change the advice – and if so, would such advice thus be dependent in terms of its quality on a particular goalgroup (usually therefore its benefits confined to the more powerful group, even when that is not desirable)?

In the above some problems were listed, seen as (important) difficulties *about* systems analysis. It seems that some of them at least allow for an easy interpretation, suggesting approaches to tackle the difficulties. For example, people not listening to systems analysts seems a direct consequence of the way the analysts design their work, especially in the case of human(s)' systems. Indeed, if they follow the standard precepts for independent scientific work they actually design for not being listened to by policy-makers and politicians! This can be understood as follows. For one thing, the systems analysts presumably would design their activities not to be direct partners to the policy-makers; scientifically they would want to act value-free, therefore only as "servants", not as political partners. But who would want to have servants then dictate what should be listened to? They should have no say whatsoever, being only part of the world of decision-makers. Secondly, if systems analysts actually provide some useful insights about the outside world, they presumably can do so only by restricting themselves to clearly defined subsystems. Then, either the policy-maker(s) plus all their opponents are in it, behaving similarly as defined in the insights – and knowing about that will cease to be interesting. Or only some are in it; and then the policy-maker would be wise to behave as if he or she is not in it. Indeed, he or she should behave as part of a different subsystem – possibly of his or her own making, to maintain some leverage against other opponents. That also means not listening. The solution to this difficulty of not listening seems clear, given this interpretation: do not design your work so as not to be listened to! Be a real opponent yourself, especially to the rulers (presidents, bureaucracies, parliaments) of this world. Or design advice so as to be acceptable, seen from all potential users' points of view – to involve them more, to have them all take advantage of the advice at the same time, and to prevent them from creating opposing subsystems to themselves.

We will come back to this type of solution. First however we will discuss somewhat more generally the assumptions, presently seeming to underly most work in systems analysis (see Churchman, 1980).

SOMETHING ABOUT EXPERIENCE

If one wants to realize X, i.e. something new or necessary, of course one would like to do it well. For that however, usually one needs to know various things: one's own and others' resources, quality criteria to be able to judge whether or not one is still doing well or has to start to choose alternatives, data to work with, procedures to order one's activities, etc. All these one may already know, or still have to acquire. It is in the latter case that the activity of *research* may be of help – to acquire the data, to build models of (parts of) the situation in which one wants to realize some X, or X', to compare alternative actions on the basis of the model's predictions (and thus on the basis of the data), or to compare allocations of resources. Preferably all this should be done at the same time that the design of the new combinations is realized.

This research activity can be structured in various ways. One general way to do so is via the so called predictive cycle: observation, induction of regularities, deduction of testable consequences, testing, evaluation in a more general context of the still acceptable inductions ... to get the desired knowledge, possibly via repetitions of this cycle. Another way is formulated in the regulative cycle: problem definition, diagnosis, development and comparison of alternative plans for actions, intervention on the basis of one of the plans, evaluation ... again, with possibly some repetitions.

These cycles are well known, in one form or another (Bemelmans and De Boer, 1981). They are based on the assumption that people will act better, to get some X, when they acquire knowledge that somehow reflects what happens in certain parts of reality. That is to say that it is assumed that such parts can be distinguished or separated from other parts, and can be described, independently from describing such other parts. Thus one should be able to build a descriptive model of for example an organization, even find input-output relations, without really taking cognizance of the co-existence of other such organizations, or of the purposes for which one does the modelling, or of the possible changes themselves brought about in reality and in the latter's partitioning, by using the modelling description. This assumption of separability may be useful, but it of course can also lead to problems. In fact it even is at the heart of what we earlier called our first meta-difficulty (meta-problem A), i.e. knowledge being generated so that it seems designed to leave people free to use it or not. The policy-maker or contractor of the research specifically is not usually one of the parts to be modelled, and thus no knowledge will be found about the relation between this policy-maker and the model. Similarly, it seems improbable that one will be acquiring knowledge with revolutionary power (meta-problem E), by assuming from the beginning that the real world can be partitioned so that a change in one part does *not* affect changes in other parts (which indeed is just the opposite of revolution).

On the basis of this type of argument it seems safe to conclude that the meta- or 2nd order problems of systems analysis may be at least partly due to the concepts and precepts themselves, used in systems analysis and in its necessary and accompanying research. These concepts apparently sometimes restrict in a way where such restrictions become impediments instead of useful tools.

To overcome these restrictions (and the engendered meta-problems A to E, and possibly others) therefore, we apparently need a change in such basic assumptions. Many possibilities suggest themselves. Most obvious would be to loosen and extend the concepts used somewhat – i.e. to generalize them. This is what I will try.

Indeed, the following generalization may do the trick. *In order to do or realize something (X, X', Y) well or better, one needs to use more of (people's) experience.* That is: more than systems analysts are wont to do at present.

This suggestion for overcoming the difficulties of the 2nd order by itself is imprecise. I will make it more precise in what follows. But something should be indicated now. That is that the usual assumption for inquiry has been changed in a fundamental way – even though one is dealing with a simple generalization. For via it we leave out the restriction that we accept as (tested) knowledge only that which, as part of our experience, relates to well-delineated and -delineable parts of reality. That implies that we will accept as knowledge much more than what is usually accepted, e.g. via the predictive cycle. The claim I want to argue of course is that systems analysts would actually do better, on the 2nd order level, if and when they would thus base themselves differently.

As a first step, let me enlarge somewhat on this concept of experience, and what I mean by it. Each individual can be construed as having an enormous store of remembered experiences, adding to it all the time. Contrary to what is usual, this store should not be seen only as something inside people's heads; it is also something external to this. For example: it is necessary, to continue walking, to experience and to remember where one is. Streets may provide clues and signals for this. That is, they are actually supports for memory: where to walk, where to cross. Similarly: in schools, in the structure of society, in habits, in crafts, in religion – in each one will find support systems for individual memory, for building up experience. Experiences remembered in this (external) way also help to organize actions, and to improve upon them (Schilpp, 1940).

This may all seem obvious. What I want to emphasize is that "knowledge" is usually seen as only a part of the many different experiences that people store via such external and internal support systems. Looking for it, one restricts oneself to what is "the same" for everybody – to what is related to clearly separable and delineable parts in reality, and thus to what does not allow for individual variation in remembered experiences. This type of knowledge of course is often useful and necessary – e.g. as it concerns the course of the moon and planets as "same" experiences, used to support navigation. But a lot more than such "same" experiences may have the quality of being useful to act and to improve actions, as external memories or memory supports.

Consider the case of decision analysis, as an example of what *not* restricting oneself to "same" experiences may do. In decision analysis one is interested in comparing and evaluating alternative plans for action. For each plan one needs data: possible consequences, probability estimates and evaluative statements about whether or not the decision-maker likes the consequences (Vlek, Stallen, 1980). In the traditional situation these data are collected to start a process of reduction: to find out what is "shared" and "the same" in the experiences of some people (e.g. experts, or participants in the decision-making process). The more "shared" the data are, the better (or "harder", or more valid) the data are believed to be – and hence the better able to support the decision-making. The "sharing" is thought possible and necessary due to something "real" in reality, of which the various experiences of people may be mere glimpses. In the sharing these glimpses are then supposed to be pieced together, to form a "decision support system".

But what when there is no such "real" thing in reality, to guide the piecing together, when nothing more than something accidental is involved? Then the sharing is no longer a guarantee for quality – even though the experiences of the various people involved may be still relevant to improve the decision-making. In this case a sensible decision support system must be built on different lines than those of "sharing", of "sameness". It may be like the ones developed by Humphreys, 1980; Pearl *et al.*, 1980. In these systems the decision-maker him- or herself is asked to state alternatives, preferences and probabilities – and these are then repeatedly checked for consistency and completeness ("is this all; would you like to reconsider . . ."). Thus the support system here in principle is empty (although it will record what is happening). It can help however in selecting parts of the experiences of a particular decision-maker. What is important is to find the experiences that help the decision-maker to choose the alternatives that are preferable – not in a general sense, but in terms of what is relevant to a particular context. Hence, nothing of "sameness" or of "sharing" is implied. Only if the system is used by someone else, he or she may use what experiences have been recorded, but there is no need to consider looking for similarities or "samenesses", in relation to the previous user. In the case of this type of decision support system it is therefore the process of cutting and selecting in a particular person's experiences that is supposed to help the decision-maker's activity – not the piecing together of general experiences to get at some part of reality that could be separated and independently described. This alternative decision support system therefore is indeed based on using all kinds of experience, not only "knowledge" in the traditional sense.

Such less restricted cutting and selecting in (general) experiences is meanwhile producing something that practically also may be called knowledge. For indeed, one is helped to approach X (or X′, if one wants), implying the use of something like knowledge; knowledge of a more general type than is usually accepted as such. It was and is my claim that this generalized concept of knowledge and the precepts that derive from it will be of help in overcoming most or all of the 2nd order difficulties of systems analysis. I have now tried to indicate more precisely what the proposed generalization means; later I will argue the claim itself somewhat more technically.

ENLARGEMENT. MORE EXAMPLES

One will realize that this generalization does not relate to the cutting into parts itself, but to what the cutting is relative to, respectively to what the quality of what results is required to be. For example, in research based on the predictive cycle most cuttings (of experience) are rejected as not fitting the general criterion of being the "same", and fitting "reality". One may therefore call this type of cutting "cutting relative to reality". In my generalization one is also cutting relative to experience. But one would reject cuttings only when their realization would have *no influence* on the improvement of activities – when they provide no support to improvement. But cuttings that have this improvement-property will have the effect of changing experiences, i.e. of becoming part of the latter while being experienced (as opposed to a situation where what matters are experiences of what is independent – in reality – from the user; i.e. "same" experiences). One would therefore like to call this type of cutting "relative to experience".

Such experience may be the whole existing conglomerate of experiences, as it is stored via individual brains, or via streets, schools, rituals; i.e. everything that may be changing and be partly ephemeral, not only that which may have some permanency over time, the "real". It should be clear of course, that cuttings relative to experience and relative to reality may overlap, one being the generalization of the other. The boundary between the two itself however is variable (this boundary is also the result of a cutting, of course; it is an example of cutting relative to experience).

To make these ideas more concrete one may think of the following. Suppose one wants to climb to the top of a mountain. To do so well, one might want to have a support system, in this case a description of the mountain area (map) – i.e. a valid description of a fixed part of reality (the result of cutting relative to reality). Plans will be made and evaluated on the basis of this "knowledge". On the other hand, one also simply might want "to have a go at it" – to go ahead and to learn as one goes along. The support system now may consist of a set of rules: to observe certain things, and then to act in a certain way (check which direction is upward from where you are now; take that direction . . .). These rules imply a cutting relative to the existing, as one experiences it over time; where one is, what can be seen. The observations provide the changing content of the support system.

The latter approach is based on the more general concept of knowledge. This concept in effect implies the former, exemplified in the idea of a map. For, if continuously taking account of the existing leads to building up a map, the two approaches are similar. This applies even when the situation arises where there are local maxima in the mountain. The point of course then is that such differences between the approaches can only be detected if one has a map – and thus already has selected a fixed part of reality (a mountain with a top, to which other tops can be defined as local maxima). But the latter cutting itself depends on experience – and thus actually is a case of cutting relative to experience.

It should be noted that these two types of approaches can be recognized in many of the formal systems that nowadays are in use to change or improve activities. For example, there are various types of statistical support systems to improve choice, e.g. in research. One of them is the well-known Neyman–Pearson approach for hypothesis testing. This is a formal system, the primitives of which must be identified anew for each choice situation. One of these primitives is the concept of "population", requiring identification of a certain part of reality. The concept of population thus cuts up relative to the real (its position is analogous to that of the concept of a map, in the paragraph above – summarizing what is known, in the traditional sense). Another type of approach is the less well-known Bayesian support system for induction. Here one bases oneself on a rule to review probabilities, i.e. a rule to change the existing representation of one's experience in terms of beliefs or probabilities. In this case we deal with a cutting up relative to experience, the cutting being the recognition of certain new events or experiences as relevant to the change in beliefs. The Bayesian system is especially geared to the use of such relevant experiences, from step to step, i.e. contextually. It does not imply any traditional "knowledge", like what is represented in the idea of a population, to which one has to relate. But it does imply the possibility of improving one's actions by using (some) experiences, as one goes along. A similar example may be found in the interpretation of probability itself – either frequentistic (cutting relative to the real) or subjective (cutting relative to experience); see Phillips, 1973.

In other support systems the two approaches may be recognized too (traditional measurement versus contextual measurement, etc.). But there are also mixtures. Consider for example the rituals of any religion, or society. Clearly, these may serve to cut up experience for individuals, for them to be morally or conventionally "good" and thus to act better. But the rituals or behaviour rules themselves usually are claimed to cut up relative to reality (to be based on the "real and living god", "social reality", etc.). This mixture of claims presumably arises out of the need to justify the rituals and rules somehow "externally". We do not need to consider such mixtures here.

Using experience in the sense of the more general approach may be called the process of "experiential redesign". For indeed, the cutting up involves a process of redesigning. One tries to find, design and construct new experiences on the basis of earlier experiences, better suited to support what one is doing.

Methods for such experiential redesign can be exemplified as follows. Suppose that one wants to improve an organization (be it a small one, or a large one) – i.e. make it possible for the organization (as such) to do its work better, and at the same time to justify the value of that (improved) work. Let us assume this is the type of X', one would like people to help approach.

As a first step one would have to organize the activities of the helper (the "you", who wants to help the organization) into those of a researcher. The latter's activities should become the desired support system. As a second step one can take one of the individuals in the organization, and analyse what he or she is doing. The analysis may involve listing activities and how they hang together (as one possibility of a method for redesign). For example, two such activities may be "therapy" and "administration", partly coupled to each other. As a third step the researcher may try to find procedures (suggestions, rules), to change some or most of these couplings between activities. Such a procedure might be: "get more administrative help", or "let the client do the administration by having him or her fill out forms", or "get a different representation of the data necessary for administration". Such procedures would of course change the relation of "therapy" and "administration", for those involved (and of course lead to new experiences).

The procedures may be thought up by the chosen individual, or by the researcher. The source for ideas, concerning possible procedures is free to choose. But in all cases the procedures should be checked, in terms of the extra quality they may provide. The checking involves two parts. First the individual can be asked to indicate which procedure(s) have the most positive (and fewest negative) effects on his or her own work and activities, i.e. which recouple and help reformulate those activities, with most positive consequences in terms of his or her own quality criteria (which can be left implicit), and least negatively on other people's (presumed) criteria (the latter criterion is introduced for various reasons: one of them to guarantee that positive effects will not be endangered via the defensive actions of the negatively affected). The individual's experience here is used as a control. The second type of checking is done by selecting a second individual, and asking him or her similarly to indicate which of the now available procedures is most helpful for the redesign of their own activities, and least harmful for those of others in the organization and possibly outside of it. The second individual may moreover be a source for new procedures, like the first, to be checked in the same way (by a third individual, etc.). And so on, with other individuals, a procedure possibly leading even outside the organization (Van Bercum *et al.*, 1979).

In practical situations of course the above procedure still requires some problems to be solved. It is not a recipe. For example, I talk here about "individuals", but also some more general sub-systems of the organization may be taken as "individuals" (e.g. "the administration", "the clients"). A choice must be made. Similarly, an appropriate aggregation level has to be found for the list of activities: one might prefer to have not more than some 15. Also the number of "individuals" whose experience is used as checks or as sources is a point for debate. In principle of course there is no limit to this number. But there are practical limits: time, manpower, administrative ability. Hence, the constructing and checking should be designed so as to help the individuals interviewed start their intended improvements promptly – thereby making it possible for others also to start thinking about change. This will imply designing an amplification of the improvements in the original group or organization. In this way the whole structure of the organization involved, seen as the (formal) link between individuals' activities and those of their collectives may start to change in the desired direction, triggered by the researcher (as a support system for using and providing experience, relevant for the research activity).

The main reason for giving this example is not this plethora of practical difficulties, of course. It is to point out the following:

(a) The activities of the individuals are based on, and therefore represent, their experience – in terms of their interactions with the organization and with other individuals.

(b) The new procedures are designed to change this experience (and its various memory supports), and to use the effects of such changes as further stimuli for change (with other individuals or activities). This is what systematic "experiential redesign" implies.

(c) The new procedures are meant to help realizing improvements, both in terms of different individual quality criteria, as well as in terms of the relation between those criteria. That is, if one individual would try to improve on his or her own criteria via the procedure(s), then that activity itself should help others to improve – and vice versa.

(d) The researcher is seen here to be a "change support" (similar to the system for questioning and answering for decision-makers; Humphreys, 1980). He or she must initiate (part of) the construction and checking of changes (that is he or she is providing Y's, for X's – to use an earlier terminology). But in principle that is all done by the participants in the change process themselves. The checking and constructing therefore is *in vivo*. It helps participants to be better able to overcome difficulties, which are due to the way their experience is organized in the first place.

As already suggested, there will be other ways of "cutting relative to experience" to start an "experiential redesign" process – apart from changing the couplings of activities (as above), or from having people express their own preferences and probabilities (as in the decision support system). After the examples given these may be easily surmised. One can think for example of redesigning the stories that people tell about themselves, in their relation to others (Van den Berge *et al.*, 1980). Or of redesigning what everyone sees of what others are doing (changing control structures). Or one can also think of redesigning streets and public places, so as to make different uses of experience possible (architects are not yet very good at this, although they want to and do sometimes succeed; Zeisel, 1981). Designing new laws to support improved activities (not restrain them) would similarly be an example of "experiential redesign", in the jurisdictional domain.

TECHNICAL MATTERS: ROUNDING UP

In the previous paragraphs I took time to develop the idea of "cutting relative to experience", as a generalization of the more traditional "cutting relative to reality". In a concrete form this generalization would lead to looking for "experiential redesign", as a process of inquiry. And I claimed that this process of experiential redesign is particularly useful in overcoming the 2nd order difficulties of "straight" systems analysis (as formulated in problems A to E). Let me now briefly develop why I hold this claim. While doing so I will raise some related, more technical points. I will follow the previous order of presentation. That is, point A′ is akin to 2nd order problem A, etc.

A′. In the process of experiential redesign two things (should) happen; one is that participants in the process of inquiry are redesigning their own experiences (and the support systems for those); the other is that at the same time they should be providing themselves with more options for choice – choice in terms of new alternative actions (the increased possibility for such choice is the improvement). Both changes imply that the participants are now more or less forced to heed the research process of the systems analysts and their results. For the changes are now more or less their own doing and their own responsibility. Among the participants must be the policy-maker(s), and/or the research contractor(s). Thus the result of the study now actually can be designed so as to be listened to by such policy-makers.

B'. In most practical situations the policy-maker is not the only "problem owner". There will be many others, like when a policy-maker wants to do something about drug abuse, or about enlarging an airfield: due to the activities of the policy-makers (and others) the peddlers may become problem owners (if they are not already), as may the drug-users, or the environmentalists, etc. Usually one can not say that there is "a deeper problem" or dominant problem, covering the problems of all these problem owners. Thus one will have to solve all such problems at the same time, vicariously. The 2nd order problem however seems to derive from the assumption that one can only solve such a dominant problem. What is eventually taken as such will always fall short, when there is no such dominant problem. According to my proposal this difficulty is overcome by providing some suggestions that may help any problem owner, even future ones, to solve one's own problem, by helping one another. The researcher hence is no longer "the" problem solver (via inquiry) for the dominant problem, formulated by the research contractor – but is actually one of the many problem owners, only with the (special) task of finding something to make overcoming everyone's difficulties easier. This implies that each problem owners' own resources and creativity (and experience) are taken as context and used – and not neglected (as is usual in inquiry). And that again implies that the researcher actually looks for procedures (Y) that leave intact any relation between X and X' (what policy-makers want and what others want), and even will strengthen such relations, when positively conjugated. This relation thus may be left implicit, but it surely is not neglected (see problem B). As a further clarification we may also refer to a frequently used formulation in the social sciences: if one would collect "what people need", and would then try to find something to satisfy those needs, one is not solving all problems "at the same time", as I suggested is necessary to prevent one problem to become dominant (e.g. of one powerful problem owner). In our proposal such an "inventarization of needs" is never necessary. That is the desired improvement (on the 2nd order level).

C'. The results of a process of inquiry (in the sense of my proposal) will consist of rules and of plans for procedures (as "empty support systems; see earlier). These will not always be abstract, in the sense that they will be implemented only later, after the study is done. Most times the implementation starts directly, with the participating individuals and during inquiry. Even then results can be formulated as rules and plans: direct changes in the way one does things. Thus the results may indeed be of the general form of plans or suggestions.

Such suggestions by the way sometimes are also arrived at via the other process: cutting relative to reality. The idea then is to separate some part of reality and to indicate its possible variations, given variations outside that part. The latter usually are expressed as A (antecedents), the former as C (consequents) – and the relation between the variations as statements or propositions like "If A, then C", or "the more A, the more C", etc. After that, if one wants a suggestion for improvement one specifies the desired C, and the resulting suggestion then follows directly: change A to the level, appropriate to the desired C. The 2nd order difficulties of course stem from the necessary separation not being possible, nor the inversion of the statement therefore. I mention this type of thinking again, to try and say something about the general form of results when "experientially redesigning".

For surely this form will not be something like "under conditions B, do D", as might be expected in analogy to "If A, then C" (and is often accepted). For I stressed earlier the context dependency of advices – and "conditions" of course serve more as a fossilized context, than as a context. What may be expected in terms of the form of advices seems more like "If you want to be able to do more than you do now, do E"; where "more" is defined in terms of participants' own quality criteria. In particular cases this form may become somewhat paradoxical or contradictory: "If you want to do F, do not do F" (or even to "..., do the reverse of F"). This latter type of advice may apply when one temporarily should desist from doing F, as when continuation of doing F itself would obstruct doing F. A simple example can be found in an advice to improve on present running ("take a rest, in order to run better later"). Another example would be to go in the reverse direction of where one wants to go – in order to be better able to jump across (e.g.) a crevice. These changes indeed imply having knowledge – but of the more general form, as indicated.

The next point to be considered is the concept of "generalization", as the quality criterion for (good) knowledge. In the more standard interpretation "generalization" is used to indicate that one wants to find the outmost boundaries of that part of reality where a certain description may apply. Thus one will try to insure to be able to change A's (in sentences like "If A, then C"), in a range of situations as wide as possible. But when we try to "cut relative to experience" the concept of generalization must mean something else: to find procedures for experiential redesign, such that even distant participants will experience its power of improvement. By "distant participants" I mean for example people not yet born, or not as yet a client of an organization, or not yet a user of certain services. This seems to be a difficult quality criterion. Can one actually find suggestions for improvement, generated in this sense? The answer is yes: we already have many of such plans or procedures. One is for example embodied in the concept of plane geometry, one in that of the formal theory of decision-making, one in that of statistical inference – each of which "theories" may serve as improvement supports, even for distant participants (as far as we know up till now). Another such procedure is embodied in the use of a bicycle: to take it and use it implies a suggestion for experiential redesign in terms of muscle movements. This redesign will work for all kinds of distant participants.

These (generalized) procedures or suggestions indeed will help overcome the 2nd order difficulty considered here: of not controlling what is taken to be the partitioning of reality, nor of the precise type of quality increase that follows. In the approach suggested here this is made into an asset: procedures should have different supporting effects for different participants.

D'. When one assumes that problems must and can be solved directly, it easily follows that one should do so wherever they occur. For if not, solving a problem may also have all kinds of effects elsewhere, even unpleasant ones (as follows from the fact that one can also solve somewhere else). But it was argued earlier that such direct solutions will in principle not be possible (due to the restricted usefulness of cutting relative to reality; hence the 2nd order problem). From that derives the need to look for "entrances", weak spots not necessarily directly related to the problematic area, where small changes will have larger effects in the attack on the problems. This need can be satisfied via the proposed design: finding such weak spots (different from where problems occur) can be made part of the interaction with the chosen individuals. For example, looking for possible changes in the couplings of activities implies that such couplings are seen as the desired weak spots. Similarly, weak spots also presumably may be found in the "visibility" between activities, or in the stories that give meaning and form to activities, or in the consistency and completeness of what one may use as experience relevant for improved decision-making, etc.

E'. To help gather knowledge in the usual way, so a policy-maker may be better able to choose (to get X), implies restricting oneself to what that policy-maker thinks is important. That will have several drawbacks: among them the ones mentioned under D'. What is necessary therefore is to be able to step out of the implied problem area – to leave the definition of where to look for a suitable "entrance" to the participants. This then will introduce the possibility of some increased revolutionary power, in the sense of changes with widely distributed positive effects. Examples of changes with high revolutionary power are the introduction of the Arabic notation for numbers, the introduction of bicycles, etc.

One can distinguish several procedures or plans to attach at least some revolutionary power to the results of inquiry (without fully guaranteeing its acquisition, of course):

(a) one tries to identify an area or system (as "entrance", see D′), aspects of which one can describe as a formal system (i.e. a set of axioms and primitives). Such formal systems are not always easy to recognize. In fact however, the usual procedure for research and inquiry is geared to finding such formal systems as descriptions of the identified area. This procedure therefore will help, even though of course it is usually not meant for what here we want to use it for. The idea then is first to find such a formal system, and second to find one that is equivalent to the one found in the first place, but having some other properties too. One then replaces the earlier system by the latter – as was done with the Roman and Arabic notations mentioned above (equivalent, but implying different computational structures). This type of replacement may introduce results with strong revolutionary power. One should note that we deal here only with partial replacements, replacements of (temporarily) identified subparts of the experience of participants (via cutting relative to experience).

(b) one first tries to find what it is that maintains some area or part of reality, *as if* it were a fixed subpart of reality (and not of experience); we call such maintained partitioning organizational closure (Pask, 1978). For example, what is it that holds together an organization (and prevents deviations), or what is it that maintains a committee, or that maintains a policy-maker in his or her position, etc., as an identifiable entity? To change and improve in the case of organizational closure one may try to mobilize such maintenance procedures – to use their power. One may for example introduce conflicting demands or set up random sequences of threats to a self-maintained identity. These will tax the maintenance procedures – and may lead to a change in them. Thus one helps such an identity to grow (to be more robust), which again may help users of what one tries to change, to be better able to do better what they are doing, or to choose what they want to do.

There are others, of such general procedures, to increase revolutionary power. The ones formulated above however should satisfy as examples.

The points A′ to E′ summarize my arguments for the claim as to why "cutting relative to experience" may be preferable to "cutting relative to reality", when it comes to solving so called real world problems in a social setting, with a minimum of 2nd order difficulties. They also are meant to elucidate some technical points – like those involved in questions about the form of knowledge, about revolutionary power, about generalization and the like.

MULTIPLE POINTS OF VIEW

It is one of the miraculous phenomena of human life that people indeed are able to design activities that are much better (in a variety of senses) than anything they have done before. Research as it was developed for example in the European Renaissance did indeed give power and truth to anyone with eyes to see and wisdom to interpret. Systems analysis later on did point out some of the bad parts that arose out of the very strength of such research. Ah, and there we have one of the strange phenomena of human life: whatever one designs, in the end its very qualities may turn it into a hindrance, into an obstacle, because valued. Research even as it was redesigned again and again shares this same fate. I have tried to show this via the enumeration of some second order difficulties, when trying to do research to help improve on social functioning.

If this phenomenon – the thing itself becoming a danger to the thing – is so widespread, what can we do about it? And indeed, is there something to do about it? Can it be changed or prevented?

Presumably not; there are some good reasons for that negative answer. But it seems we do have the ability to ameliorate its consequences, at least as far as research to support social change is concerned. In the paper I restricted myself to the problem of amelioration and presented a design for such research, and a justification.

The justification hinges mainly on the said phenomenon itself. Nothing should be accepted as given, but all as produced by the past in some kind of jumping out act. That jumping out is the basis of our ability to see drawbacks to what exists and is valued, to see that strange phenomenon; and it can therefore also be the basis for improvement – the old becoming part of the new and supporting it, not being replaced by it. Thus this jumping out – formulated as particular type of cutting relative to experience – was built into the research method presented. This is why the method can be argued to have less of those curious negative side-effects most good designs introduce. The weakness is used to become more like a strength.

Another way of formulating this would be to say that such second order difficulties stem for the most part from assuming the existence of a preferred point of view: from it the world presumably can be seen as it is (objectively, validly, etc.). When such a point of view however turns out to be produced rather than appears to exist, other points of view become equally valid. Thus, as I indicated in the beginning of the paper, the researcher actually designs himself not to be listened to when he or she assumes such a preferred point of view. It is only when he or she becomes a real opponent that something may happen – but that implies taking the politicians' point of view seriously, and indeed admitting multiple and parallel points of view for all the actors concerned. The researcher thus becomes only one of the observers, and has to behave accordingly to have any effect. The researcher cannot take on the role of a super-observer.

I have tried to show that this very multiplicity of points of view does not mean the end of serious science. But it does mean the implementation of research methods that base themselves on this multiplicity – on the fact that there is no clear reason for assuming some "final" goal for humanity, some "underlying" and objective world similar for all individuals, some single "best" utopia where we will all know it all. The proposed research method implies that the world is produced by itself in all its variety, and that therefore some preferred productions (preferred from many different points of view) can be helped to come into existence, via the production process itself.

The method considered has been used extensively by me, and thus has grown in scope and precision. I have tried to sketch some of this. But my main aim in this chapter is to demonstrate that there are some inherent defects to all that is good, and that even so these still may be overcome. To find (other) ways to do so seems to me to be the main challenge for systems analysts, especially when interested in practical change, supported by research – more of a challenge than designing something that is (only) good.

REFERENCES

Bercum, F. van, W. Houwing, J. Vermeulen and H. van der Zaken (1979) Onderzoek in het Dercksencentrum. Memo I.W.A., University of Amsterdam.
Berge, F. van den, W. Bossewinkel, S. Groenewold, M. Muis and H. Wildschut (1980) Flikkers en agressie. Memo I.W.A., University of Amsterdam.
Bemelmans, T. M. A. and J. G. de Boer (1981) Ontwikkelingsmethoden I. Het ontwikkelen van informatiesystemen. *Informatica* 23/2, 67–76.
Churchman, W. (1980) *The systems approach and its enemies*. Basic Books, New York.
Groen, P., A. Kersten and G. de Zeeuw (1980) *Beter sociaal veranderen. Een onderzoeksaanpak.* Coutinho, Muiderberg.
Humphreys, P. and W. McFadden (1980) Experiences with MAUD: aiding decision structuring versus bootstrapping the decision maker. *Acta Psychologica* 45/1–3, 273–301.
Jungermann, H., G. de Zeeuw (eds) (1977) *Decision making and change in human affairs*. Reidel, Dordrecht.
Pask, G. (1978) "Against conferences" or "The poverty of reduction in Sopscience and Pop-systems". In: R. Ericson (ed.), *Silver Anniversary Meeting SGSR 1978*, SGSR, Washington.
Pearl, J., A. Leal and J. Saleh (1980) GODDESS: a goal-directed decision structuring system. Memo UCLA-ENG-CSL-8034, Los Angeles.
Quade, E. S. and H. J. Miser (1980) The concept, nature and use of systems analysis. Working Paper WP-80-58, IIASA, Laxenburg, Austria.
Schilpp, P. A. (1940) *The philosophy of George Santayana*. Open Court, La Salle.
Vlek, C. A. J. and P. J. Stallen (1980) Rational and personal aspects of risk. *Acta Psychologica* 45/1–3, 273–301.
Zeeuw, G. de (1981a) Philosophy of change. In: R. Trappl (ed.), *Proc. of the 5th Intern. Meeting on Cyb. and Systems Res.* Hemisphere Publ. Cy, Washington.
Zeeuw, G. de (1981b) Speeding up improvement. In: G. Lasker (ed.), *Proc. Quality of life and how to improve it* (Acapulco).

13

Rethinking the Process of Systems Analysis and Operational Research: From Practice to Precept – and Back Again

ROLFE TOMLINSON

INTRODUCTION

There is an old saying "You should practise what you preach" – which is sometimes stated in more formal language "From precept to practice". It implies, not only that what we do should be determined by our philosophy and our beliefs, but also that we should develop and state those beliefs with a view to their application.

In the early days of systems analysis and operational research this approach was very much adopted. A set of precepts were taken over from the natural sciences and adapted as guidelines for the practice of ORASA (Operational Research and Applied Systems Analysis). Some deviation from the ideal was necessary, of course, but this was at first seen as a departure from perfection, inevitable in an imperfect world – but not giving cause to question the basic thesis. Only gradually did it appear that the discrepancies were so great that doubts needed to be cast on the precepts, not on the practice. There had been many saying this from the 1960s on, but it was a long time before it was realized that these statements were more than the sour grapes of curmudgeonly old men. It was in the light of this that in reviewing the state of OR and Systems Analysis for the Royal Society in 1977, I took as my title "From Practice to Precept".[1] The time had come, I suggested, to take a look at successful practice having removed the scales over our eyes imposed by inappropriate precept. We needed to examine what is really happening – and restate appropriate precepts in the light of good practice.

This rethinking process has been going on in most countries which have seriously attempted to make use of ORASA as an aid to policy development

205

and organizational decision-making. Discussions in line with those held in the IIASA seminar have recently taken place, e.g. in the Methodology Working Group of the European Association of OR Societies. Although the experiences and approaches used vary greatly, there is extraordinary agreement with regard to the main conclusions. The reformulation of our precepts – our beliefs and ideals – is not a matter of simple academic interest. It has the deeper purpose of improving the general practice of the subject – a development that is now possible because we have a firmer, more systematic, philosophical foundation. No longer need we be defensive about apparent departures from precept. At last, we should be able to train newcomers to the subject as it is, and properly advise them as to the means of achieving effectiveness. The circle is complete – from practice to precept, and back again!

This final chapter, then, examines the practical implications of what was said in the seminar, what was learnt by those present, and what can be passed on to others. There is something here for all the actors involved in ORASA; not just practitioners, but also for their clients, for those who teach and for those who do research.

Before we go on to discuss the likely impact of these ideas on the various actors concerned, it may be helpful to set out what seem to be some of the most important practical points that came out of the discussion.[2] They are not prescriptions. The wheel which has now turned once, will turn many times before we can be prescriptive about the subject. Indeed, its very nature makes prescription almost impossible. But already we believe that the ideas stated here can, and do, change practice.

1. The need to understand the *nature* of the system that is the subject of study. In particular the analyst should be aware of the aspirations of, and the demands placed upon, the human actors in the system, whether they are involved directly or indirectly.
2. The need to understand that if the analyst's work is to be of value, he will be *intervening* in this sytem, and indeed, become an element within it.
3. The need to explore the *"hidden assumptions"* which underlie both the analyst's approach and the systems response.
4. The need to develop an awareness of *"process"* both in organizational decision-making and in the analysis, and the importance of the interaction between the two.
5. The need to understand the ways in which *change* can take place, and that in most cases the analyst has to be content with "change for the better" rather than "change to the best" – if indeed that latter phrase has any meaning at all.

Many practitioners may claim that they already take these factors fully into account – some certainly do. Since we have developed our arguments from good practice it could hardly be otherwise. We are saying that if we accept these factors as part of the fundamental structure of the subject, rather than seeing them as departures from the "pure" methods of science, there will follow certain basic changes in practice, in the attitude and behaviour of our clients, in our teaching, and in our research. Let us now examine each in turn.

IMPLICATIONS FOR THE PRACTITIONER

In the traditional image of scientific research, the practitioner is a god-like creature, remote and separate from the world of things and artefacts that he observes and experiments with. He can be, indeed must be, totally objective; the answers he produces are "right" in an absolute sense. If he has to descend from this god-like position in order to "sell" his product, it may affect his personal integrity but should not modify the "rightness" of his results. He will certainly receive little professional praise for such activity, even though it may be accepted as necessary. In this tradition the ORASA worker would be logical and dispassionate, developing coherent hypotheses based on verifiable data of known precision which he has subjected to critical validation. His work will be openly available for criticism by his peers, who will be as logical and dispassionate as himself.

The reality as we now see it is very different, and at first sight it may appear that every one of the foundation stones of the scientific tradition on which the ORASA scientist has tried to build his career is broken or despoiled. Indeed, if the classical scientific paradigm were retained, it would be possible to view the discussions on which this book is based as an attempted justification of failure. That would be wrong and totally misleading. On the contrary, the concepts are based on success – the real failure against which it is directed is a failure of theory, not practice. There have been failures in practice, of course,[3] for the same reasons that there are failures in all forms of activity. There is nothing in the nature of the trained ORASA worker that guarantees his or her freedom from human failings such as incompetence, inexperience, over-confidence, intolerance and incomprehension. Starting from success, however, we have identified those elements that successful practitioners have known to be important, and then fitted them into a general methodological framework which enables us to identify *why* certain factors are important. Only from this basis can we develop our methodology.

Perhaps the key word in this whole question of rethinking is "process".[4] Instead of visualizing the problem situation as static and unchanging, we must understand it as dynamic. If the work is related to organizational decision-making, it is necessary to understand that in any living organization there are frequent changes in the personnel, developments of opinion, changes in the environment, changes in policy. Thus the analyst has to be aware of the organizational process – the actors, the pressures to which they react, the information they receive and the channels through which it comes, and the actual processes by which discussions take place and ideas are codified. In particular a good deal more attention needs to be paid to the structure of information, its accessibility and its point of entry into the process of decision.

These factors may seem relatively unimportant when the study is of an apparently more abstract nature directed towards public policy. But this is not so; opinion develops over time and a variety of political processes are inevitably going on. The analyst who works in ignorance of the "process" underlying public decision-making is in turn in serious danger of being ignored by that "process" when his report is available.

Equally, attention needs to be paid to the process of investigation. Too often this is described in sequential terms, involving the successive major steps of problem definition, data collection and verification, model building and verification, solution formulation, and implementation. When this simple description is found to be unsatisfactory, reality is approximated by introducing multiple feedback loops – to allow for problem redefinition, reformulation of models, etc. etc. Although, in theory, this apparently enables one to reconstruct any actual process of investigation, I can no longer believe that it is an adequate representation of the ORASA process, (anymore than I can believe that a sinusoidal oscillation, as the amplitude and wave lengths reduce to zero, approximates satisfactorily to a straight line). To understand the ORASA process we need to restructure our thinking. For any study that is not of a standard format – and it could be argued that ORASA workers are not, by definition, concerned with standard format problems – the approach is akin to that of the climber traversing new ground through the process of trial and error,[5] whereas classical science tends to describe his work as if he has a map on which he can plot an optimum path. The analogy cannot be taken too far, since the analyst will have additional sightings beyond those he can acquire from his own experience (some of which will, of course, be wrong). But the investigation does need to be seen as a journey based on the analyst's understandings and the perceptions that develop as he proceeds. And of course we must assume that he possesses a compass to check direction.

The question then follows – what compass? The IIASA seminar had a subsidiary title "The Hidden Assumptions of Systems Analysis" which is extremely relevant to the question. If the assumptions, whether of the analyst or the decision-maker, remain "hidden" the analyst's "compass" is likely to prove a dangerous and defective instrument. Indeed, the development of an adequate compass is one of the first and major steps that the investigator must undertake. He cannot do it on his own, away – to maintain the analogy – from the mountain. The only way to develop and test the compass is in the field by interaction between the analyst and those involved in the organizational process. But interaction at a single point in place or time is not adequate. Testing has to be continuous – for things change with place, within the organization, and with time. We must therefore think of the interaction itself as a shared process common to the organizational process and the analytical process. It is as a result of this interactive process that the manager can acquire the understanding that makes it possible for effective implementation to take place, because the organization believes itself to be adopting its own solution. Incidentally, when we talk in these terms we find the analyst very much involved in implementation; he cannot reject it as a "managerial responsibility". But this concept of implementation is very different from the "salesman" concept which implies that the organizational world and analytical world are separate, and that the solution is an "analytical" solution (based on the hidden assumptions of analysis) which has to be foisted on to the organizational world (with its different, and often contrary, assumptions).

However, even though the new approach rejects the reductionist, sequential approach associated with classical scientific methodology, the elements used to describe the classical process do have reality. Problems do have to be formulated, data collected and analysed, models built and verified, and solutions formulated and implemented. Skills have to be developed in them all. But that is how they should be considered; as skills (i.e. elements of human ability) to be drawn upon as required, rather than a formally structured foundation to the investigational process. Seen in this light, the mathematical methods of operational research and systems analysis constitute one important part of the set of tools that have to be mastered in the development of a skill. Let us then look at these four essential skills and determine how our understanding and practice of them should be modified by our rethinking.

Let us start with problem formulation. Classical statements of ORASA imply that the problem must be clearly defined in any study – in organizational language we refer to "terms of reference". We can accept, as we must,[6] that there are many ways in which a problem can be formulated – depending on the analyst and the internal and external environment at the time of study – without altering this fundamental requirement. Nevertheless, the results displayed during the seminar force us to modify even this simple requirement. The first step in formulating a problem is to identify the problem owner. But in real life situations we often find that there are many problem owners, owning different, though overlapping, problems – all of which have to be solved to some degree if the problem of the principal problem owner is to be satisfactorily dealt with. At first sight this simply appears to be a matter of optimization under multi-objectives. But the dynamics of the relationships involved and the conflicting nature of the objectives, as well as their fuzzy definition, lead us realistically to a more sophisticated appreciation of the problem situation. From the search for optimization, we move to a search for feasibility and for improvement. But what is "improvement"? The danger here is that in operationalizing "improvement" the analyst is likely to do this using his own, sometimes hidden, assumptions. In fact, if one looks realistically at many apparent ORASA successes, e.g. in the field of stock individual problems was diverse, and that peer criticism was doubly effective since the critics did not share the same hidden assumptions as the investigators. Although this interdisciplinary approach has remained an ideal, the need for some formal training in ORASA has tended towards a more uniform mode of thinking and approach. It is now possible to see this as a danger, which will be increased rather than overcome by agreeing on a common formal approach to the formulation of problems and the conduct of investigations. The development of any science depends upon original thinking, and this is most easily done by drawing into the subject people from many different educational backgrounds and with varying experience. Peer criticism should be the prime means of ensuring horizontal thinking. Indeed the question remains as to how far an isolated ORASA worker, without benefit of divergent peer criticism, can maintain effectiveness. Nevertheless, if the peers speak too much with one voice, they can have the reverse effect. (Many see this as the basic failure of the "professions".)

To return to the main issue, the new thinking forces us to realize that problem formulation is not only complex and imprecise, but that it depends to some extent on time and on the information available. It may be possible to define the problem adequately only at the end of a study. This means that the investigator needs to exercise particular care in defining his original terms of reference, and then in making sure that the client's requirements (and his own) do not alter significantly during, and as a result of, the study. Terms of reference are not intended to be a safety barrier between the analyst and reality.

We now come to the question of data. The accepted precepts of the ORASA worker relating to data collection and analysis have been those of the statistician. There is a search for quantification, a concern with reliability of sources, an insistence on measuring uncertainty – all these, combined with a realistic understanding that data will never be perfect, that there is a balance between cost and effectiveness, and that when the time comes the best advice must be given on the evidence available.

This, so far as it goes, is wholly admirable – and analysts who spend their time spinning models in the absence of data deserve the criticism they too seldom get. BUT, numerical data is only a small part of the data available to the ORASA worker. It is like the tip of the iceberg; however visible and even menacing the tip may appear to the layman, it is not the largest or most dangerous part of it. Similarly, although decisions may appear to be made on the basis of the visible, often economic, facts – acceptance and implementation will certainly depend on proper account having been taken of the hidden, qualitative, reality underlying the situation.

Statisticians are, of course, often aware of this hidden mass of data – particularly when it relates to human experience or belief. Bayesian statisticians, games theorists, decision analysts and others have worked hard to discover means by which such hidden data can be made visible and to develop a methodology whereby non-quantifiable factors can be inserted into numerical equations. This remains one of the most potentially exciting, but also potentially dangerous, areas for mathematical statisticians to extend the range of tools available to ORASA workers. The danger lies of course in the presumption that all usable data can be reduced to numerical form – or, conversely, that analysts can only use numerical data.

To a large extent this thinking joins up with what has been said in the previous section on problem formulation and objective setting. Just as the objectives of a study often cannot be set in the traditional multi-objective programming formulation, because of complexity, fuzziness and changing relationships, so the appropriate data cannot be confined in this way. We assume that concepts such as "efficiency" can be adequately described in numerical terms, but it may not always be possible. Certainly, we do not pay sufficient attention to "structure" and "process". Too many studies, and too much data collection, assume a static situation. Time and relationships create a dynamic situation that must be fed into the analyst's data bank. Even here, of course, quantification remains an important tool, but it is never sufficient. In particular, the interpretation of numbers in a dynamic system needs a deep understanding of the structure of the system. But it also requires an understanding of how that structure may change if some of the "hidden assumptions" alter.

We come now to the question of model building and verification. So many text books have been written on the subject that it might be thought that there is no more to say. For all the rethinking that is going on, the building of a model remains at the heart of the ORASA process, and is perhaps its most distinctive feature. But whereas, in classical theory, the importance of the model was the ability to undertake formal experiments and determine optima, it is now seen to be much more:

(i)   as providing an open statement of belief about structure and relevant relationships for discussion between interested parties, and

(ii) as an instrument for exploration, to answer "what-if?" questions.

Its importance lies much more in the ability to create understanding, and to suggest relationships, than in making numerical predictions.

The repercussions of such an approach are considerable, but they are not always obvious. In my experience, the changing awareness of this was related to a move from large optimization models in planning, towards small "what-if" models. But the question is not "big/small" or "optimization/simulation", nor even "hard/soft"! (where a "soft model" is one that makes use of qualitative relationships as well as quantitative ones). Increasingly the question is not "Which model?" or "How Large?", but rather "What should our modelling strategy be?". Some 20 years ago I was responsible for what appeared to be a straightforward linear programming problem at a chemicals plant. We started by working on weekly data, but the marketing people could not use our results because of short-term, day-to-day, capacity requirements and the production people said that they could not efficiently switch their plans as often as this. The work was never implemented because we could never find a single model that would adequately reconcile the two sets of requirements. With modern computer facilities, we might have steamrollered ourselves out of trouble, but in retrospect, we were looking at the wrong problem. There was no way that a single model could satisfy all the requirements. So, just as we have had to give up the idea of the single client with a single objective and a unique problem – just as we have had to give up the idea that all data is numerical and concerned with the state of the organization at a point in time – we must also give up the idea of a single model. We need mixes of models, some simple and some complex; some for the analyst and some for those in the organization. And the skill we need to acquire is not simply one of model classification and manipulation, but of modelling strategy – a very different skill.

Finally, we come to the question of solution formulation and implementation – a question that brings us to ask questions such as "What is a solution?" and "What do we mean by implementation?". How, in fact, do we judge the success of a study? Do the organization and the analyst have the same criteria? Should they? The only satisfactory definition of success must be very general in form. As a result of the analysis some changes should occur which is accepted by the "problem owner" as effective and beneficial. (Incidentally, this gets over the question of whether a recommendation "Do nothing" is change. It does not change action, but it does change attitudes and understanding.) Thus, a study of production control, in which the manager rejects a proposed computer support system but develops an improved understanding of the relative importance of different factors in the production process, thus enabling him to make changes leading to higher output, must be judged a success. Equally, a report on energy policy may have an initial impact on a government committee, but is unlikely to create a change in policy unless the study provides a link to action in the form of appropriate information and models which can enable the officials to translate ideas into practice. Because of this, it is impossible to separate the question of solution formulation from that of problem formulation. We have to remember that it is the owner of the problem that must own the solution, and if there are many problem owners the question of solution ownership will be equally complex. It hardly needs to be said that a mathematical formulation is not a solution formulation, and the bridging of the gap needs to be seen as part of the science of ORASA, not as an unscientific, demeaning addition to it.

At our seminar, the consensus of how this could be done was through involvement, and we shall be discussing some of the problems that arise from this in the next section of this chapter. Before we leave the practitioner, however, we need to say something about the ethical problems forced on him by this rethinking. As a substitute for the professional standards of behaviour followed by doctors, lawyers, etc. etc. the ORASA worker has tended to claim that he follows the "scientific" ethic – which in practice has meant two main things, objectivity and verifiability. It is difficult to reconcile these two factors with the processes described here (indeed, their validity for the scientific world as a whole is under criticism) but they should not be discarded too lightly. Both practitioners and their clients will demand something in their place, and perhaps we would do better to define more closely what we mean rather than try to invent some new concept.

Objectivity in the strict philosophical sense means a total lack of bias in undertaking the study and presenting the results. In this strict sense it is unattainable, for, even if they do not start with "assumptions", analysts inevitably develop a belief about their ideas and understanding in the course of the work and they certainly have to employ advocacy in getting those ideas accepted. The usual answer to this is that the analyst must at least "know himself" – and that he has also to explain his assumptions and uncertainties when reporting to his client. (It is not always realized that the client is not at all interested in what appears to be a process of self-justification and avoidance of responsibility.) More seriously, however, it is doubtful whether, in this strict sense, objectivity has any real meaning when dealing with a complex situation which has many problem owners. There is, for example, no way of presenting conflicting value judgements without implying relative values. In practice we find ourselves in a situation of "relative" objectivity. In my experience in the OR team in the National Coal Board, the stance taken by members of the team in a particular study would generally be strongly pro-National Coal Board (though not necessarily pro- a particular policy), and, less strongly, pro- the immediate client (in relation to some other level of authority in the Board). Yet one of the most frequent comments made on our work was its "objectivity". Relative to the problem owner we were able to take a birds-eye view of the problem, without being constrained by adherence to local policy or prejudice or from threats relating to promotion prospects, etc. Nevertheless, there were constraints upon us – we would not wish to offend the client unnecessarily, for fear we were not able to work for him again, nor would we lightly make a recommendation against declared HQ policy. So the idea of objectivity remains a desirable ideal – a guide for action to ensure that when a decision-maker acts on "objective" advice, the full consequences of that action are known to him, so far as they can be known. Legalistically and philosophically, therefore, objectivity may mean very little. In practice, objectivity remains a powerful guiding force, despite the inevitable partiality that arises in relation to the client's affairs and the advocacy that goes into the acceptance of a solution. Incidentally, even this qualified objectivity stands in contrast with other professional ethics. For example, most ORASA professionals would deny that the freedom of the legal advocate to suppress evidence in support of his case is available to the ORASA worker.

The question of verifiability is even more difficult to support in rigorous terms – it implies:

(i) open data, cross-checked,
(ii) a model in which every element has been verified and tested for sensitivity,
(iii) a rigorous checking of results against data independently collected.

When much of the data is drawn from people's statements rather than from checked documents; when many relationships are, at the most, good guesses; when the only people who can check on validity are the people who have assisted in developing the model – when all these occur – the rigorous concept of verifiability is quite inapplicable. But, in some broader sense, the concept of verifiability remains vital to general acceptability of the ORASA process. Data must be checked, even if it is based on opinion or personal observation. The model(s) must be open, and the main areas of sensitivity explored. There must be validity checking. Clients satisfaction is clearly essential for success, but client satisfaction may not be enough. The change must be for the better. In the classical concept, "better" could usually be equated with the minimization or maximization of a single index – cost, profit, journey time, etc. No longer. "Good" is a vector of many factors, some only qualitative, but we must have some means of judging the areas of progress and regress. The ORASA worker who does not concern himself with verifiability – deliberately offering himself to criticism both by his clients *and* his peers, is on a dangerous and slippery slope.

Because the process we have described started with practice, the statements set out above may not appear to be different from the best practice in operation today. Indeed, they are not. But they are very different from much that is undertaken in the *name* of ORASA, and it is to be hoped that increasingly practice will follow the guidelines laid down here. More importantly, the new focus provided by the rethinking process should encourage the practitioner to concentrate the attention of researchers to these points where progress needs most to be made. It could well be argued that the world does not so much need new solutions to old problems, as a new formulation of its problems.

IMPLICATIONS FOR OTHER ACTORS

The Client

Little attention has been given in the foregoing discussion to the major implications of these ideas for the client of an ORASA study, and to the changing behavioural patterns that they seem to demand. At first sight the new ideas might be expected to receive enthusiastic support from those involved in the decision-making processes, in ensuring that the work will be fully relevant, but they imply, *inter alia*, very different client-analyst relationships. It cannot be taken for granted that such change will be welcomed. In exploring this area systematically, we have to consider:

(i)   the compatibility of the proposed method of operation with the expectations of the (individual) clients involved,
(ii) the compatibility of the analytical process with the management or decision-making process of the organization concerned.

We shall first consider the individuals. Clearly the approaches that have been discussed involve a very different relationship between the client and analyst than exists in the "classical" situation. This change in relationship could well place a burden on the client's shoulders that he is not willing to bear. In the classical relationship the client would discuss the problem with the analyst, and give him access to relevant people and data sources. The analyst would then make a formal proposal setting out terms of reference, statements of resources required (notably money!) and a postulated completion data. The job would then be done and reported, with recommendations, in due time. In all this the client's position and relationships within his organization remains unaltered and unthreatened. He has neither associated himself with the results of the study, nor given up any of his authority. He may, without loss of face, accept all, some, or none of the recommendations. In the new relationship, postulated in the "rethought" analytical process, something quite different is proposed. It is now expected that the client (or some of the clients) will be involved at the problem-formulation stage, that he will be involved in the building and verification of models, and that he will take personal responsibility for the proposed decision. Can we seriously assume that he will be prepared to accept such a relationship, or indeed that he *should* be so prepared.

In the classical situation the analyst is clearly cast in the role of the "expert" — one who cannot be *contradicted*, within the very clearly-defined limits of his expertise, but who can be *ignored*, largely because his advice as an expert only carries weight within those clearly-defined limits. Thus the client can always claim that factors outside that expertise are over-riding! If he accepts this "expert" relationship the analyst places himself with the engineer, the doctor, the lawyer, the accountant — in the role of professional adviser. It is, of course, a role that has its compensations; e.g. it gives him the right to speak without responsibility for decision, and he can avoid the difficulties of serious problem formulation. On the client side, many managers and politicians would prefer that the relationship should be of that form. It is both a comfortable and familiar situation for them. Not the least advantage is the freedom to ignore advice that proposes action contrary to their wishes. The new situation implies a commitment from the beginning.

If the problem were to be posed in the form of such simple relationships, "rethought" ORASA would have no chance of success; the client would simply not be interested. However, the picture we have just given implies the grossly oversimplified assumption that decisions are taken by one man (or one client group) at a point of time, whereas an essential element in our rethinking has been an appreciation of the fact that we are dealing with *processes*, involving many problems involving different problem owners, each with their own attendant decision-making processes. The unitary client becomes a complex "client-system".

One of the major difficulties that may arise is the conflict that may occur between cooperation and commitment. Organizationally this may often be resolved by a formal separation of the two functions between, say, manager and executive. The same may be reflected in the ORASA side. This is illustrated by the following diagram, developed by Lockett and Poulding,[8] in a continuing study of OR implementation. They postulate three levels of staff involved, both at the client and the ORASA level, and study the interactions between them occurring in a sample of OR studies.

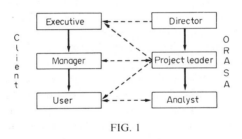

FIG. 1

Figure 1 shows the level and the most likely interactions. The research showed that a very great variety of interaction patterns occurred in practice. For our present purposes it does indicate how "commitment" can be delegated. Thus if the executive is the "problem owner", and if he delegates to the manager responsibility for supervision of the project, *and* responsibility for an implementable (or implemented) solution, he may ensure that the spirit of the "rethought ORASA" process is maintained without losing his freedom of action. Similarly, the existence of an ORASA executive above the project leader may make it possible to bring in the other problem owners without violating the project leader-manager relationship. Hence, by proper organizational relationships, it will often be possible to introduce the new methodology in an acceptable manner to the client executive (problem owner). However, it only does this by creating a problem of a different kind at the level of client manager/project leader.

This whole field requires further study. The implication of the relationship described above is that the level of responsibility for the final solution becomes blurred. The ORASA worker becomes, so to speak, a "thinking extension" of the manager himself. They have to build a dialogue between them in which each, to some degree, moves away from the traditional client/expert relationship. It is not a situation for which the manager is likely to have been trained, nor in which he will have experience. Moreover, he may simply not wish for such a relationship – seeing it as incompatible with his managerial responsibilities. How then does one describe the compromise? One thing is clear – there is no approach which is "ideal" in any absolute sense. The manager is part of the system, and the analytical process needs to be designed to match the managerial process.

This brings us to the second of the compatibility requirements mentioned at the beginning of this section. The "investigation style" must match the "managerial style". A study directed towards government policy will be conducted quite differently in the UK, USA and USSR, because the decision-making processes are quite different in the three cases. Similarly the style needs to be different in a strongly-decentralized organization from that where the central control is absolute. Within the same political system and national culture, there are extreme differences in the way in which decisions can be taken and implemented within organizations – differences that depend on history, technology and, above all, individual behaviour patterns. A critical element in a successful study is an understanding of what knowledge is available, what information is used and required – by whom and when – and the continual appreciation of process that can only be acquired by strong personal contact. Some decision-making processes are of a very formal style, giving little apparent opportunity for analytical input except at critical decision points, by which time most of the "informal" opinion formation may have been completed. This means that the "informal" process must be understood and penetrated.

Neither the manager nor the managerial process are likely to be redesigned for the benefit of the analyst. He must initiate the process of designing a fruitful method of interaction with his process of investigation. But too often he received no training relating to this, which passes some of the responsibility on to the teachers.

Teaching

It is clear that there are major implications in what has been said above, concerning the teaching of analysts and also of managers. So far as analysts are concerned it implies a greater knowledge of social behaviour in organizations and a formal training in methodology, i.e. the science of how to undertake an ORASA study. Currently it has to be admitted that – under pressure from students, from other academics and even from the non-academic world – teachers of ORASA tend to teach what is both readily-teachable and examinable – this means an emphasis on tools rather than skills, and even less on general methodology. Part of the reason is that most formal training is given to people without experience in a field where appreciation of the truth requires some experience. Another reason is more deeply philosophical in that there is an inherent difficulty in teaching a subject which is so strongly related to the structure of individual problems, in a general, non-problem specific, environment. Indeed, the very attempt to produce a teaching format is likely to impose a structure on the subject which is not a true representation of the reality. However we may overcome the difficulties, it is clear that the currently available philosophical and methodological bases for teaching are inadequate.

There is no place here for full discussion of the issues involved. These are better discussed elsewhere[9] than would be possible in the short space available in this paper. There is ample scope for more debate. One thing is clear – most courses as they now exist are inadequate – if the typical product is expected to be expert in the craft of ORASA. (To be fair, most courses do not claim this.)

Even more inadequate, however, is the teaching in this subject and on courses for prospective managers. Why, you might ask, should managers be trained to make use of systems analysis – they don't get specific training in making use of lawyers, engineers and other professional advisers? Surely it is the adviser's job to learn to speak to them. It is a legitimate reaction, which drives the question deeper. The question is not one of the manager understanding the analyst better – as we have said, "Why should he?" But the manager does need to *understand* the organizational processes within which he operates and the way that these can improve. Such understanding will inevitably lead to an awareness of interactions with the analytical processes, so that decisions can incorporate that analysis so as to create positive changes and increased efficiency. That this is *not* done can be seen from the limited success of very many attempts at organizational change – whether the proposals for change come from within the organization or from external consultants. So, part of the problem lies in the fact that management education as a whole gives too little attention to the systems behaviour of organizations.

But, beyond this, we have the fact that although organizational problem-solving remains a vitally important activity of management (we must remember that the analyst only helps with a small subset of all management problems), it is given little if any attention on formal courses. It is seen as an acquired gift. At the moment it is – because it has to be. But the lessons are hard learnt and, in many cases, ill-learnt – i.e. people misunderstand their experience and then transfer their deductions inappropriately. Without a background of understanding derived from such knowledge, the task of the ORASA intervener will remain hard, and uncertain. Thus, the ORASA teachers have a dual task – to restructure their teaching of methodology for prospective and experienced analysts – and to develop more effective teaching programmes for managers in general problem solving.

Research

If what we know provides a challenge for practitioners, for managers and for teachers – our lack of knowledge provides just as great a challenge for researchers. The unknowns are so many that it is almost presumptuous to make a personal selection. Individual researchers will, as always, follow a line that seems to them to be of interest and potentially useful. We shall only make two main points.

The first of these is that there is a great need to lay emphasis on process, to understand that any study of ORASA which ignores the dynamics both of the investigational process *and* of the managerial process under investigation is ignoring the substance of what ORASA and decision-making are about. Much more research of this kind is needed. In making such research studies, however, it is important to accept that any observation is unrepeatable, and that even the most meticulous applied research needs to be theory-driven. Much of the research in this field is either static, or implicitly accepts the classical reductionist paradigm of hard science. This is partly because much of the data is collected by relatively inexperienced students brought up in this paradigm. Yet if experienced staff are employed – a much more costly process, particularly when considered in opportunity-cost terms – the implicit theories which they bring to their observations affect the whole course of the investigation. In order to get valid observation, therefore, peer criticism of the underlying theories is of vital importance. Even with well-structured theories it is difficult to reduce the number of primary observations to a manageable level – which is, of course, no excuse for unstructured data collection. Many basic issues in research methodology need reexamination.

This leads to a second point of issue, namely the need for collaboration. Individual researchers cannot hope to tackle the area adequately. They need to get together and coordinate the approach. The results of the seminar already indicate that the same principles are appearing in work from many cultures – so by careful design we can collaborate to our mutual advantage.

Conclusion

To have obtained a general consensus of opinion with the very diverse group of scholars and practitioners who attended the seminar was something of a miracle, and gives rise to a hope that we are seeing a substantial move forward towards the design of a soundly-based ORASA methodology, which will be of major value to decision-makers at organizational, national and perhaps even international levels. Then, and then only, will it be possible to discuss rationally – between the analysts themselves as well as between analysts and the problem owners – the part that ORASA can be expected to play as an aid to complex decision-making.

REFERENCES

1. Tomlinson, R. C. Operational Research and Systems Analysis: from Practice to Precept. *Philos. Trans. Roy. Soc.*, London, Ser. A 287, pp. 355–371, 1977.
2. The list is obviously a personal one, although references to the particular elements are easily found in the individual papers. The notion of "hidden assumptions" is strongly associated with Kindler, Kiss and Farkas, "intervention" with Boothroyd, but it is difficult in general to identify the general ideas put forward here with one author.
3. Some of these are brought out by Moscarola, Dror and Larichev in their chapters.
4. "Process" has been one of the key words in the authors thinking about the subject, e.g. in Tomlinson, R. C. "Some dangerous misconceptions concerning Operational Research and Applied Systems Analysis", *European Journal of Operational Research*, 7 (2), pp. 203–212, 1981.
5. This concept follows the argument by de Zeeuw in his chapter in this volume.
6. See Tomlinson, ref. 4 above, 1981.
7. The terms "vertical" and "horizontal" thinking have been popularized by Edward de Bono in a series of books on creative thinking.
8. Lockett, A. G. and Poulding, E. OR/MS Implementation – a Variety of Processes. *Interfaces*, 9, pp. 45–50, 1978.
9. Education in Systems Science. Ed. Bayraktar *et al.*, Taylor and Francis, London (1979) presents the results of a searching conference in this area.

Appendix

About the Authors

Igor Viktorovich BLAUBERG born in 1929, Cand. Sc. (Philos.), is Head of the Laboratory at the Institute for Systems Studies, the State Committee for Science and Technology and the USSR Academy of Sciences. He specializes in philosophical and methodological problems of systems research. Main works: *Problem of Integrity in Marxist Philosophy*, Moscow, 1964; *Systems Approach: Prerequisites, Problems, Difficulties*, Moscow, 1969 (together with Sadovsky, V. N. and Yudin, E. G.) in English (translated by A. Rapoport: General Systems/Yearbook) Vol. XXV, 1980, pp. 1–31; *Concept of Integrity and its Role in the Scientific Knowledge*, Moscow, 1972 (together with Stefanov, N. K., Sadovsky, V. N. and Yudin, E. G.) (in Bulgarian); *Systems Theory: Philosophical and Methodological Problems*, Moscow, Progress Publishers, 1977 (together with Yudin, E. G. and Sadovsky, V. N.), in English.

Hylton BOOTHROYD, is Reader in Operational Research at the University of Warwick, UK. As a graduate mathematician he moved straight into the practice of on-site investigative studies with the Operational Research Executive of the National Coal Board in the UK. He and his teams were concerned with a wide variety of questions, particularly those relating to the construction of new mines, the supply of spares and the maintenance of underground equipment. Their studies led to widely-implemented and sometimes controversial recommendations. After 10 years his deepening interest in the theoretical foundations for offering OR/Systems advice led him to look to a university environment for the freedom to follow-up such issues without the need to make client interests paramount. He is still a competent mathematical/computational/investigative practitioner when he puts his mind to it, but that is not often!

Peter CHECKLAND, is Professor of Systems at the University of Lancaster and a member of the UK National Committee for IIASA. After reading

Chemistry at Oxford he joined ICI Limited in 1954. When he left to move to the University in 1969 he was manager of a research group developing new products in the synthetic fibre industry. At Lancaster he has led an action research programme aimed at developing systems methodology for tackling the unstructured problems of the real world (as opposed to the well-defined problems of the laboratory). The 12 years of this research have led to "soft systems methodology" and to a re-thinking of the fundamental basis of systems thinking. An account of this, together with an account of the action research, is given in "Systems Thinking, Systems Practice", published in 1981 by John Wiley and Sons.

C. West CHURCHMAN, is Acting Chairman of the Center for Research in Management and Professor Emeritus of Business Administration and Public Health at the University of California, Berkeley. He received his Ph.D. degree in Philosophy from the University of Pennsylvania and, together with Russ Ackoff, started the first academic graduate programme in operations research at Case Institute of Technology. His chief intellectual interest is in the application of management science and operations research to the improvement of the human condition. He expresses this interest both in practical work for government and in philosophical work in books.

Yehezkel DROR, is Professor of Political Science and Wolfson Professor of Public Administration at the Hebrew University of Jerusalem. He has served as a Fellow at the Center for Advanced Study in the Behavioural Sciences, Paolo Alto; a Visiting Scholar at the Wilson Centre in Washington, DC; and a Fellow at the Institute for Advanced Study, Berlin. His academic work concentrates on the advancement of policy sciences, with application to the improvement of governance and policy-making. He has also worked for and in governments, including the RAND Corporation in the USA and the Israeli government. In addition to his academic research, he serves as a consultant to a number of governments and international organizations.

János FARKAS, sociologist and philosopher, is Head of Science and Technology Department, Institute of Sociology, Hungarian Academy of Sciences. His research deals with methodological questions of science studies, sociology of science and technology. Main publications: (in Hungarian): Az ötlettól a megvalósulásig (From the Idea to the Realisation, 1974); A modern tudomány szerkezete (Structure of Modern Science, 1981); A tudomány társadelmi tényege (The Social Substance of Science, 1982).

József KINDLER, is Professor of Management and Industrial Engineering, Technical University of Budapest. He received a B.S. in chemical engineering, M.S. in industrial engineering, Ph.D. in managerial economics all from the Technical University of Budapest. He holds a scientific degree in economics from the Hungarian Academy of Science. Prior to joining the faculty of the Technical University of Budapest, Professor Kindler was in different managerial parts in the field of Hungarian Food Industry. He is the co-author of a book on techniques of decision methodology, co-editor of books in systems theory and systems research in addition to a number of papers in the fields of management, and decision-making. His research interests include applied statistics and systems research. He is currently doing research in decision theory, decision methodology and various aspects of evaluation research. Prof. Kindler is a member of the Society for General Systems Research.

István KISS, is Director of the Bureau for Systems Analysis, State Committee for Technical Development, Hungary. He received his first diploma in control engineering, and wrote his D.E. thesis in Systems Engineering. Prior to joining the State Committee, Dr Kiss was assistant Professor in Operational Research and Systems Engineering at the Technical University of Budapest, and later Head of Department, R and D Management at the Central Research Institute for Physics. In 1973 he was a guest scientist at IIASA, and at present serves – amongst his other duties – as secretary of the Hungarian NMO to the Institute. He is the President of the Hungarian Division of Society for General Systems Research. He has published several papers and co-edited books in systems research and related fields. Member of editorial boards of the *International Journal of General Systems*, and *Human Systems Management*. He is currently editing a book in English on the introduction of systems thinking in general education in Hungary.

Oleg Ivanovich LARICHEV, born in 1934, D.c.S., is Head of the Laboratory of Research and Development Planning at the Institute for Systems Studies, the State Committee for Science and Technology and the USSR Academy of Sciences. He specializes in the methodological problems of decision-making and systems analysis, has practical consulting activity in the field of decision-making. Larichev is author of many papers and the book "Science and art of decision-making" (Nauka, Moscow, 1979)

Giandomenico MAJONE, is Professor of Statistics in the Faculty of Economic and Social Sciences of the University of Calabria, Italy, and a research scholar at IIASA. His present interests in the conceptual foundations of systems and policy analysis are an extension of previous concerns with the foundations of statistical inference and decision theory, but also the result of this experience in consulting and policy advising. Such experiences have revealed the artificial nature of the traditional distinctions between description, prescription and persuasion, and the need for a metalanguage capable of dealing with all three aspects of analysis.

Eduard Mikailovich MIRSKY born 1935, Cand. Sc. (Philos.), is Senior Researcher at the Institute for Systems Studies, the State Committee for Science and Technology and the USSR Academy of Sciences. He specializes in philosophical and methodological problems of systems research and science of science. Main works: Systems Approach to Science; Methodological Comments – In: *"Systems Research, Yearbook 1977"*, Moscow, 1980; The Systems Articulation of the Interdisciplinary Subject-Matter – In: *Systems Research, Methodological Problems, Yearbook 1980*, Moscow, 1981 (all in Russian); Philosophy of Science, History of Science, Science of Science – In: J. Hintikka, D. Gruender and E. Agazzi (eds) *Theory Change, Ancient Axiomatics and Galileo's Methodology.* Proceedings of the 1978 Pisa Conference on the History and Philosophy of Science, Dordrecht–Boston–London, 1981.

Iain I. MITROFF, is currently the Harold Quinton Distinguished Professor of Business Policy, in the Department of Management and Policy Science, of the Graduate School of Business, University of Southern California. His qualifications are in engineering science and he took a minor in the philosophy of science for his Ph.D. at Berkeley, under West Churchman. His dissertation was one of the first computer simulations of human behaviour. His subsequent research is especially concerned with the development of methods which are both theoretically sound and practically effective to aid decision-makers in coping with messy, ill-defined problems. He has been exceptionally critical about naive assumptions about the objectivity of science and scientists. He has published a number of books and over a hundred papers in professional and scientific journals on such topics as: 1. The decision and problem solving styles of managers and scientists, 2. The philosophy, psychology, and sociology of science, 3. Knowledge acquisition and use, 4. The design of management information systems, 5. Management and strategic planning, 6. Organizational psychology.

Jean MOSCAROLA, is a Maître Assistant in the Institut Universitaire de Technologie d'Annecy. As a researcher he belongs to the research group LAMSADE in PARIS Université Dauphine, under the leadership of Bernard Roy. He is involved both in active operational research practice and in empirical observation of decision processes as well as methodological reflection about efficiency of OR. J. Moscarola was leader of an AFCET working group on decision processes. He is active in European Working Groups of EURO.

Vadim Nikolayevich SADOVSKY, born in 1934, D.Sc. (Philos.), is Head of the Laboratory at the Institute for Systems Studies, the State Committee for Science and Technology and the USSR Academy of Sciences. He specializes in the logic and methodology of science and in the methodological problems of systems research. Main works: "The Deductive Method as a Problem of the Logic of Science", In: P. V. Tavanets (ed.) *Problems of the Logic of Scientific Knowledge*, Dordrecht, D. Reidel, 1970, pp. 160–211; *Foundations of the General Systems Theory, Logical and Methodological Analysis*, Moscow, Nauka Publishers, 1974 (in Russian); *"Problems of a General Systems Theory as a Metatheory"*, *Ratio*, Vol. XVI, 1974, No. 1, pp.

33–50; *Systems Theory. Philosophical and Methodological Problems*, Moscow, Progress Publishers, 1977 (together with Blauberg, I. V. and Yudin, E. G.); Logic and the Theory of Scientific Change – In: J. Hintikka, D. Gruender and E. Agazzi (eds), *Theory Change, Ancient Axiomatics and Galileo's Methodology*. Proceedings of the 1978 Pisa Conference on the History and Philosophy of Science, Dordrecht–Boston–London, D. Reidel, Vol. 1, 1981, pp. 49–62.

Rolfe TOMLINSON, was, at the time of the seminar, Chairman of the Management and Technology Area at IIASA, and is now Professor of Systems and Operational Research at the University of Warwick, UK. He is also President of the European Association of OR Societies. Originally qualified as a mathematician, engineer and statistician, he joined, in 1960, the Operational Research Executive of the British National Coal Board and was its Director from 1965–1977. In this position he had to develop a methodology for the planning and control of his 100-strong team, and this led to a concern about the discrepancies between the Executive's successful practice and popular descriptions of the subject. This expression found outlet in a number of published papers, and in the joint organization of this seminar.

Gerard DE ZEEUW, born 1936, is Professor for General Andragology, the study of design for social change, at the University of Amsterdam. After finishing studies in mathematics, statistics and econometrics in Leiden and Rotterdam he studied mathematical psychology in Stanford. He worked afterwards in psychology, decision-theory, theory of science, systems research and in artificial social systems – both as researcher and as teacher – in Amsterdam. He has edited and written 5 books, and contributed more than a hundred scientific papers. He is one of the co-founders of the International Federation for Systems Research.

3 5282 00122 6656